Gender and The Labor Market

Meltem İnce Yenilmez / Ufuk Bingöl (eds.)

Gender and The Labor Market

Key Facts and The Trends in Equal Employment

PETER LANG

Bibliographic Information published by the Deutsche Nationalbibliothek
The Deutsche Nationalbibliothek lists this publication in the Deutsche Nationalbibliografie; detailed bibliographic data is available online at http://dnb.d-nb.de.

Library of Congress Cataloging-in-Publication Data
A CIP catalog record for this book has been applied for at the Library of Congress.

Cover illustration: © Fokusiert/istockphoto.com

ISBN 978-3-631-81791-9 (Print)
E-ISBN 978-3-631-84156-3 (E-PDF)
E-ISBN 978-3-631-84157-0 (EPUB)
E-ISBN 978-3-631-84158-7 (MOBI)
DOI 10.3726/b17832

Peter Lang – Berlin · Bern · Bruxelles · New York · Oxford · Warszawa · Wien

This publication has been peer reviewed.

www.peterlang.com

Preface and Acknowledgments

This book covers deep researches from different perspectives and disciplines upon women in labor markets by successful and expert researchers in their field. In this book, different and rigorous analyses of all areas influenced by gender researches were made in order to be one of the new reliable sources about the women studies in labor markets with various dimensions.

This book consists of six parts. After the introduction, in the first section, there are two chapters about qualitative and theoretical researches related to the concept of women in labor markets and gender theory. In the first chapter, a qualitative evaluation was made between Women and Social Policy in terms of postgraduate dissertation theses by Prof. Verda Özgüler. Her aim in this chapter is to gauge how the topic of women and social policy within the discipline of labor economics and industrial relations is evaluated through an analysis of graduate theses. To this end, graduate theses that were written under the Department of Labor Economics and Industrial Relations and obtained from the thesis archive of the Council of Higher Education (CoHE) of Turkey were examined with document and content analysis. Scrutinized data were shown and interpreted with percentage and frequency tables with fruitful results. In second chapter of first section, Assoc. Prof. Yeliz Yeşil studied a multi-perspective theoretical framework of women in education and employment and revealed and valuable suggestions were developed. According to her study, women's positions in economic, social, cultural and political life should be strengthened. Education of women is important to be successful in tackling poverty and to achieve country development.

The second section of this book is directly related to the women and career concepts of gender studies. In the first chapter of second section, Asst. Prof. Gaye Özçelik scrutinized women's work and careers under COVID-19 pandemic with a boundary theory perspective. As you know, the global COVID-19 pandemic has had an unprecedented impact on societies not only leading to health crises, but also giving rise to a global economic downturn, accompanied by a sharp increase in unemployment levels that are likely to have long-run repercussions for gender equality regarding work and career outcomes. The pandemic has further challenged existing micro boundaries to the detriment of women. In particular, women have to shuffle between work and housework-related role boundaries in order to fulfill the daily demands of these two distinct, but interconnected domains. Drawing on boundary theory, the aim of her chapter is to illustrate the severity of women's boundary-crossing activities in the form of role transitions between work and home during a pandemic crisis. In the second chapter, Asst. Prof. Betül Yılmaz evaluates the female manager in academia focused on Turkish universities. In this context, the number of female academics taking part in academia has approached the number of male academics but the number of female academics working in administrative positions has been increasing; it is not yet at the desired level.

The third section of this book aims to show researches related to parental issues of women in labor markets. In the first chapter of this section, Asst. Prof. Zeynep ELİTAŞ describes the effect of parents' education on time spent with pre-school children aged between 0 and 5. She utilizes 2014–2015 time-use survey data and diaries of daily activities conducted by Turkish Statistical Institute (TurkStat) for Turkey. These diaries contain the information about time spent in child's physical care and educational activities. Parental time equations are estimated separately for each parent in the household on their education levels and other control variables. Results of the analysis show that (i) there are differences in time allocation by the education levels of parents and (ii) the effects of education on parental time allocation differ between mothers and fathers. These differences support that policy making should place additional emphasis on the subject. According to literature, low female labor force participation rate and employment rate in Turkey have been linked to many factors by researchers. One noticeable factor appears to be the childcare burden of women with small children. Turkish women are traditionally the primary care providers of their children. The next best alternative childcare option is getting help from relatives, especially from grandmothers. On the other hand, formal (or institutional care) use in Turkey is not high enough compared to many other countries. Thus, the work-family conflict remains a critical issue for many women in Turkey. Asst. Prof. Didem Pekkurnaz aims to investigate the important socioeconomic and demographic factors related to employment status and childcare choices of Turkish women with small children. For this purpose, she used a nationally representative survey data. Estimation results reveal that low-educated women are less likely to be in the labor force and use formal or paid childcare. A high number of small children are also associated with a lower probability of labor force participation, but it has a positive impact on the use of formal care. It is also observed that women working with social security, working at regularly paid jobs and from high-wealth households have higher probabilities of using paid childcare.

The fourth section of this book contains entrepreneurial researches on women in employment with two chapters. In the first chapter, Assoc. Prof.

Berna Balcı İzgi analyzes Women's entrepreneurship and Youth Female Labor Force Participation in Turkey with econometric model. According to the findings, the increase in female labor force participation increases the female employer ratio after the third period. It is therefore important to encourage women's participation in paid work. As a conclusion of her research, Syrians had clustered at a certain place for survival and for their safety, but when they began to feel safer in recent years, they began to spread all over the city for approaching their workplace or for improving their quality of life. Prof. Verda Özgüler and Assoc. Prof. Fatma Kocabaş emerge the outlook of home-based female entrepreneurship in academia in Turkey. In their study, articles in academic journals and graduate theses written in Turkey from the perspective of gender roles and from the perspective of labor economics are presented with document analysis from qualitative research methods in which "home-based women entrepreneurship" is addressed.

In the fifth section of this book, there are four chapters related to macroeconomic impacts of women in labor market on poverty and finance. In the first chapter, Asst. Prof. Dilek Murat and Asst. Prof. Betül İnam carried out a quantitative field study in order to determine the effects of public spending on poverty. In their study, 36 OECD member countries were grouped according to poverty levels, and the data compiled were evaluated by discriminant analysis. The results found that all variables included in the analysis were effective when the analyzed countries were divided into low or high poverty groups. In the second chapter, Res Asst. Dr. Gülsüm Akarsu, Asst. Prof. Reyhan Cafri and Asst. Prof. Hanife Bıdırdı discussed female labor force participation and poverty with the evidences from Turkey. They aim to demonstrate the impact of female labor force participation on poverty at the regional level for Turkey between 2014 and 2017 using panel data techniques. Unlike the studies conducted with micro data, it is thought that the variables that reveal the economic and social structure of Turkey included in the model and use of regional level data will contribute to the literature. According to the empirical findings, female labor force participation, male labor force participation, income inequality, inflation and urbanization should be considered as important factors affecting poverty. In the third chapter of fifth section, Dr. Hasan Bakır examines the relationship between finance and labor in Turkey, as a developing country, through consumer credit. According to his findings were considered, it is determined that the amount of consumer loans used by lower income groups and wage earners increased, meaning that the levels of indebtedness increased. In the last chapter of this section, Asst. Prof. Hakan Ulucan analyzes the experiment of violence prevention centers (SONIMs), which are founded in 2013 in 14 pilot regions in Turkey and extended to countrywide implementation, possibly after having proven its success in the following years. The nine cities where SONIMs are founded are compared with the neighboring cities without SONIMs in a difference-in-differences approach. According to results, the SONIMs made differences in both reducing the violence and increasing the work rate among the women in the whole country.

In the sixth section of this book, there are two chapters related to international and institutional studies regarding the women in labor market. In the first chapter of this section, Asst. Prof. Omca Altın evaluates the EU's regulations aimed at preventing gender discrimination in labor markets and examines the extent to which these regulations are effective in preventing gender discrimination. As a result of the study, she observed that the EU made many arrangements to prevent gender discrimination in the labor market and developed various policies and programs, but all these arrangements, policies and programs did not reach their full purpose, and that inequality toward women in labor markets remains an important problem. In the second chapter, Assoc. Prof. Pınar Çuhadar and Res. Asst. Behiye Körpe examine the Middle East, as prominent on gender inequality and violations of women's rights, in terms of the effect of social norms on women's employment and gender politics, and evaluate the period after the Arab Spring, which was born as a freedom movement, in terms of gender politics. According to their evaluation and data they used, shows that the Arab Spring did not improve women's conditions in most Middle Eastern countries as expected; women's social, economic and political demands were still not met.

We would like to thank all the authors and researchers who are experts in their field for their devotion and diligence and hope to help our readers. It is also important to note that all chapters of this book underwent a serious both cross and external double-blind review process. We would also like to thank our external reviewers for their expertise and contribution to our book. We especially appreciate the valuable insights and guidance that has further helped shape our ideas. We also thank the publishing team for their immense support through the phase of publication. It has been an amazing journey so far. Thank you for helping this manuscript bloom from proposal to final publication. At the end of our saying, we also offer our endless gratitude to the families and children who are the source of motivation for us and our authors with their patience and support during the conduct of these valuable works.

Our respect.

Editors; Assoc. Prof. Meltem İNCE YENİLMEZ & Asst. Prof. Ufuk BİNGÖL

Contents

List of Contributors

Prof. Verda ÖZGÜLER
Anadolu University, Turkey

Assoc. Prof. Yeliz YEŞİL
Trakya University, Turkey

Assoc. Prof. Gaye ÖZÇELİK
İstanbul Bilgi University, Turkey

Asst. Prof. Betül YILMAZ
Bandırma Onyedi Eylül University, Turkey

Asst. Prof. Zeynep ELİTAŞ
Anadolu University, Turkey

Asst. Prof. Didem PEKKURNAZ
Başkent University, Turkey

Assoc. Prof. Berna BALCI İZGİ
Gaziantep University, Turkey

Assoc. Prof. Fatma KOCABAŞ
Anadolu University, Turkey

Asst. Prof. Dilek MURAT
Uludağ University, Turkey

Asst. Prof. Betül İNAM
Bilecik Şeyh Edebali University, Turkey

Dr. Hasan BAKIR
Uludağ University, Turkey

Res. Asst. Dr. Gülsüm AKARASU
Ondokuz Mayıs University, Turkey

Asst. Prof. Reyhan CAFRİ
İskenderun Technical University, Turkey

Asst. Prof. Hanife BIDIRDI
Kocaeli University, Turkey

Asst. Prof. Hakan ULUCAN
Pamukkale University, Turkey

Asst. Prof. Omca ALTIN
Kastamonu University, Turkey

Assoc. Prof. Pınar ÇUHADAR
Mardin Artuklu University, Turkey

Res. Asst. Behiye KÖRPE
Mardin Artuklu University, Turkey

Meltem İnce Yenilmez and Ufuk Bingöl

Introduction of Gender and the Labor Market: Key Facts and the Trends in Equal Employment

Today, human capital lies at the center of sustainable economic growth and development. Owing to the vast advances in politics and the economy, it has become a necessity to enact clear social, labor and economic policies, which will bear to mind the role of women as central players in the rapidly advancing world. There is no doubt that the skills and attitudes of the female gender could become the driving force for the growth of businesses and overall, the nation.

However, looking at the level of inequality across diverse societal demographic categories within the labor market, there is no doubt that many people may look to discrimination as a possible reason. This has resulted in an abundance of experimental and theoretical studies on social control issues. However, the only advancements social scientists and economists have gleaned in their studies is that it is an enormous challenge measuring discrimination, which is beyond their imaginations. First is the issue of defining discrimination; the other is discerning the technology of measurement. Already Milton Friedman, a Nobel Laureate and economist at the University of Chicago, has warned that researchers must always carefully distinguish between equality of opportunities and equality of outcomes.

The current guide provides a tour de force on segregation issues, especially in the labor market. However, it is important to emphasize that although discrimination and segregation may seem similar, they are not entirely the same. In truth, society's enforcement of discrimination is segregation. However, segregation may also occur from deliberate choices concerning differences in orientations and labor divisions within the home. In the present book, the researchers provide a counter study to orthodox gender discrimination study, particularly in areas such as labor market segmentation and segregation. Therefore, the authors carefully addressed empirical and theoretical grounds, especially on gender segregation in the rapidly advancing labor market. A method of analysis is created to measure wage derivatives, gender inequality and human capital, concerning their occupational segregation contributions. However, there seems to be a dogging phenomenon of inequality between the male and female, alongside social and ethnic groups in the labor market. This event has been displayed in many ways, including flaws in career growth opportunities, industrial or occupational segregation and pay differentials.

Nevertheless, sociologists show particular interests in gender occupational segregation issues, as women are most likely isolated to lower-paying positions and work status. These occurrences have prevailed continuously throughout history and in diverse nations, are the most prominent reasons behind unequal wages between men and women. Therefore, these segregations must be given adequate attention. However, before that can happen, there is a need to understand that discrimination is not always the same as segregation. In reality, segregation only means that the genders are treated differently, particularly within job positions across industries or occupations. Therefore, the career or academic choices men and women make can equally fuel the growth of these disparities. When these choices are placed in the limelight, the resulting labor market would not have such impacts of discrimination.

However, concerning occasions where employers particularly prefer working with the male gender than the female, this may be eloquently seen as an act of discrimination. Nevertheless, even in these particular occasions, segregation may sometimes result from the choices men and women make. Hence, such disparities are consequences of the socialization process, which on its own has some levels of discriminatory practices but occurs before entry into the labor force.

The purpose of this book is to deliver insights and discourse about women in management and the labor market while considering the different theories and approaches across nations and economies, alongside its consequences. The book reviews all global forms of positions on the matter including theoretical, organizational, empirical, comparative, evolutionary, country, sectoral and individual studies. The book provides insights into the principal areas, including women within developing and developed countries labor markets, as well as considering geographic similarities. Furthermore, it aims to expand on the general and scientific knowledge about women in the labor markets while sharing insights on emerging studies and discussions among policymakers, academics, research communities, national and international development facilities.

Section 1 Conceptual Researches on Women in Labor Markets

Verda Özgüler

Women and Social Policy: An Evaluation of Labor Economics and Industrial Relations in Turkey in Terms of Postgraduate Theses

1 Introduction

Social policy is a very rich field covering social protection regimes for human beings in national and international contexts (Esin, 1982: 125; Altan, 2017: 11). Whereas it only dealt with workers' problems at its inception, with time it expanded conceptually in the face of global developments and increasing social problems (Yüksel, 2014: 129).

Social policy was taken up as a scientific concept for the first time in Germany in late 19th century by Riehl, and later emerged again as a widespread scientific discipline when the "Social Policy Society" was founded in Germany (Güven, 1972: 1). Another scholar who has made an effort to develop terminology besides Riehl was Adolf Wagner. However, the concept matured with the work of Otto von Zwiedineck-Südenhorst published in 1911 (Erkul, 1983: 1).

Following a different line of development in each country, social policy is mainly carried out by public authorities in order to compensate and eliminate to a possible extent the negative consequences that arise during the functioning of the current economic and social system (Özgüler, 2020: 7).

While the social policy in its narrower sense has the purposes of eliminating conflicts that arise between workers and employers in the capitalist system, the instability and conflicts of interest, and of ensuring social harmony between the classes, in its broadest sense, it takes interest in the problems of all social groups in order to produce a solution. Social policy includes protection of employees and their families against social risks, as well as institutions and rules that provide protection for the entire society (Erdut, 2004: 36–37).

Born and developed in parallel with the need to seek solutions to the social problems encountered in social life, the discipline continues its academic development within the Departments of Labour Economics and Industrial Relations in Turkey[1].

---

1 In its broadest sense, social policy, which is defined as activities to reduce conflicts between the labour and capital classes, has a long-established tradition in Turkey.

Labour Economics and Industrial Relations Departments have strong interdisciplinary aspects (Özkaplan & Selamoğlu, 2005). While the contents of the discipline of social policy and labor economy and industrial relations departments do not match each other, there is a complementary structure to them (Akan, 2011: 1953).

This research includes a partially detailed overview of the subject by analyzing the graduate theses, and aims to answer the following questions:

- What is the distribution of the dissertations examined in the scope of the study according to the years, the levels of postgraduate study, and the universities?
- To what extent is the participation in working life and economic situation in terms of women discussed in the thesis?
- What concepts are the different views of women's labor discussed in the thesis?
- In what dimension is the importance of education in women's participation in social life and labor markets covered in the treatises examined?
- What topics are covered in the thesis on public regulations and women's rights for women?

These questions are answered within the framework of the dimensions created by using the studies examined under the following heading.

2 Studies on Women and Social Policy

The first developments concerning social policy in higher education in Turkey began in the 1920s with the words of Tuna and Yalçıntaş (2011: 9). But Erkul

---

Social policy studies initiated by Gerhard Kessler at Istanbul University in 1934 have continued at Ankara University under the leadership of Cahit Talas since the 1950s. Today, there are 32 universities continuing their academic studies in the Department of Labour Economics and Industrial Relations, with 7 of these universities also providing evening education (education starting in the morning at universities in Turkey usually lasts until 5 pm. However, some universities can provide training in the evening outside these hours. The word second instruction is used for evening classes to emphasize that they provide this education.) 1 providing distance education, and 1 providing online education alongside the traditional face-to-face mode of instruction. When Kessler was founded it, social policy focused on issues such as population, urbanism, labour matters and housing policies. Nowadays, it deals with a wide range of issues that create social disadvantages such as unemployment, poverty, social exclusion, domestic violence, and climate-related problems.

expresses that social policy in Turkey from 1915 onward is available under names such as "Politics of Society," "Social Policy," "Public Politics," "Social Politics," "Welfare Economy," "Public Economy," "Conventional Economy," and "Labor Economics" (Erkul, 1983: 4).

It is observed that the "Social Economics" course was added to the program with the instruction of August 1, 1924, of the higher education institution, whose name was "Ulumu Aliyel Ticariye Mektebi (Ulumu Aliyel Commercial School)" in 1883, and was first renamed "Higher Economics and Trade School" and then "Academy of Economic and Commercial Sciences." This course was later called "Social Economy" (Tuna and Yalçıntaş, 2011: 9). In 1928, even though the Faculty of Law at Istanbul University intended to teach a Social Economics course, it could not be implemented.

Social policy education in the Western sense started in 1933–1934 university reform in Turkey under the leadership of German professor Gerhard Kessler in İktisat ve İçtimaiyat Enstitüsü(Institute of Economics and Social Studies) within the Faculty of economics of Istanbul University. The institute started with "Kessler belonging to the social liberal movement who is a moralist and actionist economist, sociologist, historian and social politician rather than a doctrinal scientist" (Tuna & Yalçıntaş, 2011: 13). Prof. Dr. Orhan Tuna and his students (also called "first generation social politicians" in the field of social policy, Prof. Dr. Sabahaddin Zaim, Prof. Dr. Nusret Ekin, Prof. Dr. Nevzat Yalçıntaş, Prof. Dr. Turan Yazgan, and Prof. Dr. Toker Dereli [Altan, 2017: 17]) initiated social policy conferences, which are considered to be the first social policy collection in Turkey.

The conferences, which were published in June 2020 as the Journal of Social Policy Conferences, Number 78, constitute one of the first reference sources in the field of social policy in Turkey.

As of the first issue of the Journal of Social Policy Conferences, published in 1948, there are 11 articles with the word "woman" in their title. The proportion of studies with the phrase "woman" in the title has a share of 1.33 % in a total of 830 articles in the journal.

The first work with women in the title is dated 1950. Penned by Arol, it is stated that in order to reveal the general status of working women living in Istanbul, a survey was made with the article titled "Status of Working Women," including women working in various official and private organizations. Participation in the surveys was very low; especially, women who were civil servants were hesitant to participate in the survey due to privacy concerns (1950: 85). In Arol's own words:

> Very few women, especially civil servants, probably because they did not trust the privacy of the survey, have answered, only about 20 to 30 of them. Working women, on the other hand, showed greater courage in this regard than female civil servants and 255 of them answered the questions in this survey. Faced with this situation, I had to study only the 255 working women's answers by not taking the civil servant women's answers into account. This amount, although small, may give an idea of those who work in this field. (1950: 85)

In this first article about women in working life, it is stated that the place of women in social life varies according to times and culture; while there is a more egalitarian structure between men and women, with the development of social life, increasing population and the emerging division of labor in primitive societies, women took place in home and the men took place as wage worker in the social life. Arol (1950) emphasized that the foundations of this development are based on economic power, while the relations of wealth and property owned by men put them in a higher priority position in society than women, and expressed the issue as "the roots of the issue of victimization, bondage and abuse of women are based directly on economic reasons" (1950: 86).

A 1984 translation article entitled "Development and Increasing Scarcity" is the second article entitled "Women in the Journal of Social Policy Conferences" (Dumont, 1984: 329). The study, authored by Dumont and translated by Ekin, emphasizes the importance of women's role in social life and describes the idea that the development of a society is directly related to the education of women in different countries. After examining the world agricultural potential in the study, views such as "I concluded that the total population of the world should not exceed 7 or 8 billion with any view, and the smaller this figure, the better the results it would bring together. Once the climax is reached, even the reduction of the world's population can be considered and the best target one day for a planet with limited resources would be a population of 2 billion" were included. Emphasizing a strong link between wealth, standard of living, population, and education, the study highlights that women's education is of key importance.

The 1992 study "Female Labour Force in the Structure of Employment in Turkey " analyzes the status of female labor force based on data from the 1988 State Statistical Institute[2] household labor force survey of 1988 (Kutal, 1992: 45). As of 1988, 50.40 % of the population is male and 49.60 % is female. It can be said that this ratio has not changed much today. According to the 2019 data from the Address-based Population Registration System 2019, the

---

2 Named today as Turkish Statistical Institute (TurkStat).

Turkish Statistical Institute (TurkStat), 50.2 % of the total population are men and 49.8 % are women (TurkStat, 2019). It is stated that women's labor force participation rates are low in urban areas, there are differences between female and male labor force participation rates and that women working as unpaid family workers are very high compared to 75.26 % among employed women. The knowledge that 75 % of women employed in Turkey are excluded from protective labor law legislation and that they are also outside the scope of social security institutions is one of the findings of the study (Kutal, 1992).

In the study "The Problem of 'Invisibility' in Women's Productive Activities in Economic Activities," dated 1995, it is emphasized that women's work generally being taken into account within the framework of traditional economic and non-economic distinction and being compared with men's participation in the workforce and economic activities is important to explain the state of "inequality" (Acar, 1995: 195). Women's participation in economic activities is low compared to men's and they are in a "secondary" position in terms of position and status. Studies on women's participation in working life often focus on this aspect. Women are not as "at the forefront" as men in economic activities that have economic value and are included in statistics and are considered "visible" in this sense. In Acar's own words:

> The home work of productive nature being fulfilled mostly by women, however, this work being called non-economic activities, and the women who fulfil them being called "economically inactive housewives" and counted as "out of employment", raises the issue of 'the invisibility of women'. The reason that this invisibility is a "problem" is that, besides the truth not being revealed, it also has important effects and consequences for the social and economic status of women. (1995: 196)

In the article dated 2005, named as "The View of Working Women on the Concept of Work in the Example of Comparison Between Academics and Textile Workers," it is expressed that within the workforce there is a classification for jobs as "masculine" and "feminine" because of the preferences of women as well as the gender roles, and thus the views of women on the concept of work were tried to be determined in the phenomenon of "women who work as laborers in textile factories and scholars" (Kumaş & Fidan, 2005: 507). From the traditional point of view, jobs in labor markets are divided into "men's jobs" and "women's jobs." However, the processes of deregulation and inflexibility experienced in today's societies have blurred the boundaries of this distinction between jobs. Although the flexible working life as a result of globalization has facilitated the entry of women into the working life, including in jobs that are considered to be men's work from the traditional perspective, the employment of women is concentrated in nonstandard forms of work. In part-time work, short-term or temporary employment, subcontracting, working at home, job sharing, teleworking, etc., the most distinctive feature of working styles is the weight of women's employment (Kumaş & Fidan, 2005: 511).

In the same issue of the journal, "Evaluation of the Provisions of the Labour Law Concerning Occupational Health and Safety of Women, Children and Young Workers," the legal dimension of the subject is addressed (Uşan, 2005). Under the New Labour Law, protective provisions for child-young workers and women workers in special groups that need to be protected in working life are evaluated.

The article published by Urhan in 2015 addresses intra-union democracy and inter-union women's organization (Urhan, 2015). Changing social and economic conditions makes it necessary to rethink the position of women who do not/cannot play a sufficient role in the trade union field while discussing the role and duties of trade unions in representing workers. The problem of representation and participation in trade union democracies results from the lack of adequate participation of women in trade unions and their exclusion in the context of demands and interests (Urhan, 2015: 31). The position of women in trade unions arguing over the secondary data of qualitative research conducted in 2014, Urhan emphasizes the trade unions forced the issue as they'll accept the agenda of the women's movement, women's demands of gender inequities concrete demands to drive back general stresses the need to find a place among trade unions. In the writer's own words:

> Because union democracy is almost reduced to the election of managers, and the vertical-hierarchical organizational structure is insisted on for various reasons. In this case, the union managers set policy and agenda by assuming that the general interests of female members are similar to their own. Efforts to determine what is in the interests of ordinary members are deemed unnecessary. Therefore, in the face of "severe and general problems" for male managers such as severance pay for unions, job security, subcontracting, protection of wages; the issues of equality remain trivial to them. (Urhan, 2015: 56)

In his study, Davutoglu discusses the effects of second wave feminism in Turkey starting after the 1980s through the first female employment article in the Journal of Social Policy Conferences (2015: 159); he argues that the 1990s were the years when second wave feminism in Turkey began to make great gains. The author considers the 1992 work of Gülten Kutal, a prominent female academic in the field of social policy, as "the beginning of mainstream social policy to acquire a gender-based quality" (Davutoğlu, 2015: 160). However, if the author's assessment is taken in the context of the articles that have been written so far, it can be said that with 11 articles in 830 studies, steps have been taken toward gaining a gender-neutral character of social policy, but the developments are sufficient. Although the only publication address for academics working in the field of social policy in Turkey and focusing on the issue of women is not the Journal of Social Policy Conferences, it is an important and respected publication in the field of social policy.

The 2016 study "Factors Affecting Women's Participation in Labour Markets in Turkey: an analysis on TurkStat data" examined women's participation in the labor force in Turkey using 2007–2016 data (Akgeyik, 2016: 31). According to the data, women's participation in the workforce tends to increase. This rate increased from 24 % to 33 % during the study period. Education is an important variable that explains women's participation in the workforce. In addition, the economic status of the family, the fertility rate, the education level of the spouse, and cultural values are other variables that affect women's labor force participation rates (Akgeyik, 2016: 48).

In the study "The Problem of Non-Maternal Care Caused by Female Employment and the Possible Consequences of Turkey's Women's Employment Policy," institutional childcare services are analyzed based on the data. The development of work and life skills targeted in Turkey's social policies during the industrialization process will be possible in a social peace environment where the benefits of children are brought to the fore (Büyükcoşkun, 2018).

A long-term observation paper titled "Determination of Women's Will in Migration Decision: Young Girls Opportunity to Move from the Village to the City" by Şahin, Çiftyıldız and Evkaya (2018), about migrating to cities from rural areas, published in 2019, examines the effects of marriage on migration. The study said:

> Many young men in Turkey recently are unable to marry because they reside in the village. Young men living in the village are forced to migrate to the city because they cannot get married and young women who feel they are forced to become urban force the men to become urban and they create the opportunity to become urban themselves.

The National Library, Anadolu University Library and Documentation Center, Bilkent University Library and Rare Book web pages were searched with the keyword "social policy" in order to reveal other studies focusing on "women and social policy" in a way that would reveal the dimensions of the research subject. At this stage, women academics publishing in this field were focused on considering that it would be appropriate to the core of the subject.

The book "Social Policy of the European Community," translated by Melek Eğilmez in 1978 and published by the press and Information Bureau of the European Community, is the first source found as a result of an Internet search. It was determined that the first Social Policy book written by a female social politician in Turkey belonged to Meryem Koray and Alper Topcuoğlu (1987).[3] The Social Policy book, written by Aysen Tokol (1995), is also the first single-authored book.

The dimensions used in the analysis of social policy theses were determined based mainly on the articles and books published in the Journal of Social Policy Conferences. In this context, the dimensions used for the analysis are given in Tab. 1.1.

Policies for women play an important role in the expansion of social policy both in scope and in practice. In the last quarter of the 20th century, sensitivity toward women has increased all over the world and equality policies have started to be introduced in order to promote discriminatory attitudes and behaviors (Koray, 2003: 313). The development of social policy is closely related to the development of human rights. The development of women's rights, which are considered to be third generation rights, is different according to countries, but is based on the acceptance that women are human before they are women. In this context, it is hoped that the inequality between men and women will be eliminated through legal arrangements, especially social values and policies to eliminate discrimination (Koray, 2003: 319).

"The Convention on the Elimination of All Forms of Discrimination against Women," which has the main purpose that could be summarized as acting as a barrier to prevent gender discrimination and inequality, providing arrangements to be made in the field of women's rights, and at the same time regarded as an integral part of the Universal Declaration of human rights, dated 1979, was ratified by Turkey in 1985. While legal arrangements are being made with the addition of women's dimension to human rights, arrangements such as participation in education, encouraging women to enter certain professions, and participation in political and nonpolitical (trade unions and bureaucracy) decision-making bodies are on the agenda. In this context, because the place of

---

3 The work was published in 1987 co-written with Alper Topçuoğlu, and the subsequent editions in 1993 and 1995 had two authors, whereas the 2000 and the subsequent editions were published as single authored. https://www.nadirkitap.com/kitapara_sonuc.php?kelime=%22sosyal%20politika%22&siralama=yayinyiliaz&bks=181&page=2 (18.07.2020).

Tab. 1.1: Dimensions and Bases Used in the Analysis of Graduate Theses within the Scope of Research

The Dimensions Determined from the Studies Examined under the Heading "Studies on Women and Social Policy"	**Dimensions Taken from the Study "The Evaluation of Graduate Theses in the Context of 'Social Policy' in Labor Economics and Industrial Relations in Turkey"**[a]	**Dimensions Used in the Analysis of Dissertations within the Scope of This Research**
• Economic level • Education • Labor Markets • Unseen labor • Women's work–men's work • Flexibility	• Harassment due to economic dependence • Social security • Social peace • Social balance (worker–employer/narrow sense, employer–all dependent employees/broad sense)	• Participation in working life and economic situation • Free labor, unseen labor, and care-giving labor • Education, widespread education
• Representation in trade unions • Feminism • Non-maternal care • Marriage • Migration • Poverty	• Threat of poverty • Social exclusion • Disease, old age • Comment favoring the worker • The road to prosperity, prosperity/happiness	• Family and woman's place in family institution • Marriage, children and non-maternal care labor • Representation in trade unions, politics and decision-making bodies • Women benefiting from equal opportunities
	• Employment • Improvement of material and cultural living conditions (housing, cooperative etc. to include areas) • Economically weak people	• Threat of poverty, migration, social exclusion • Improvement of women's place in society, material and cultural living conditions (including housing and cooperative etc. areas),
	• Fusion of social classes with society (minimizing class contradictions) • Non-formal education • Measures taken by the state to protect workers (institutions, practices)	• Feminism • Legal regulations • Measures taken by the state to protect workers (institutions, practices)

[a] Özgüler, 2020.

women in society is closely tied to social values, it is very important to ensure change in society. The presence of women who are able to receive education in accordance with the requirements of the age and work in the labor markets in the relationship of paid employment plays a key role for social development and progress (Koray, 2003: 322).

Universities, an important institution of society, are important institutions in terms of their transformative role in society. The type and extent of the academic work carried out here contributes to the accumulation of knowledge in different areas of the social sense and ensures social progress. The examination of the graduate thesis, which is one of the main products of academic knowledge production, makes visible the academic effort behind it and determines the literature development and direction in the fields it is concerned with. It is an area worth examining, especially because of the monitoring stages and juries in the writing process of doctoral theses and the ability to "enable the student to continue his/her academic life as an independent researcher" with the title of a Doctor as a result.

The study of graduate theses written in Turkey on women and social policies is based on this basic idea.

3 Method

This study has a qualitative research pattern that enables the presentation of research results based on code and categories by reading the data one by one. The subject of "women" is covered in a wide range of topics, from English language and literature to social services, from economics to folklore. According to the statistics obtained from the Council of Higher Education (CoHE) (National Thesis Centre) web page in the Internet search dated July 16, 2020, there are 8,056 graduate theses with the word "woman" in the field of Social Sciences.

Within the scope of the research, a database of graduate theses written in the fields of Labor Economics; Labor Economics and Industrial Relations; Labor Economics, Industrial, and Organizational Psychology; Human Resource Management;, Occupational Health and Safety, Labor and Social Security Law; Social Policy; Social Psychology, Management and Labor Sociology; and theses with Labor Economics and Industrial Relations were established. Among these theses, which can be considered as the universe of the study, 298 theses with the word "woman" in the title were included in the scope of the research.

The database used in the study covers 5,302 graduate theses. The graduate theses with the concept of "women" in the title were downloaded to the computer on June 10, 2020, and June 15, 2020, from the CoHE (National Thesis Center) web page.

Tab. 1.2: Dissertations Examined within the Scope of the Research

Department of Labour Economics and Industrial Relations	Number of the Thesis	Percent (%)
Labor Economics and Industrial Relations	163	54.73
Labor Economics and Industrial Relations (in the subject area)	112	37.58
Social Policy	6	2.01
Human Resources Management	5	1.68
Labor Economics	5	1.68
Social Psychology	3	1.01
Industrial and Organizational Psychology	1	0.34
Occupational Health and Safety	1	0.34
Labour and Social Security Law	1	0.34
Sociology of Management and Work	1	0.34
Sum of Theses about Labor Economics and Industrial Relations	**298**	**100.00**

The data in Tab. 1.2 are based on the department and subject areas. The aim of this course is to teach the basic concepts of Labor Economics, Labor Economics and Industrial Relations, Labor Economics and Social Politics, Labor Psychology and Human Resources, and Sociology of Labor. The dissertations in these branches of science are completely covered by the department and subject area searches, and they were determined by comparing them one by one in the excel database. There is only one thesis that is not covered and it has been added to the database.

The theses related to the research questions were transferred to a different excel file, and the records from different departments and duplications were eliminated; the final form was given to the database. The database was examined by a researcher with the title of a Doctor who has studied on the subject, and the database was given its final shape. "CoHE Code, Name, Year, Keyword, Thesis Name, University, Language, Type, Advisor, Abstract" columns are included in the database file.

The theses were classified in terms of year, graduate level, and the institute where they were written. MAXQDA Analytics Pro 2018 qualitative analysis program was used to analyze and visualize themes, keywords, and codes by reading the dissertations on the axis of basic dimensions covered under the heading "Women and Social Policy."

In determining the theses on women and social policy within the scope of the research, it can be said that taking the graduate theses of the Departments of Labour Economics and Industrial Relations constitutes an important limitation of the study. However, the selection of Labor Economics and Industrial Relations Theses, which continue the tradition of Social Policy and have interdisciplinary aspects, provides a useful framework for answering research questions.

The theses that are subject to the research are included in the analysis by applying the document review stages, which can be listed as "reaching documents," "obtaining documents," "analyzing data," and "using" by means of the document review method.[4] In document analysis, word, theme, character or person, and sentence or paragraph can be analyzed.

In this study, content analysis was used to examine the topic of women in the context of social policy, which is among the fields of study of different social sciences such as gender and women's studies, sociology and psychology, primarily in the "Labour Economics and Industrial Relations" sections. The stages of content analysis were "selection-reduction," "grouping," "generalization-abstraction," and "association with theory/literature." Frequency and percentage values were taken into consideration in tabulation of thesis data examined in content analysis.

The analysis was conducted based on the dimensions in the third column of Tab. 1.1 of the dissertations written in relation to the theory:

- Participation in working life and economic situation,
- Free labor, unseen labor, and care-giving labor,
- Education, widespread education
- Family and woman's place in family institution,
- Marriage, children, and non-maternal care labor,
- Representation in trade unions, politics, and decision-making bodies,
- Women benefiting from equal opportunities,
- Threat of poverty, migration, and social exclusion
- Improvement of women's place in society, material, and cultural living conditions (including housing and cooperative, etc., areas),
- Feminism,
- Legal regulations.

4 80.251.40.59/education.ankara.edu.tr/aksoy/eay/eay/b0506/ymetin.doc (04.05.2019).

4 Findings and Discussion

In this part of the study, findings with quantitative and qualitative dimensions related to the graduate theses examined within the scope of the research are included. Within the scope of the study, 298 theses with the title "woman" were included within the scope of research out of 298 graduate theses written in the field of 5,302 Labor Economics and Industrial Relations, and 37 doctoral theses were examined through document review and content analysis out of 298.

Of the 298 theses studied, 37 (12.42 %) were doctoral and 261 (87.58 %) were master's theses. Although the number of doctoral dissertations is very small, the reading and examination of the full texts were done through the doctoral dissertations due to the importance and weight it carries in terms of academic studies. Thirty-two PhD theses with full text access were examined with content analysis while the master's level theses were dealt with their basic bibliographic features.[5]

Within the scope of the study, 97.32 % (290 theses) of the theses were written in Turkish and 2.68 % were written in English. When Tab. 1.3 is examined, it is seen that 2019 is the year in which the most theses are written in terms of both master's and doctoral theses. The other two years in which the highest number of theses is written are 29 in 2017 and 28 in 2018. For doctoral theses, the years 2015 and 2017 follow the year 2019.

Theses with a frequency of 5 and more are given in Tab. 1.4. Other than Ankara Yıldırım Beyazıt University, all of these universities have departments related to the Department of Labor Economics and Industrial Relations and the departments of graduate education correlating with the departments. There is a Department of Social Policy in graduate education at Yıldırım Beyazıt University in Ankara.

Tab. 1.5 shows the subjects written for theses in the detailed scan section of the theses within the scope of the research. Detailed scanning subject section contains more than one title for each thesis. The table was created based on the topics written in the first order.

---

5 (1) Protection of Working Women (With European Community and Turkey Dimensions); (2) Investigation of First Aid Training Models in Home Accidents Given to Mothers with Children of 0–6 Years of Age; (3) Qualifications and Job-Related Views of Women Working in Household Cleaning Jobs; (4) Essays on Female Labor Supply in Turkey; (5) Full-text access to five theses entitled Empirical Analysis of the Relationship between Social and Demographic Factors, Liberties, Institutional Factors, and Female Labor Force Participation could not be attained.

Tab. 1.3: Distribution of Graduate Theses with the Keyword "Woman" in the Title between 1986 and 2019 by Years and Types

Years	Masters		PhD		Total	
	Number	Percent (%)	Number	Percent (%)	Number	Percent (%)
1986	1	0.34	–	–	**1**	**0.34**
1987	1	0.34	–	–	**1**	**0.34**
1991	1	0.34	1	0.34	**2**	**0.68**
1992	2	0.67	–	–	**2**	**0.67**
1994	–	–	1	0.34	**1**	**0.34**
1995	1	0.34	–	–	**1**	**0.34**
1996	2	0.67	–	–	**2**	**0.67**
1997	2	0.67	3	1.01	**5**	**1.68**
1998	4	1.34	–	–	**4**	**1.34**
1999	5	1.68	–	–	**5**	**1.68**
2000	4	1.34	–	–	**4**	**1.34**
2001	2	0.67	–	–	**2**	**0.67**
2002	4	1.34	1	0.34	**5**	**1.68**
2003	2	0.67	1	0.34	**3**	**1.01**
2004	4	1.34	–	–	**4**	**1.34**
2006	9	3.02	–	–	**9**	**3.02**
2007	4	1.34	–	–	**4**	**1.34**
2008	2	0.67	1	0.34	**3**	**1.01**
2009	6	2.01	3	1.01	**9**	**3.02**
2010	12	4.03	–	–	**12**	**4.03**
2011	4	1.34	1	0.34	**5**	**1.68**
2012	6	2.01	3	1.01	**9**	**3.02**
2013	10	3.36	–	–	**10**	**3.36**
2014	8	2.68	1	0.34	**9**	**3.02**
2015	20	6.71	4	1.34	**24**	**8.05**
2016	17	5.7	2	0.67	**19**	**6.37**
2017	29	9.73	4	1.34	**33**	**11.07**
2018	28	9.4	2	0.67	**30**	**10.07**
2019	69	23.15	9	3.02	**78**	**26.17**
Total					**298**	**100.00**

Tab. 1.4 Distribution of Graduate Theses with the Keyword "Woman" in the Title between 1986 and 2019 by Universities

University	Number	Percent (%)
Istanbul University	27	9..06
Gazi University[a]	24	8..05
Sakarya University	22	7..38
Marmara University	21	7..05
Ankara University	20	6..71
Yalova University	16	5..37
Çanakkale Onsekiz Mart University	15	5..03
Dokuz Eylül University	15	5..03
Süleyman Demirel University	15	5..03
Muğla Sıtkı Koçman University	10	3..36
Kocaeli University	7	2..35
Uludağ University	6	2..01
Akdeniz University	5	1..68
Anadolu University	5	1..68
Yıldırım Beyazıt University, Ankara	5	1..68
Cumhuriyet University	5	1..68
Pamukkale University	5	1..68
Universities with 5 and more theses written	223	0.75
Universities with fewer than 5 theses written	75	0..25
Grand Total	**298**	**100..00**

[a] With the decree dated 18.05.2018 and numbered 30425 published in the official gazette, No. 7141, with the date of acceptance of 09.05.2018, "Law for Amendments on Some Laws and Decrees with Higher Education law" (with additional Article 183), Hacı Bayram Veli was founded as being a unit of Gazi University. The Department of Labour Economics and Industrial Relations has also moved to the new university.

Tab. 1.6 can be examined in order to express the thesis in the context of the titles and topics covered by the research in short key words and to get an idea of which subjects 298 theses are focused on.

Tab. 1.6 shows that a significant proportion of the studies are concentrated in the field of women's participation in labor markets. In the literature, the labor force participation rate and its determinants are quite important. The labor force participation rate, which represents the relative weight of the total of employees and unemployed in the active population, is very low in Turkey in terms of women. It is not surprising that the subject, which is also on the

Tab. 1.5: Distribution of Graduate Theses with the Keyword "Woman" in the Title between 1986 and 2019 by Subject

CoHE Thesis Detailed Survey Subject Area	Number	Percent (%)
Labor Economics and Industrial Relations	182	61.06
Sociology	30	10.07
Economy	26	8.72
Law	11	3.68
Training and Education	6	2.02
Public Administration	6	2.01
Psychology	6	2.01
Social Services	6	2.01
Econometric	4	1.34
Journalism	2	0.67
Business Administration	2	0.67
Banking	2	0.67
Health Institutions Management	2	0.67
Political Science	2	0.67
International Relations	2	0.67
Demographics	1	0.34
Religion	1	0.34
Home Economics	1	0.34
Public Health	1	0.34
Public Relations	1	0.34
Finance	1	0.34
Insurance	1	0.34
Tourism	1	0.34
Agriculture	1	0.34
Total	**298**	**100.00**

research agenda of the International Labour Organization (ILO) and various international organizations, is also in the first place in written theses. In fact, indicated by separate keywords in the table, labor force and unemployment (which was among studies with a frequency below three), are also related to labor force participation. As a natural result of the selection of the working economy and Industrial Relations theses universe, the theses focus on different aspects of working life. When Tab. 1.6 is examined in general, it is quite common for women's employment and women's participation in working life to be expressed with "problems" or with negative aspects. The "problem," which

Tab. 1.6: Distribution of the Theses with the Keyword "Woman" in Its Title between 1986 and 2019 according to the Keywords Determined by the Author

Keyword	**Number**	**Percent (%)**	**Keyword**	**Number**	**Percent (%)**
Joining The Workforce	13	4.36	Gender and Society	5	1.68
Problem	13	4.36	EU	4	1.34
Poverty	13	4.36	Bank	4	1.34
Union	12	4.03	Maternity	3	1.01
Initiative	10	3.36	Mother	3	1.01
Migration	10	3.36	Divorce	3	1.01
Promoting employment	10	3.36	Gender	3	1.01
Agriculture	9	3.02	Working life	3	1.01
EU	8	2.68	Education	3	1.01
Legal regulations	8	2.68	Informal	3	1.01
Home-axis operation	7	2.35	Home services	3	1.01
Textiles	7	2.35	Business life	3	1.01
Family	6	2.01	Labor	3	1.01
Flexible operation	6	2.01	Women who work in public service	3	1.01
Career	6	2.01	Part-time	3	1.01
Vocational course	6	2.01	Globalization	3	1.01
Violence	6	2.01	Welfare	3	1.01
Business family	5	1.68	Stress	3	1.01
Studies with a frequency of 3 and more				213	71.55
Studies with a frequency below 3				85	28.75
Grand Total				**298**	**100.00**

* The table is based on the statements in the thesis titles.

ranks second in frequency, includes theses about the problems women face in their working life and suggestions for solutions. Following this, the keyword "poverty" is one of the negative things women face. The theses include "taking part in the working life because of poverty and economic difficulties" and "not being able to get out of poverty despite working because the jobs worked are low-paid and have poor working conditions that do not bring high income."

The keywords not included in Tab. 1.6 due to their frequency being lower than three are observed to have a wide range of topics regarding women taking part in the working life and social policies regarding women, such as being an academic, discrimination, glass ceiling, double load, children, emotional labor, feminism, job satisfaction, unemployment, mobbing, and positive psychological capital.

The 298 theses in the scope of the research have been analyzed together, without showing a regard for master's degree or doctorate degree.

As of this part of the study, 91.89 % (34 theses) and 8.11 % (3 theses) of the 37 doctoral theses planned to be examined within the scope of the research were written in English. Since 5 of the 37 doctoral theses could not be accessed in full text, the content analysis for 32 theses was carried out and the results were presented in the following tables and graphs.

Of the theses in Tab. 1.7, 21 (65.63 %) were written under the Department of Labour Economics and Industrial Relations, 9 (28.13 %) are from the "subject" area of the CoHE thesis search page, and one (3.13 %) is from the Department of Human Resources Management and Social Psychology. Of the 32 theses, 30 are in Turkish and 2 are in English.

The 32 doctoral theses provided full text access were read and coded using the MAXQDA Analytics Pro 2018 Qualitative Analysis Program.

Table 1.8 gives the most frequently repeated codes as a result of the qualitative reading of 32 doctoral theses examined within the scope of the research. In this context, 85 codes and 1,209 times were repeated in the documents examined. These codes were examined in relation to the dimensions obtained from the literature and in the third column of Tab. 1.1 to determine cross-theme transitions and it was determined that the dimensions of "family and woman's place in the family institution" and "marriage, children and non-maternal care labor" were covered by the dimension of "free labor, unseen labor, and care labor." It has been assessed that the code of women's problem, which was thought to be included within the dimension expressed as "Improvement of the position of women in society, improvement of material and cultural living conditions (housing, cooperative, etc. the fields included)," is closer to the code of "free labor, care-giving labor, and invisible labor"; and the code expressed as roles is closer to "Feminism" dimension and the code expressed as cooperative is closer to "to participate in working life and economic situation" dimension.

In this study, which has a qualitative pattern, the stages of determining the relevant code and themes, determining the transitions between themes, re-examining and writing the themes in the context of research questions and determined dimensions were also coded by a coder other than the researcher and controlled in terms of validity and reliability. However, since qualitative research has a structure that by its nature cannot be generalized and abstracted

Tab. 1.7: Distribution of Doctoral Theses with the Keyword "Woman" in the Title between 1991 and 2019 by Years and Universities

Year and University	Number	Percent (%)
1991	**1**	**3.13**
Anadolu University	1	3.13
1997	**1**	**3.13**
Selçuk University	1	3.13
2003	**1**	**3.13**
Istanbul University	1	3.13
2008	**1**	**3.13**
Dokuz Eylül University	1	3.13
2009	**3**	**9.38**
Ankara University	1	3.13
Dokuz Eylül University	2	6.25
2011	**1**	**3.13**
Sakarya University	1	3.13
2012	**3**	**9.38**
Ankara University	2	6.25
Marmara University	1	3.13
2014	**1**	**3.13**
Istanbul University	1	3.13
2015	**4**	**12.50**
Dokuz Eylül University	1	3.13
Gazi University	3	9.38
2016	**2**	**6.25**
Ankara University	1	3.13
Sakarya University	1	3.13
2017	**3**	**9.38**
Hacettepe University	1	3.13
Istanbul University	1	3.13
Marmara University	1	3.13
2018	**2**	**6.25**
Suleyman Demirel University	1	3.13
Uludag University	1	3.13
2019	**9**	**28.13**
Anadolu University	1	3.13
Ankara University	2	6.25

(continued on next page)

Tab. 1.7: Continued

Year and University	Number	Percent (%)
Dokuz Eylül University	1	3.13
Gazi University	1	3.13
Ihsan Doğramacı Bilkent University	1	3.13
Middle East Technical University	1	3.13
Sakarya University	1	3.13
Yalova University	1	3.13
Total	**32**	**100.00**

Tab. 1.8: The Most Frequently Repeated Codes in Doctoral Dissertations Written between 1991 and 2019

Code	Number	Percent (%)	Code	Number	Percent (%)
Poverty	157	12.99	Education,	25	2.07
Free labor	47	3.89	E-commerce	23	1.90
The labor force participation rate	43	3.56	Business family life	22	1.82
Feminism	37	3.06	Union	21	1.74
Gender and society	36	2.98	European Union	20	1.65
Information	35	2.89	Human rights	16	1.32
Knowledge	35	2.89	Fordism-Post Fordism	15	1.24
State regulations	35	2.89	Gender	14	1.16
Home-based working	35	2.89	Welfare	14	1.16
Discrimination	34	2.81	Work	13	1.08
Employment	34	2.81	Industrial Revolution	13	1.08
Migration	33	2.73	Family	12	0.99
ILO	31	2.56	Women in legal sense	12	0.99
Patriarchal	30	2.48	Unemployment	12	0.99
Labor economics	30	2.48	Performance	12	0.99
Globalization	29	2.40	Maternity	11	0.91
Non-formal	28	2.32	Career	10	0.84
Flexibility	27	2.23	Technology	10	0.84
Sum of codes with a frequency of 10 and more				1011	83.63
Sum of codes with a frequency below 10				198	16.37
Grand Total				**1209**	**100.00**

Tab. 1.9: Dimensions Obtained from Doctoral Dissertations Written between 1991 and 2019

Dimensions Derived from Code and Themes	Number	Percent (%)
Participation in working life and economic situation	424	35..07
Free labor, unseen labor and care-giving labor	202	16..71
Poverty, migration	190	15..72
International Dimension	98	8..11
Education, widespread education	68	5..62
Feminism	68	5..62
State regulation	61	5..05
Rights	38	3..14
Globalization	29	2..40
Union	21	1..74
Ottoman Empire Era	6	0..50
Definition	4	0..33
Grand Total	**1209**	**100.00**

from researchers' perspectives and readings in the field, when an analysis is performed again with the same theses, differences may arise.

Table 1.9 shows the new situation in which the dimensions of international regulations, globalization, and the working life regulations in the Ottoman Empire period are added and merged, which are not included among the dimensions obtained from the literature.

When Tab. 1.9 is examined, it is seen that the dimension of "participation in working life and economic situation" is the most intensively discussed. This is an expected result due to the database of theses written in the Departments of Labour Economics and Industrial Relations on which the research is based. However, it is noteworthy that "union," which is also relevant to the department, is one of the least addressed dimensions.

In the theses, women working in different sectors such as agriculture, finance and different types of work, stress, poverty, work life balance, job satisfaction, and emotional labor are discussed. In the theses, while the negative effects taking place in the labor market on women who bear a double load were studied more extensively, it was emphasized that the welfare level of women with higher education level is higher. There are jobs in which women can increase their productive capacity through home-based work, entrepreneurship, co-operatives, as well as jobs in which women in informal sectors could be identified as working poor due to the dual nature of the labor market as much as good jobs.

The different views of women's labor are addressed in very different forms, such as paid labor, unpaid labor, unseen labor, care-giving labor, secondary labor, etc.

The dimension of "free labor, unseen labor, and caregiving labor" is the dimension regarding gender and patriarchal themes and codes that emphasize the role of woman as wife and mother. As the theses in question were written under the Departments of Labour Economics and Industrial Relations, all of these issues are covered within a framework of women's working life.

The international foundation of relevant legislation and applied policies about women's participation in the working life are European Social Charter, ILO conventions and recommendations, to the activities of the United Nations.

"Education, widespread education" is a form of education in which women enter labor markets and work in jobs that are paid higher and offer them better working conditions. Within the scope of nonformal education, a good position can be achieved in the labor markets through vocational training and becoming a professional.

Under the title of "Ottoman Empire Period," the legal regulations in the relevant period and the place of women in working life are emphasized.

The dimension called "Definition" deals with definitions and concepts that are used in the expected way because the documents being examined are doctoral thesis.

The word cloud image, which consists of the most frequently repeated words in the studies researched, also allows to see all the codes in a single image.

Figure 1.1 contains the word cloud created from the word frequencies used in all 298 theses without distinction between master's and doctorate.

Since the word cloud was linked to the main subject of the study when it was formed, the most frequently repeated word was found to be "female," and was subsequently left out of the word cloud.

Alongside the word cloud above that covers all theses in general, the word cloud created from the codes contained in the doctoral theses studied is included in Fig. 1.2.

Word cloud images often allow us to see the explanations that can be expressed in many pages in a single picture. It has been used quite frequently in qualitative studies in recent years. This research also includes descriptions and statements as well as word cloud visuals.

Fig. 1.1: Word cloud derived from the theses included in the research.In its simplest definition, a word cloud is an aesthetic image of text, where words come together in mixed forms. The dimensions of the words in the visual also vary according to how often a word is used in the analyzed database. (Created by the author).

Fig. 1.2: Word cloud derived from doctoral dissertations included in the research (Created by the author).

5 Conclusion

Since the field of social policy with the most general definition is a whole of measures focusing on the solution of problems based mainly on paid labor relations and continues its academic development within the Departments of Labour Economics and industrial relations within the university structure in Turkey, it has been attempted in this research to explore under which key words, themes and dimensions the subject of "women and social policy" is taken into account.

The Departments of Labour Economics and Industrial Relations have a special place in the higher education system with its structure that takes the changing and transforming working life, emerging new forms of work and new concepts into the field of academic review, based on the tradition of social politics that started before the university reform of 1933–1934.

In the research carried out, traces of current and multidimensional structures were observed in both Master's and doctoral theses. It is in the background of almost all theses that the process of globalization has significantly affected labor markets as it has in all areas of society. Similarly, all studies referred to international institutions and organizations and the use of international experience in law, regulations, and applied policies. The theses are expected to include national and international developments. Similarly, definitions and concepts are included in a wide range of findings and are compatible with expectations. Contrary to expectations, trade unions, which are the foundations of Labour Economics and Industrial Relations departments, are limited in their work on the representation of women in trade unions.

Gender-based discrimination is based on male-female inequality, which places women in secondary positions both in social life and in labor markets, with intensive free labor provision, often making them the sole provider of home-based forms of work and home-care labor.

As is often emphasized in the research theses, education and vocational training, which will enable women to be better positioned in the labor market, are very important. The construction of gender, which is slightly highlighted in the thesis, and concepts of women and womanhood expressed as "women in language" are taken up under the major branches of science "Women's Research," "Women's Studies," and "Women's Studies and Gender" within the scope of "the Centre of Research and Practice of Women's Problems"[6] in 16

6 http://kasaum.ankara.edu.tr/?page_id=47 (21.07.2020).

universities in Turkey as of July 16, 2020. In the postgraduate theses written in this department during the course of this research, gender-based citizenship, violence, women in films, TV series, and novels, women's movements, privacy, activism, body image, sexual profile, feminine language, eco-feminism, ecological balance, patriarchy, masculinity, gender construction, and feminism types are studied intensively.[7]

The theses examined within the scope of the research showed that there are a wide range of topics, from domestic violence to the problems of women working in tea agriculture and their position in working life, in accordance with the broad use of social policy. However, it is of course important for women to take part in the working life, the double role they are assigned, and sometimes even more than two roles, and the problems they face both in the household and in the work life to be addressed in academic studies. More importantly, it is important that the knowledge created in academia can be disseminated in a way that is beneficial to social life, in the most common words, "not stay on dusty shelves." The work done by scholars on the subject of women and of social policy areas, and research about these works by relevant civil society organizations and policy makers in an effective manner, is one of the most important activities that needs to be done in this area.

References

Acar, A. (1995). İktisadi Faaliyetlerde Kadınların Üretici Faaliyetlerinin "Görünmezliği" Sorunu. *Sosyal Siyaset Konferansları Dergisi*, 0(40), 195–202. https://dergipark.org.tr/tr/pub/iusskd/issue/918/10370 (17.07.2020).

Akan, T. (2011). Sosyoloji, Politika ve Ekonomi (SPE) Bölümlerine Doğru: Çalışma Ekonomisi ve Endüstri İlişkileri Bölümlerinin Yeniden Yapılanmasına İlişkin Bir Model Önerisi. *İş, Güç Endüstri İlişkileri ve İnsan Kaynakları Dergisi*, 3, 30–48. http://www.isguc.org/?p=article&id=463&cilt=13&sayi=3&yil=2011 (15.07.2020).

Akgeyik, T. (2016). Türkiye'de Kadınların İşgücü Piyasasına Katılımını Etkileyen Faktörler: TÜİK Verileri Üzerine Bir Analiz. *Sosyal Siyaset Konferansları Dergisi*, (70), 31–53. https://dergipark.org.tr/tr/pub/iusskd/issue/33511/372379 (17.07.2020).

7 The detailed survey on the CoHE thesis screening page showed that 383 graduate theses were written within the scope of "Women's Studies" and "Women's Studies and Gender" main disciplines.

Altan, Ö. Z. (2017). Prof. Dr. Ömer Zühtü Altan, *Türkiye'de Sosyal Politikanın Çınarları* (Ed. Banu Uçkan), 1–47, Legal Yayıncılık: İstanbul.

Arol, M. (1950). Çalışan Kadınların Durumu. *Sosyal Siyaset Konferansları Dergisi*, 0(3), 85–102. https://dergipark.org.tr/tr/pub/iusskd/issue/926/10482 (11.06.2020).

Büyükcoşkun, S. (2018). Kadın İstihdamının Ortaya Çıkardığı Anne-dışı Bakım Sorunu ve Türkiye'nin Kadın İstihdamı Politikasının Muhtemel Sonuçları. *Sosyal Siyaset Konferansları Dergisi*, (73), 85–105. https://dergipark.org.tr/tr/pub/iusskd/issue/36332/414301 (19.05.2020).

Davutoğu, A. (2015). Türkiye'de İkinci Dalga Feminizmin Etkisi ve Sosyal Siyaset Konferansları Dergisi'nde Gülten Kutal'ın İlk Kadın İstihdamı Makalesi. *Sosyal Siyaset Konferansları Dergisi*, (69), 159–174. https://dergipark.org.tr/tr/pub/iusskd/issue/33251/370122 (05.03.2020).

Dumont, R. (1984). Gelişme ve Artan Kıtlık: Kadınların Rolü Ne Olmalı? Çev. (Ekin, N.). *Sosyal Siyaset Konferansları Dergisi*, 0(33), 329–336. https://dergipark.org.tr/tr/pub/iusskd/issue/933/10529 (11.06.2020).

Erdut, Z. (2004). Liberal Ekonomi Politikaları ve Sosyal Politika, *Çalışma ve Toplum*, 2, 11–37.

Erkul, İ. (1983). *Sosyal Politika Dersleri, TC.* Anadolu Üniversitesi Yayınları: Eskişehir.

Esin, P. (1982). *İş Bölümü, Yabancılaşma ve Sosyal Politika-Kuramsal Bir Yaklaşım.* Ankara Üniversitesi Siyasal Bilgiler Fakültesi Ya. No. 502, Ankara.

Güven, E. (1972). *Sosyal Politika Ders Notları.* EİTA Yayınları: Eskişehir. http://kasaum.ankara.edu.tr/?page_id=47 (21.07.2020).

Koray, M. & Topçuoğlu, A. (1987). *Sosyal Politika*, Karınca Matbaacılık: İzmir.

Koray, M. (2003). *Sosyal Politika*, (2. Baskı), İmge Kitabevi: Ankara.

Kumaş, H. & Fidan, F. (2005). Akademisyen ve Tekstil İşçileri Karşılaştırması Örneğinde Çalışan Kadınların Çalışma Olgusuna Bakışları. *Sosyal Siyaset Konferansları Dergisi*, 0(50), 507–532. https://dergipark.org.tr/tr/pub/iusskd/issue/891/9928 (04.02.2020).

Kutal, G. (1992). Türkiye'de İstihdamın Yapısında Kadın İşgücü. *Sosyal Siyaset Konferansları Dergisi*, 0(37–38), 45–61. https://dergipark.org.tr/tr/pub/iusskd/issue/921/10404 (10.06.2020).

Özgüler, V. (2020). Türkiye'de Çalışma Ekonomisi ve Endüstri İlişkileri Lisansüstü Tezlerinin "Sosyal Politika" Bağlamında Değerlendirilmesi. *Sosyal Siyaset Konferansları Dergisi*, (78), 1–45. https://dergipark.org.tr/tr/pub/iusskd/issue/53124/708386 (01.06.2020).

Özkaplan, N. & Selamoğlu, A. (2005), Amerika Birleşik Devletleri'nde Çalışma Ekonomisi ve Endüstri İlişkileri Eğitimi Üzerine, *İş, Güç Endüstri İlişkileri ve İnsan Kaynakları Dergisi*, 7(1). http://www.isguc.org/?p=article&id=235&cilt=7&sayi=1&yil=2005 (06.05.2020).

Şahin, H., Çiftyıldız, K. & Evkaya, C. (2018). Göç Kararında Kadın İradesinin Belirleyiciliği: Genç Kızların Köyden Kente Göç Etme Fırsatına Çevirmesi. *Sosyal Siyaset Konferansları Dergisi*, (75), 211–235. https://dergipark.org.tr/tr/pub/iusskd/issue/41800/504515 (03.04.2020).

Tokol, A. (1997). *Sosyal Politika*, Uludağ Üniversitesi: Bursa.

Tuna, O. & Yalçıntaş, N. (2011). *Sosyal Siyaset.*Filiz Kitabevi: İstanbul.

TurkStat (2019). Adrese Dayalı Nüfus Kayıt Sistemi Sonuçları, 2019. http://www.tuik.gov.tr/PreHaberBultenleri.do?id=33705 (04.02.2020).

Urhan, B. (2015). Sendika İçi Demokrasi ve Sendika İçi Kadın Örgütlenmesi. *Sosyal Siyaset Konferansları Dergisi*, (69), 29–58. https://dergipark.org.tr/tr/pub/iusskd/issue/33251/370114 (27.03.2020).

Uşan, M. (2005). İş Kanununun İş Sağlığı ve Güvenliği İle Kadın, Çocuk ve Genç İşçileri İlgilendiren Hükümlerinin Değerlendirilmesi. *Sosyal Siyaset Konferansları Dergisi*, 0(50), https://dergipark.org.tr/tr/pub/iusskd/issue/891/9933 (12.02.2020).

Yüksel, H. (2014). Küreselleşme Sürecinin Sosyal Politika Dinamikleri Üzerinde Neden Olduğu Değişimin Analizi . *Süleyman Demirel Üniversitesi Sosyal Bilimler Enstitüsü Dergisi* , (19) , 127–151

Internet Resources

80.251.40.59/education.ankara.edu.tr/aksoy/eay/eay/b0506/ymetin.doc (04.05.2019).

http://kasaum.ankara.edu.tr/?page_id=47 (21.07.2020).

https://tez.yok.gov.tr/UlusalTezMerkezi/tezSorguSonucYeni.jsp (20.07.2020).

https://www.nadirkitap.com/kitapara_sonuc.php?kelime=%22sosyal%20politika%22&siralama=yayinyiliaz&bks=181&page=2 (18.07.2020).

Yeliz Yeşil

Women Education and Women Employment

1 Introduction

Education is an important factor in solving the unemployment problem, which is one of the most important problems faced by countries in the globalization process, and in increasing employment. Education contributes to the development of societies and provides individuals with the necessary knowledge and skills for the continuation of social life. It plays an important role in the development of countries. In order to realize the development and industrialization process in accordance with the conditions of the age, the need for qualified and highly skilled labor is required. For this, it is essential to establish a solid relationship between education and employment.

Also education is necessary for economic and social development, and all citizens should benefit equally from education in the country. Gender inequalities should be eliminated. Women's positions in economic, social, cultural and political life should be strengthened. Education of women is important to be successful in tackling poverty and to achieve country development.

In this study, the importance of education, women education and women employment will be analyzed and future inferences will be made.

2 Education and the Benefits of Education

Education has an important share in meeting the needs of the individual to survive, improve herself/himself, become a member of the society and live in harmony with the society. This situation raises the need and right of every person to be educated. Having a right is one of the criteria of being human. The freedom of human is possible by using his rights fully and equally. Until the 19th century, education right of the man was recognized only to the nobility who held the administration; the idea of educating the people started with the French Revolution of 1789. Education right has been included in the documents more broadly such as the Universal Declaration of Human Rights, the basic principles of the United Nations Educational, Scientific, Cultural Organization (UNESCO) and the Council of Europe etc. (Özaydınlık, 2014).

In order to invest in people and prepare individuals for the future, education is necessary. By the help of the education, education–employment relationship can be established and disadvantaged groups' participation in economic and social life can be supported (Yeşil, 2019: 776).

Also according to Yeşil and Tokbaş (2018), education activities are important, because individuals who are educated in their profession and who like their profession are more productive and successful in business life, so in order to find a job, individuals must have a sufficient level of education (Yeşil, 2020: 202).

Generally, education is investment in human capital as a lasting legacy since it requires the individual with the knowledge and skills needed. Education makes an individual more productive in whatever economic activities he/she undertakes (Egbe-Okpenge & Orhungur, 2012), so education can provide the development of countries, because education has many effects such as developing awareness, providing an understanding of problems and helping progress (Mieczysław & Yeşil, 2020).

In addition to this, education is not only a prerequisite for a productive and quality life, but also an effective means of change in both social and individual contexts, and a key to minimizing inequalities between social groups and genders (Bingöl, 2019). Women need to get rid of their secondary position in social life, and education plays an important role in achieving equal opportunities for men. Any quantitative and qualitative progress in women's education provides significant economic and sociocultural gains. For this reason, advances in women's education have very positive consequences for the empowerment of women in social, cultural, psychological, economic and legal positions and taking a decisive role in society, although they are still behind men in many respects (Tor & Ağlı, 2016). Also with educational activities, individuals can develop their knowledge, skills and experience, and individuals are directed to the areas where they will be successful (Yeşil, 2015).

3 The Importance of Women Education

UNESCO's World Atlas of Gender Equality in Education published in 2012 provides a vast amount of statistical information about where women and men are as students across the globe, relating the information to international criteria. It is quite clear from the publication of a global atlas that education is a vital ingredient of economies today and that the goal of universal education for all is fast becoming a reality (David, 2015).

In order for a country to achieve sustainable development, women need economic and social empowerment. On the other hand, developments in today's world make it important to sustain and strengthen human values. Therefore, if women get stronger, they will add strength to future generations. Therefore, women's empowerment and access to their individual rights and interests are a vital goal in terms of strengthening our family and social structure (Kadın Güçlenmesi Strateji Belgesi ve Eylem Planı 2018–2023).

It is extremely important for women to take equal advantage of educational opportunities and possibilities at all levels in taking an active role in social life. Article 10, which regulates CEDAW's right to education, obliges states to take all measures to prevent discrimination against women in order to ensure that they have equal rights in education. In addition, with the documents accepted as a result of the Fourth World Women Conference (Pekin Declaration and Action Plan), 12 critical areas have been determined to take action for the advancement and empowerment of women and one of these critical areas is "Women and Education." Turkey attended the Pekin Action Plan and international commitments such as the Sustainable Development Goals; they reveal that countries should make all the arrangements to ensure that women and girls have equal rights in education (http://www.sbb.gov.tr/wp-content/uploads/2020/04/KadininKalkinmadakiRoluOzelIhtisasKomisyonuRaporu.pdf).

In addition, the education mechanism plays a key role in ending the reproduction of possible inequalities, both through the information processes offered at school and within the cultural climate offered by the school. The right to education is guaranteed to all, without discrimination, with the provisions of article 42 of our Constitution, "nobody can be deprived of the right to education and education, and primary education is compulsory for all citizens and girls, and is free of charge in public schools" (http://www.sp.gov.tr/upload/xSPTemelBelge/files/RySPo+KADININ_GUCLENMESI_STRATEJI_BELGESI_VE_EYLEM_PLANI_2018-2023_.pdf).

Additionally, there are some reasons why women should get an education. They are (Madu, 2013):

- Future Educated Generations: An African proverb says, "If we educate a boy, we educate one person. If we educate a girl, we educate a family – and a whole nation." By sending a girl to school, she is far more likely to ensure that her children also receive an education. Investing in a girl's education is investing in a nation.
- Decrease Infant Mortality: Children of educated women are less likely to die before their first birthday. Primary education alone helps reduce infant mortality significantly, and secondary education helps even more.

- Decrease Maternal Mortality: Educated women (with greater knowledge of health care and fewer pregnancies) are less likely to die during pregnancy, childbirth or during the postpartum period. Increased education of girls also leads to more female health-care providers to assist with prenatal medical care, labor and delivery, delivery complications and emergencies, and follow-up care.
- Decrease Child Marriage: Child marriage – in some cases involving girls as young as 6 or 8 – almost always results in the end of a girl's schooling. The result is illiterate or barely literate young mothers without adequate tools to build healthy, educated families. Educated girls typically marry later, when they are better able to bear and care for their children.
- Decrease Population Explosion: Educated women tend to have fewer (and healthier) babies.
- Increase Involvement in Political Process: Educated women are more likely to participate in political discussions, meetings, and decision-making, which in turn promotes a more representative, effective government.
- Decrease Domestic and Sexual Violence: Educated girls and women are less likely to be victims of domestic and sexual violence or to tolerate it in their families.
- Improve Socioeconomic Growth: Educated women have a greater chance of escaping poverty, leading healthier and more productive lives, and raising the standard of living for their children, families and communities.

In addition, educating girls today will also help future populations. According to UNESCO data, if all females in developing countries completed primary education, child mortality would drop by a sixth, saving nearly one million lives annually. Also, maternal deaths, which the U.N. vows are largely preventable, would reduce by two-thirds. Schools can provide girls with life skills, reproductive health knowledge and a social space to discuss issues (Bysiewicz, 2018).

4 Women Education in Turkey

Various campaigns, initiatives and projects have been implemented in our country in recent years within the framework of ensuring gender equality in education and 100 % enrollment in primary education. Especially in 2004 and beyond, projects and campaigns carried out by both state institutions and nongovernmental organizations and media leaders are all examples of good practice and each addressed girls' access to school in a different dimension. Education campaigns have been launched through the Ministry of National

Education, UNICEF, UNESCO, ILO, nongovernmental organizations, media, private institutions and organizations. Some of the campaigns have been concluded and some are still ongoing (Özaydınlık, 2014).

According to the National Education Statistics Database results, between 2008 and 2018, it has been observed that the proportion of people aged 25 and over and completing at least one education level in the total population has increased over the years. The proportion of individuals aged 25 and over who completed at least one education level in the total population was 81.1 % in 2008 and 90.1 % in 2018. When the proportion of those who have completed at least one education level is examined by gender, the ratio, which was 72.6 % in women and 89.8 % in men in 2008, was 84.5 % and 95.9 %, respectively, in 2018. The proportion of the population aged 25 and over, which is the least university graduate, in the total population was 9.8 % in 2008 and 19.9 % in 2018. When this ratio is analyzed by gender, in 2008, the proportion of women aged 25 and over who were at least university graduates was 7.6 %, while the rate of men was 12.1 %, this rate was 17.5 % for women and 22.4 % for men (https://www.alomaliye.com/2020/03/06/2019-istatistiklerle-kadin/).

As seen in the table, women's participation in formal and non-formal education is lower than men. In our country, in addition to the lifelong learning activities carried out by the Ministry of National Education through schools/institutions providing vocational and technical education, nongovernmental organizations offer literacy, skills and vocational courses for women; municipalities organize similar courses free of charge. Multi-Purpose Community Center (ÇATOMs) affiliated to the Southeastern Anatolia Project (GAP) Administration, the General Directorate of Turkish Employment Agency (İŞKUR) and organizations affiliated to the ministry are located in similar activities (https://www.ailevecalisma.gov.tr/media/6315/kad%C4%B1n%C4%B1n-gue%C3%A7lenmesi-strajesi-belgesi-ve-eylem-plan%C4%B1-2018-2023.pdf).

Tab. 2.1: Participation in Education and Training by Sex, Age Group, Education Attained and Labor Status – Population Age 18 and Over

	Participation in Formal Education			**Participation in Nonformal Education**		
	2007	**2012**	**2016**	**2007**	**2012**	**2016**
Male	7.2	9.8	10.9	17.3	17.5	19.8
Female	4.5	6.8	8.0	10.5	13.4	13.8

Source: http://tuikweb.tuik.gov.tr/PreTablo.do?alt_id=1018

5 Women Employment in Turkey

Women's position is essential among other disadvantaged groups. Increasing employment opportunities for women is likely to create significant progressing terms of providing gender equality. Barriers against women's access to equal education and economic opportunities with men need to be eliminated. Improving women's status is critical for development and ensuring gender equality. For the achievement of economic and social development in any country, men and women should have equal access to rights and opportunities (Yeşil, 2020: 291). The active role of women in the economy makes them more active in the society and increase their confidence. Women living in rural areas need to be supported in order to do their jobs better and obtain economic independence (Fidan et al., 2017; Yeşil, 2018a: 94).

Also it is essential to increase women employment for struggling with poverty. Increasing the participation of women in their working life and strengthening their social and economic strength are important for the development of the country's economy. Also women employment is significant for economic growth (Yeşil, 2018a; Yeşil & Fidan, 2019).

In addition to this, the Turkish Employment Agency (İŞKUR) maintains a firm belief in the potential of women's employment and entrepreneurship for catching up with the economically advanced countries and continues to pursue its efforts to this end with deep commitment, making use of innovative approaches. İŞKUR plays an important role in developing and implementing both active and passive employment policies in Turkey, and its activities and services in this area are improving day by day. The Agency stands at the center of national policies, and is at the same time engaged in a continuous process of change and transformation in line with its results-based management approach (https://www.ilo.org/wcmsp5/groups/public/---europe/---ro-geneva/---ilo-ankara/documents/publication/wcms_484714.pdf).

Tab. 2.2: Basic Labor Indicators Not Adjusted for Seasonal Effects, 15+ Years Old (1,000 People), March 2019 and March 2020

	Total		Male		Female	
	2019	**2020**	**2019**	**2020**	**2019**	**2020**
Labor force participation rate (%)	52.9	48.4	71.7	67.1	34.4	30.1
Employment rate (%)	45.4	42.0	62.4	58.6	28.8	25.8
Unemployment rate (%)	14.1	13.2	13.0	12.7	16.2	14.3
Nonagricultural unemployment rate (%)	16.1	15.0	14.5	14.1	19.8	17.1

Source: http://www.tuik.gov.tr/PreHaberBultenleri.do?id=33787

Tab. 2.3: Basic Labor Indicators Not Adjusted for Seasonal Effects, 15–64 Years (%), March 2019 and March 2020

	Total		Male		Female	
	2019	**2020**	**2019**	**2020**	**2019**	**2020**
Labor force participation rate (%)	58.4	53.7	77.9	73.2	38.8	34.1
Employment rate (%)	50.0	46.5	67.5	63.7	32.4	29.2
Unemployment rate (%)	14.3	13.5	13.3	13.0	16.5	14.5
Nonagricultural unemployment rate (%)	16.2	15.1	14.5	14.2	19.9	17.2

Source: http://www.tuik.gov.tr/PreHaberBultenleri.do?id=33787

As seen in the table, women's labor force participation rate, employment rate are lower than men for 15+ years old.

As seen in the table, women's labor force participation rate, employment rate are lower than men for 15–64 years.

6 The Importance of Women Education for Women Employment

Generally the aims of training activities are women development, strengthening women, increasing women consciousness, increasing production, women's having job and increasing women participation into economy (Yeşil et al., 2016; Yeşil, 2018b: 274).

Today, education is important to catch rapid change and development. Education is necessary for the individual to survive, improve himself and live in harmony with society. There may be problems in exercising the right to education. Also the problems related to the education of women continued in the historical process. The education of women is indispensable for the development of the country.

Strengthening women contributes to making jobs more economically, more effective and sustainable, also women can increase their self-confidence and their position in society. By improving women entrepreneurship, women employment can be increased in the job market, also women can adapt to change and development (Fidan et al., 2015; Yeşil, 2018b: 274).

According to Riaz and Pervaiz (2018)'s study, both women's education and employment play an important role in women empowerment. Educated women are more likely to participate in decision making regarding their own health care, major household purchases, spending of household earnings and decision regarding contraceptive use as compared to uneducated women.

Tab. 2.4: Labor Force Status by Educational Attainment, March 2019 and March 2020 [15+ – Age] (Labor Force Participation Rate)

	Labor Force Participation Rate					
Educational Attainment	**Total**		**Male**		**Female**	
Total	52.9	48.4	71.7	67.1	34.4	30.1
Illiterate	18.1	13.8	32.4	24.4	15.2	11.6
Less than high school	48.0	43.0	67.7	62.1	27.7	23.3
High school	55.4	49.2	71.5	65.9	36.5	29.9
Vocational high school	64.8	60.2	80.9	77.3	40.9	35.5
Higher education	80.4	75.1	86.2	83.4	73.7	65.7

Source: www.tuik.gov.tr

Tab. 2.5: Labor Force Status by Educational Attainment, March 2019 and March 2020 [15+ – Age] (Employment Rate)

	Employment Rate					
Educational Attainment	**Total**		**Male**		**Female**	
Total	45.4	42.0	62.4	58.6	28.8	25.8
Illiterate	15.7	12.1	24.9	19.0	13.8	10.7
Less than high school	41.5	37.2	58.4	53.2	24.0	20.6
High school	46.5	41.6	62.2	57.5	28.1	23.3
Vocational high school	55.0	51.5	71.4	67.8	30.6	28.0
Higher education	69.5	66.7	76.7	75.9	61.1	56.2

Source: www.tuik.gov.tr

Additionally, according to Habib et al.'s (2019) study; education and employment have high significant positive relationship with women empowerment in decision-making, control over the resources and voice. Education helps women get employment, and employment makes them financially independent and economically strong, which then leads to their empowerment. When women are empowered, they reach out and empower other women.

As can be seen in the table, as the education level of women increases, the labor force participation rates increase.

As can be seen in the table, as the education level of women increases, the employment rates increase.

7 Results and Evaluation

The rapid structural and economic changes that are taking place globally bring with them the process of transition to an information society. While increasing the importance of globalization and international standards, this transition also has a direct impact on employment. Unemployment, the underlying problem of our day, is the root cause not only of economic problems but also of many social and political challenges. The use of active employment policies aimed at increasing women's employment in combating employment is of vital importance for countries seeking to achieve sustainable development in the century in which we live. It is apparent that women's participation in the labor force, the economy and the world of entrepreneurship is not only desirable, but essential. All the indicators on which economic dynamics are based show that women's participation in the economy through employment or entrepreneurship constitutes the basic building block of our country's efforts to "take her place among the ten largest economies of the world in 2023" (https://www.ilo.org/wcmsp5/groups/public/---europe/---ro-geneva/---ilo-ankara/documents/publication/wcms_484714.pdf).

Gender discrimination prevents the realization of social and economic development. Ensuring gender equality is important for women's empowerment. Policies and programs that achieve gender equality must be produced for an egalitarian social structure. All state plans and programs should be strengthened gender equality and empowerment of women and girls in society. It should be ensured that women take advantage of decision-making mechanisms and education rights on an equal basis with men.

Countries need to end all forms of discrimination against women in order to achieve sustainable development. It is also important to remove regional differences between men and women. In addition, developing inclusive and innovative policies should be evaluated in order to reach the targets. In addition, measures should be taken to ensure the active participation of girls who have completed their vocational and technical education in employment. Besides, schooling, attendance and completion rates should be followed.

Particularly attention should be given to the education of girls and women living in rural areas. In addition, conditional education aids should be expanded and applied throughout the education life. Family-oriented training on girls' education needs to be increased. It is important to increase the support for children who have been married and have children to continue their education. Also, eliminating the differences in terms of the quality of education provided in higher education institutions and efforts to improve the quality of education need to continue. Vocational training courses should be continued to increase the participation of women in the workforce.

Also effective and efficient implementation of education and training programs should be ensured at all levels of education to raise awareness about gender equality. In order to provide education on gender equality in higher education, curricula can be changed and academic programs can be created. The proportion of illiterate women should be clearly determined.

In addition to this, necessary analyzes should be determined by determining the reasons such as early marriage, child labor and domestic work related to gender inequality that cause women and girls to go out of formal education. The efficiency of the education system should be measured.

In the provinces where early and forced marriages are high and girls have low schooling rates, social assistance and scholarship opportunities should be expanded. In order to prevent early marriages and forced marriages, families who do not send their girls to school should be sanctioned if necessary.

Also the studies on the needs of disabled women and girls, access to school and absenteeism should be carried out. Trainings providing vocational skills that will create nonagricultural employment areas for women in rural areas should be expanded. Entrepreneurship trainings for women should continue, especially in rural areas.

Distance education for women who work to gain computer skills can be expanded. In addition, activities to support and strengthen working women can be increased. Trainings can be provided for women to be included in the digitalization process to benefit from e-citizenship and similar electronic environment. As a result, it is very important to give a special importance to the education of women and girls in the society and to continue increasing the studies carried out in recent years.

References

Bingöl, U. (2019). Türk İşgücü Piyasasında Genç İşsizliği İle Mücadele Konseptinin Onbirinci Kalkınma Planı, Eğitim 2023 Vizyonu Ve Ulusal İstihdam Stratejisi Çerçevesinde Değerlendirilmesi. In Yavuz Kağan Yasım (Ed.), *İşgücü Piyasasında Dezavantajlı Gruplar* (pp. 143–165). Ankara: Türk Metal Sendikası Araştırma ve Eğitim Merkezi.

Bysiewicz, I. (2018). Importance of Girls' Education around the World, retrieved from https://borgenproject.org/importance-of-girls-education/#:~:text=Schools%20can%20provide%20girls%20with,a%20priority%20for%20her%20children (Accessed May 20, 2020).

David, M.E. (2015). Women and Gender Equality in Higher Education?, *Education Sciences*, 5, 10–25.

Egbe-Okpenge, E.G. & Orhungur, M.M. (2012). Gender Issues in Entrepreneurial Development in Benue State (Nigeria) and Counseling Implications. *Bulgarian Journal of Science and Education Policy (BJSEP)*, 6(2), 386–397.

Fidan, F., Yeşil, Y. & Arpat, B. (2015). Türkiye'de Kadın Girişimciliğini Geliştirmede Eğitim Faaliyetleri, 5.Uluslararası Kadın ve Toplumsal Cinsiyet Araştırmaları Konferansı, 25–27 Mart 2015, Gazi Magusa, KKTC.

Fidan, F., Yeşil, Y. & Karasu, F. (2017). Kadın Çiftçilerin Sosyo-Ekonomik Güçlenmesinde Eğitimin Rolü. *Uşak Üniversitesi Sosyal Bilimler Dergisi/ UUSBD*, 10(3), 409–437.

Habib, K., Shafiq, M., Afshan, G. & Qamar, F. (2019). Impact of Education and Employment on Women Empowerment. *European Online Journal of Natural and Social Sciences*, 8(3), 62–74.

Kadın Güçlenmesi Strateji Belgesi ve Eylem Planı 2018–2023, retrieved from https://www.ailevecalisma.gov.tr/ksgm/ulusal-eylem-planlari/kadinin-guclenmesi-strateji-belgesi-ve-eylem-plani-2018-2023/ (Accessed June 17, 2020).

Madu, C.F. (2013). Why We Should Support Girls' Education, retrieved from https://www.voicesofyouth.org/blog/why-we-should-support-girls-education#:~:text=IMPROVE%20SOCIOECONOMIC%20GROWTH%3A%20Educated%20women,children%2C%20families%2C%20and%20communities (Accessed May 17, 2020).

Mieczysław, M. & Yeşil, Y. (2020). Comparing the Activities to Improve the Quality of Unıversity Education between Poland and Turkey. *Journal of Social and Humanities Sciences Research*, 7(53), 1147–1157.

Özaydınlık, K. (2014). Toplumsal Cinsiyet Temelinde Türkiye'de Kadın ve Eğitim. *Sosyal Politika Çalışmaları Dergisi*, 14(33), 93–112.

Riaz, S. & Pervaiz, Z. (2018). The Impact of Women's Education and Employment on Their Empowerment: An Empirical Evidence from Household Level Survey. *Quality & Quantity*, 52, 2855–2870.

Tor, H., & Ağlı, E. (2016). Kadın ve Eğitim. *Eğitim ve Öğretim Araştırmaları Dergisi*, 5(Özel Sayı), 67–74.

Yeşil, Y. (2015). Kobilerde Eğitim ve Geliştirmenin Örgütsel Bağlılıkla İlişkisi: Çerkezköy Organize Sanayi Bölgesi'nde Bir Araştırma. Sakarya Üniversitesi Sosyal Bilimler Enstitüsü, Doktora Tezi, Sakarya.

Yeşil, Y. (2018a). Analyzing "Neighborhood houses" Which Are Applied by Çerkezköy Municipality: Veliköy Neighborhood Case. In E.Torun Gerçek & Ş. Gerçek (Eds.), Contemporary Debates In Social Sciences (pp. 93–103). İstanbul: Ijopec Publication.

Yeşil, Y. (2018b). The Importance of the Development of Women Cooperatives in Turkey and Analyzing The Activities about Women Cooperatives' Development in the Recent Years. In M.K.Namal, M. Koçancı & M. Karataş (Eds.), *Strategic Researches II: From Local to Global, Working Life and Social Policy* (pp. 258–279). İstanbul: Ijopec Publication.

Yeşil, Y. (2019). İnsan Kaynaklarının Geliştirilmesi Operasyonel Programının Önceliklerine Göre Değerlendirilmesi. In Z. Gölen & H. Babacan (Eds.), *Sosyal, Beşeri ve İdari Bilimlerde Akademik Çalışmalar-2019/2* (pp. 775–788). Cetinje: IVPE, Stamparıja.

Yeşil, Y. (2020). Assessment of the Importance of Vocational Education: Investment in Human and Employment. In Abdullah Bağcıoğulları (Ed.), *Current Studies in Social Sciences* (pp. 199–207). Ankara: Akademisyen Kitabevi A.Ş.

Yeşil, Y. & Fidan, F. (2019).The Importance of Entrepreneurship Training Activities for Increasing Women Employment in Turkey. In C. Akar & H. Kapucu (Eds.), *Contemporary Challenges in Business and Life Sciences* (pp. 175–180). İstanbul: Ijopec Publication.

Yeşil, Y. & Tokbaş, M. (2018). Mesleki Eğitimde Öğrencilerin Motivasyonlarının ve Beklentilerinin İncelenmesi: Honaz meslek yüksekokulu'nda bir araştırma. *Elektronik Sosyal Bilimler Dergisi*, 17(67), 938–948.

Yeşil, Y., Karasu, F. & Alpaslan, K. (2016). Amacı, İçeriği ve Yararlılığı Bağlamında Türkiye'de Kadın Kooperatiflerinin Eğitim Faaliyetleri. *Akademik Sosyal Araştırmalar Dergisi*, 4(35), 501–512.

Internet Resources

2019 İstatistiklerle Kadın, retrieved from https://www.alomaliye.com/2020/03/06/2019-istatistiklerle-kadin/ (Accessed June 7, 2020).

Action Plan on Women's Employment, retrieved from https://www.ilo.org/wcmsp5/groups/public/---europe/---ro-geneva/---ilo-ankara/documents/publication/wcms_484714.pdf (Accessed June 17, 2020).

İşgücü İstatistikleri, Mart 2020, retrieved from http://www.tuik.gov.tr/PreHaberBultenleri.do?id=33787 (Accessed July 3, 2020).

Kadının Güçlenmesi Strateji Belgesi ve Eylem Planı. (2018–2023), retrieved from https://www.ailevecalisma.gov.tr/media/6315/kad%C4%B1n%C4%B1n-gue%C3%A7lenmesi-strajesi-belgesi-ve-eylem-plan%C4%B1-2018-2023.pdf (Accessed June 13, 2020).

On Birinci Kalkınma Planı (2019–2023) Kadının Kalkınmadaki Rolü, retrieved from http://www.sbb.gov.tr/wp-content/uploads/2020/04/KadininKalkinmadakiRoluOzelIhtisasKomisyonuRaporu.pdf (Accessed July 3, 2020).

Türkiye İstatistik Kurumu, retrieved from www.tuik.gov.tr (Accessed July 3, 2020).

Section 2 Career-Based Researches for Women in Labor Markets

Gaye Özçelik

Women's Work and Careers under COVID-19: A Boundary Theory Perspective

1 Introduction

The global COVID-19 pandemic has had an unprecedented impact on societies leading not only to health crises, but also giving rise to a global economic downturn, accompanied by a sharp increase in unemployment levels that are likely to have long-run repercussions for gender equality regarding work and career outcomes. While pre-existing inequalities are being exacerbated worldwide, women are particularly among those most severely affected by the pandemic (United Nations, 2020a) in all facets of society. The type and the severity of the pandemic's impact on them are various, depending on the context and their social status. Acknowledging the inequality that women have had to face even at the best of times, the pandemic has intensified challenges to their boundaries in the context of the work/home life dichotomy (OECD, 2020).

Under COVID-19, the most impacted occupations have been nurses, carers, cashiers, waitresses, etc. from sectors, including health, education, food and real estate, in which women are disproportionately employed (Alon, Doepke, Olmstead-Rumsey, and Tertilt, 2020; Coates, Cowgill, Chen, and Mackey, 2020). On the one hand, the closure of many service businesses, such as cafes, restaurants, hairdressers, etc., has led to their dismissals or being laid-off, while on the other, critical businesses, such as hospitals, pharmacies or grocery stores, where the nature of work does not allow telecommuting, have put women at high risk (OECD, 2020).

Many countries have ended up closing schools and day-care centers. In addition, many families have abstained from asking for childcare help from grandparents or other close elderly relatives due to the fast virus spread and higher death rates among this group. Nor have they been able to seek outside help for domestic work – "work performed in or for a household or households" (ILO, 2011; Convention No. 189). For these reasons, working parents have found themselves forced into carrying out both work-related responsibilities and housework tasks (such as cooking and cleaning) at the same time (Alon et al., 2020). As has always been the case, women when compared to men, carry a disproportionate burden in the care economy (ILO, 2018), which has been exacerbated under COVID-19 (ILO, 2020a, 2020b).

The onset of the COVID-19 pandemic along with the pre-existing inequalities faced by women has further challenged the existing micro boundaries – "frequent and usually recurring transitions, such as the commute between home and work" (Ashforth, Kreiner, and Fugate, 2000; p.472) – to the detriment of women. In particular, they have to shuffle between work- and housework-related role boundaries in order to fulfill the daily demands of these two distinct, but interconnected domains. Furthermore, role boundaries have been found to be important determinants of work and career outcomes (Cho, 2020): when these boundaries become permeable, this can negatively impact these outcomes (Ashforth et al., 2000), especially for women (Desilver, 2020). As women comprise around half the population worldwide, their level of participation in the workforce is very imperative for boosting economic growth and sustainable development in all countries (Karaalp-Orhan, 2017). Drawing on boundary theory, the aim in this chapter is to illustrate the severity of women's boundary-crossing activities in the form of role transitions between work and home during a pandemic crisis.

2 Boundary Theory

Boundary theory is a relative new development in the work-family research field (Gudeta and Engen, 2018; Bianchi and Milkie, 2010; Harrington, 2007). The theory is defined as a framework that describes the process of negotiating and maintaining boundaries between the work and nonwork domains to simplify and order such structuring (Ashforth et al., 2000, Nippert-Eng 1996). "Work" and "home" are two examples of domains created by boundaries (Nippert-Eng, 1996). Research on interaction between work and nonwork focuses on the components of the work and home roles or domains, respectively, each of which consists of a set of various activities, carried out in line with an individual's work- or nonwork-related goals. These domains can be separated or integrated. This means that when individuals develop and manage work and home boundaries, they develop strategies that can be described as falling along a continuum from high segmentation to high integration (Ashforth et al., 2000; Nippert-Eng, 1996). When boundaries are explicit, clear and definite, the domains are segmented (Nippert-Eng, 1996). Segmentation strategies help to reduce the blurred lines between the work and home domains or roles, which enables individuals to cope with multiple role expectations (Hewlin, 2003) and diminishes the interference between work and home (Rothbard and Edwards, 2003). In contrast, when the boundaries are blurred, the domains are integrated, thus giving rise to an overlap between them (cf. Nippert-Eng, 1996). An extended version of boundary management strategies has been proposed by Kossek and Lautsch (2007), where, according to them, individuals can choose to separate work and life domains (segmenting), or integrate work and life domains (integrating) or they can shuffle between the two.

The literature portrays three types of boundaries, namely spatial, temporal and, sometimes, psychological/mental. In conventional forms of work, spatial boundaries can be represented by the workplace, the wall or door at the workplace, etc., where the individual establishes her/his role boundary and segments it from the nonwork domain. In the context of home-based telework, a spatial boundary may be a wall, or a door, etc., which divides the workplace from other parts of the home (cf. Ahrentzen, 1990). A temporal boundary refers to the end of the official working hours or shift, while psychological boundaries are those "rules created by individuals that dictate when thinking patterns, behavior patterns and emotions are appropriate for one domain and not the other" (Clark, 2000: 756). According to Clark, "borders are lines of demarcation between domains, defining the point at which domain-relevant behaviour begins or ends" (2000: 756).

There are two mechanisms that influence an individual's decision to choose among different boundary strategies, namely flexibility and permeability (Kossek and Lautsch, 2012). The former is defined as "the degree to which temporal and spatial boundaries are pliable" (Ashforth et al., 2000: 474). For example, an individual may leave work early to pick one's child from school. Permeability refers to an individual being physically present in a certain domain, but psychologically or behaviorally involved in another role (Ashforth et al., 2000: 474). For instance, when an individual can call one' parents or kids, arrange a doctor appointment or order household-goods from the Internet, while being present at work during office hours, he/she has a relatively high permeable boundary. In contrast, when a person finds no time to attend to other roles, e.g., making private and family-related arrangements, he/she has an impermeable boundary.

The theory also takes into consideration the transitions between the roles within the work and nonwork domains (Ashforth et al., 2000; Kossek and Lautsch, 2012). It describes role transitions, such as that between work and home, as a boundary-crossing activity, where one exits and enters roles by surmounting boundaries (Ashforth et al., 2000: 472). When someone leaves the office heading off to lunch, the crossing of a physical boundary may give rise to the crossing of a mental one, whereby that person starts to think of home and personal issues. However, in the case of remote working, the use of information and communication technologies (ICT) during nonwork hours may not allow an individual to detach from thoughts of work to those of home (Yang, Zhang, Shen, Liu, and Zhang, 2019). When there is a misalignment between work and family/home demands, a role conflict can arise (Greenhaus and Beutell, 1985), which can be alleviated by the individual's self-initiative enabling him/her to make a flexible and permeable role boundary transition (Ashforth et al., 2000).

However, the current unprecedented and extreme circumstances of the pandemic have caused many people to have almost no control over their work and home/family boundaries as these boundaries have become intermingled due to lockdowns (Cho, 2020; Blustein, Duffy, Ferreira, Cohen-Scali, Cinamon, and Allan, 2020). When we consider women, the pandemic has been compounding the burdens placed on them: from such as taking on care giving and domestic work responsibilities at home, needing to prioritize the well-being of family members as well as sacrificing time dedicated to their paid work and careers. The situation is even worse for women working in the most adversely affected sectors (i.e., health care) under the pandemic, who are disproportionately engaged in these, thus being subject to extremely permeable role boundaries in very large numbers. As Cho (2020) has pointed out, this health crisis has been giving individuals little opportunity to gain perceived control over the situation. In the next section, the frequently encountered challenges women face in both the outside work and home contexts, as well as their exposure to an uncertain labor market and risks of pay reductions are discussed.

3 Women's Career and Work Boundary Challenges under COVID-19 Pandemic

3.1 The Challenges of Working outside the Home

With the onset of the pandemic and the urgent need for social distancing, the day-to-day boundaries of individuals have been challenged, i.e., affecting individuals' work and career outcomes (Cho, 2020). While many organizations have put remote work policies into practice that enable individuals work from home (Gallego Gomez and Roca, 2020; Harter, 2020; Restubog, Ocampo, and Wang, 2020), others operating in essential fields, e.g., health and social care, by their nature, have to send employees to work outside in the field, thus exposing them to various threats (Alon et al., 2020). Despite the serious implications of the pandemic for all, a higher negative impact will continue to be the reality for many vulnerable groups (OECD, 2020), among which are those women who have to bear the brunt in terms of restricting their options by virtue of their gender (United Nations, 2020a).

A higher share of women than men are employed in those sectors (e.g., health care) and occupations (e.g., nurses and midwives), being at the front line dealing with the pandemic (Alon et al., 2020; ILO, 2020a). In fact, women today constitute two-thirds of the workforce of health and social services worldwide. Despite their low numbers among physicians, dentists and pharmacists, data drawn from 104 countries show that women represent 85 % of the nursing and midwifery population (Boniol et al., 2019). While health-care workers are in a relatively better position in terms of securing their jobs (Coates, Cowgill, Chen, and Mackey, 2020; OECD, 2020; United Nations, 2020a), they are at higher risk of being severely infected, as the degree of severity of the disease heavily depends on the amount and density of the virus that people are exposed to. In this regard, due to the nature of health professions, nurses and midwives are more likely to be required to physically touch, treat and care for infected people (Financial Express, 2020; ICN, 2020). Many have to work exhausting shifts and barely get enough sleep or rest, if any (Financial Express, 2020). Because they all have high levels of fear of contaminating their family members with the coronavirus, many have had to make the decision to sleep in hotels, basements, borrowed apartments and even cars (Bowen, 2020; Bryant, 2020). Even under normal conditions, it has been argued that women in the health industry, employed in highly stressful occupations, for example, nurses and midwives, experience particular difficulties, especially when they have children at home (Morehead, 2001). These hardships can vary from high job demands, long irregular working hours, staff shortages and low control over the situation. As a consequence, they are hardly likely to experience clear role boundaries, as they are on call 24 hours a day, seven days a week, and hence, cannot simply shut everything down and go home (Firmin and Bailey, 2008).

Considering the life-threatening pandemic, many women health personnel fighting the virus in hospitals by treating patients have been making a deliberate choice to stay away from their children and spouses in order to save them from any contamination. So, from a boundary perspective the pandemic has impacted their flexibility to contract their work domain boundary, which in turn, negatively affects their physical and psychological participation in their private domain. In this regard, as Cho (2020) claims, their perceived control and management over work–nonwork boundaries have diminished.

3.2 The Challenges of Facing an Uncertain Labor Market and Unemployment

Industries and organizations are and will be differentially affected by COVID-19. Notably, airlines, real estate, accommodation, tourism and the food industries have been hit the hardest (Bapuji, Bakker, Brown, Higgins, Rehberin, and Spicer, 2020). Frontline workers employed in these industries cannot work from home as can knowledge workers in managerial or professional jobs who do most of their work on computers. These frontline workers have been affected more than others in the form of full or partial job losses or higher risks of being infected (Bapuji, Patel, Ertuğ, and Allen, 2020). Above all, women have to face the starkest employment losses as these industries have been greatly affected by the pandemic. For instance, those low-wage workers at risk of cuts to wages or unemployment are found to be disproportionately minority women, particularly women of color, in most developed countries (Bahn, Kohen, and Rogers, 2020).

Drawing on boundary theory, employees faced with the threat of job loss are more likely to allow work to permeate into their personal/family domain in order to alleviate their susceptibility to job insecurities (Boswell, Buchanan, and Harris, 2014). As Boswell and Olson-Buchanan (2007) demonstrated, employees with feelings of job insecurity have to let work interfere with their personal and family life. Under these negative labor market implications due to COVID, similar reflections can be made regarding the female labor force, who might have to let work demands impact their nonwork domain in order to alleviate their vulnerabilities to potential job loss. This flexibility created by allowing permeable boundaries may give rise to increased role conflict.

The ILO has reported that in 2020, 527 million women, representing 41 % of total female employment, are employed in these sectors, compared to 35 % of males. Women are likely to be under higher risk than men in terms of unemployment by the current crisis (see Fig. 3.1) (Bapuji et al., 2020; Coates et al., 2020; ILO, 2020a). The Institute for Women's Policy Research (2020) has reported that around 60 % of those becoming unemployed have been women, and they have lost more jobs than men in many sectors impacted by cutbacks due to the coronavirus pandemic. According to gender analysis by the United Nations (UN), women (2020b) in Palestine have found that the lockdown and closures of schools have caused an increase in the burden of unpaid care work on women and girls. A report by United Nations Development Programme (UNDP) (2020) has also stated that women and girls are much more burdened with domestic chores and care responsibilities than men. Hence, even under conditions of

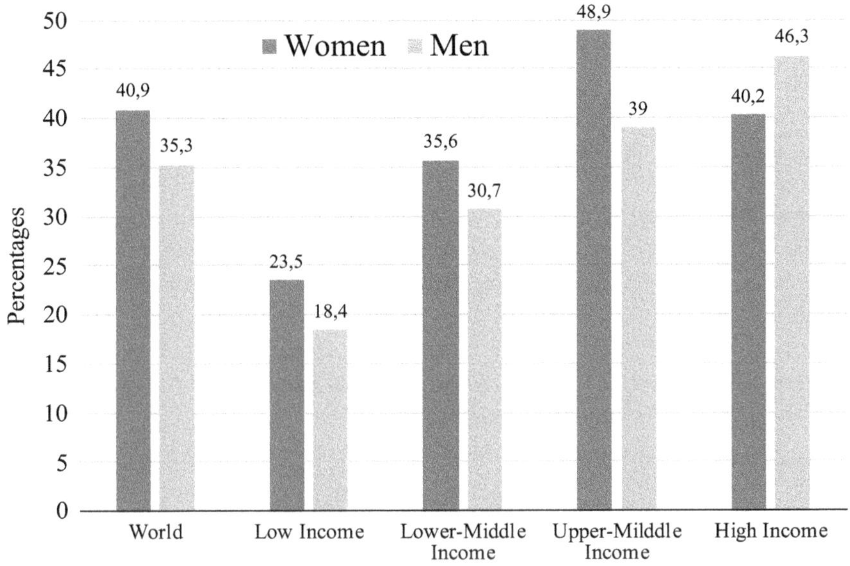

Fig. 3.1: Share of employment currently at high risk* of reduction in working hours, cuts to wages and layoffs, by sex, 2020.

* Accommodation and food services; real estate, business and administrative activities; manufacturing and wholesale/retail trade **Source**: ILO calculations based on ILO (endnote 12) and ILOSTAT (endnote1)

unemployment, because women have to manage proactively their micro boundaries of job seeking and family care, they have fewer opportunities less time to find suitable outside work than their male counterparts (Blustein et al., 2020). The disproportionate responsibilities of women for handling domestic labor time can limit the scope of their job searches and the maintaining of necessary network ties (Fuller, 2008), notwithstanding the labor market contractions in many industries due to COVID-19.

3.3 The Challenges of Working from Home

Given the life threatening and chaotic nature of the pandemic along with the need for social distancing due to its infectious nature, many organizations have decided to deploy remote employment practices that necessitate individuals working from home (Adalja, Toner and Inglesby, 2020). The use of modern ICT, such as e-mail, online conference platforms, smart phones, which have already been present in the workplace for a long time (Yang et al., 2019), has vastly increased with the onset of COVID-19. The utilization of ICT has allowed many to connect to work during nonworking hours and at the weekends. This has increased many employees' working time, with both employees and employers tending to assume that they must be available at all times. Hence, the use of ICT involves the interference of work and life domains (APS, 2020). Some recent research has argued that the use of ICT provides benefits to employees as it allows them to have a greater sense of control over their work or family roles (Ninaus et al., 2015), thereby being able to fulfill their responsibilities in both domains (Derks et al., 2016). However, in extreme situations, team supervisors and managers have been found to make greater demands on their subordinates, which limit their opportunities to use their self-initiative to maintain control over their work environment (Desilver, 2020).

Another implication of the sudden crisis and remote work may be career shock, whereby people cannot swiftly realign their planned career needs and aspirations with the changes in the work context and new dynamics in the nonwork one (Akkerman, Richardson and Kramer, 2020). This unprecedented shift to working-from-home practice has become even more critical with the closing of schools and childcare facilities. Gender and children in the home have an influence on how boundaries are managed (e.g., Myrie and Daly, 2009). It is, for the most part, "women" who have to take up the challenge to undertake multiple role boundary transitions. Due mostly to gendered norms, women are still perceived to be the main care giver of the family (spouse, children, and elderly) independent from their academic credentials or high labor market participation level (Flaherty, 2020). For many women, it has become constraining to pursue their career aspirations work from home, while at the same time attending to various nonwork demands (e.g., assisting children's home schooling and handling domestic labor, such as cleaning and cooking or running errands for elderly family members, who have been advised to stay home at all times (Moore, 2020; Schomer, 2020). As for the lines between work and family roles, these have become blurred and people's accustomed day-to-day behaviors have had to change, which has been a huge challenge for many, particularly in maintaining work and family boundaries (Senior, 2020; Verbeemen and Bujwid D'Amico, 2020). Women have little, if any, individual opportunity to segment these domains and are forced to integrate them, thus having to manage multiple role transitions (Ashforth et al., 2000). One domain might easily take up the time of the other, thus creating further disruptions and stress on the well-being of female employees. In this respect, deep-rooted gender norms can limit women's career choices and aspirations and build barriers to their career progression (Bukhari, Manzoor, Rasheed, Nayyer, Malik, and Babar, 2020). Similarly, under the coronavirus, women have been found as being less likely to report positive benefits from remote work, accompanied by psychological (i.e., decline in well-being and feelings of distress) (Zhou, Hertog, Kolpashnikova, and Kan, 2020) and social costs (reduced mutual learning, loss of visibility and restricted career development) (Desilver, 2020).

A worker's cross-role domain boundaries are created not only by the individual oneself, but also, by other members of role domains, including supervisors, peers and/or family members as they are also affected by these boundaries (Allen et al., 2014). It is almost always women who are expected to sustain high productivity by different stakeholders, such as supervisors, colleagues and family members, when faced with all the boundary crossing challenges (Cho, 2020). For instance, most men are reluctant to share domestic chores and care responsibilities even when they are unemployed, seeing this as the dispositional role of women. This is not only true for women from lower socioeconomic groups, for it is also the case for those of higher socioeconomic status. Notably, regarding academic communities, men submitted 50 % more papers than they did before the coronavirus, while there was sharp reduction in the number of those submitted by women (Kabeer, 2020). If women are perceived to be underperforming in the work and family domains, this might dissatisfy or disappoint work colleagues and family members. If they are not able meet these stakeholders' expectations in full, they can easily be pushed into withdrawing from work and return to the place society expects them to reside in – their gendered position in society.

4 Conclusion and Recommendations

The onset of the COVID-19 pandemic all around the world has further exacerbated the evident social and economic challenges as well as the inequalities imposed on women, who either work outside the home, or from within it. Moreover, the pandemic increased the precarity of the labor market and hence, the risk of long-term female unemployment. Many are having to deal with oppressive working conditions, such as increased work demands, irregular working hours, reduced pay, risks of becoming unemployed, limited availability of social support due to school and childcare facility closures as well as taking on further domestic chores and care responsibilities. Relative to men, the burden in most cases falls on women, who experience a blurring of the boundaries between work and home, thus making it particularly challenging to fulfill the daily demands of these two distinct but interconnected roles or domains, which bring further pressure on them. Role boundaries have been found to be important determinants of work and career outcomes. Drawing on boundary theory, this chapter has demonstrated the severity of women's boundary-crossing activities in the form of role transitions between work and home during the current pandemic.

Comprising the majority of the workers in the higher risk sectors, women, especially those who work from outside the home, have been disproportionately exposed to COVID-19 due to their employment in such as the health, food, accommodation and real estate sectors. Under the current uncertainty, clear work/home life boundaries have become harder for women to implement and this inability to practice distinct roles is adding extra burden to their lives domains. Moreover, the coronavirus has resulted in more people working from home than ever before. Further, the female knowledge worker segment of women has to confront role boundary conflicts during this time. One might think that the sudden expansion of remote work would end up benefiting women in terms of enabling them to integrate and manage work and home domains in a more flexible way. However, the evidence is to the contrary, with the onset of the crisis having increased their unpaid care work and domestic labor loads in addition to their paid work responsibilities, thus exacerbating their inequalities. The pandemic has blurred the boundaries of two domains between which many women shuffle to meet the requirements of both.

It would not be surprising, if women were to be profoundly influenced by this crisis in the long run, for the pandemic may not disappear soon and thus give rise to further contraction of many negatively influenced industries that tend to employ them. This will result in it being difficult for them to acquire economically satisfying jobs, if any at all. So, the pandemic carries the risk of diminishing women's possibilities to participate in the labor market, and many may decide to detach themselves from it permanently. It goes without saying that this outcome is not without its implications. Knowing women's potential for economic growth, equalization of their opportunities with those of men by reducing barriers to their participation in the labor force boosts welfare and economic growth across all societies. Further research on the cross-domain boundaries of women will provide new insights and could be utilized to guide organizations and societies in establishing strategies for developing gender-responsive economic and social policies and programs aimed at achieving more equal and sustainable societies with economic prosperity for all.

References

Adalja, E. T and Inglesby, T. V. (2020), "Priorities for the US health community responding to COVID-19", *JAMA*, 323(14), 1343–1344.

Ahrentzen, S. (1990). "Managing conflict by managing boundaries: How professional homeworkers cope with multiple roles at home", *Environment and Behavior*, 22, 723–752.

Akkermans, J., Richardson, J., and Kraimer, M. L. (2020), "The COVID-19 crisis as a career shock: Implications for careers and vocational behavior", *Journal of Vocational Behavior*, 113, 1–5.

Allen, T. D., Cho, E., and Meier, L. L. (2014), "Work family boundary dynamics", *The Annual Review of Organizational Psychology and Organizational Behavior*, 1, 99–121. doi:10.1146/annurev-orgpsych-031413-091330.

Alon, T. M., Doepke, M., Olmstead-Rumsey, J., and Tertilt, M. (2020), "The impact of COVID-19 on gender equality", NBER Working Paper Series, No. 26947, Northwestern University, http://faculty.wcas.northwestern.edu/~mdo738/research/COVID19_Gender_March_2020.pdf (Accessed 29 May 2020).

Ashforth, B. E., Kreiner, G. E., and Fugate, M. (2000), "All in a day's work: Boundaries and micro role transitions" *The Academy of Management Review*, 25(3), 472–491. https://doi.org/10.2307/259305.

Australian Psychology Association (APS) (2020), "Managing hazards to employee mental health during coronavirus (COVID-19)", https://www.psychology.org.au/getmedia/7e615d8c-5469-4111-a3b4-c36a0f50d240/APS-IS-COVID-19-Managing-hazards-to-emplyee-(1).pdf (Accessed 9 June 2020).

Bahn, K., Cohen, J., and van der Meulen Rodgers, Y. (2020), "A feminist perspective on COVID-19 and the value of care work globally", *Gender, Work & Organization*, 1–5.

Bapuji, H., Bakker, F. G. A., Brown, J. A., Higgins, C., Rehberin, K., and Spicer, A. (2020a), "Business and society research in times of the corona crisis", *Business & Society*, Editorial, 1–12.

Bapuji, H., Patel, C., Ertuğ, G., and Allen, D. G. (2020b), "Corona crisis and inequality: Why management research needs a societal turn", *Journal of Management*, Research Collection Lee Kong Chian School of Business.

Beghini, B., Cattaneo, U., and Pozzan, E. (2019), *ILO: A quantum leap for gender equality: for a better future of work for all*, International Labour Organization, Geneva.

Bianchi, S. M., and Milkie, M. A. (2010), "Work and family research in the first decade of the 21st century", *Journal of Marriage and Family*, 72(1), 705–725.

Blustein, D. L., Duffy, R., Ferreira, J. A., Cohen-Scali, V., Cinamon, R. G., and Allan, B. A. (2020), "Unemployment in the time of COVID-19: A research agenda", *Journal of Vocational Behavior*, Editorial, 1–4.

Boniol, M. et al. (2019), "Gender equity in the health workforce: Analysis of 104 countries", Health Workforce Working Paper, No.1, World Health Organization, http://apps.who.int/bookorders (Accessed 24 March 2020).

Boswell, W. R., and Olson-Buchanan, J. B. (2007), "The use of communication technologies after hours: The role of work attitudes and work–life conflict", *Journal of Management*, 33, 592–610.

Boswell, W. R., Olson-Buchanan, J. B., and Harris, T. B. (2014), "I cannot afford to have a life: Employee adaptation to feelings of job insecurity", *Personnel Psychology*, 67: 887–915. doi:10.1111/peps.12061.

Bowen, A. (2020), "'I tell my wife to get away.' Facing coronavirus fears, Chicago nurses and doctors try to protect their own families." *Chicago Tribune.* https://www.chicagotribune.com/coronavirus/ct-life-doctors-nurses-protect-patients-family-20200402-4p5tbklbafgrxl3pbw45fvwama-story.html (Accessed on 5 June 2020).

Bryant, M. (2020), "I can't hug my kid': How coronavirus is upending medical workers' lives", https://www.theguardian.com/world/2020/apr/16/us-medical-workers-lives-upended-coronavirus (Accessed 4 June 2020).

Bukhari, N., Manzoor, M., Rasheed, H., Nayyer, B., Malik, M., and Babar, Z. (2020), "A step towards gender equity to strengthen the pharmaceutical workforce during COVID-19", *Journal of Pharmaceutical Policy and Practice*, 13(15), 1–5. https://doi.org/10.1186/s40545-020-00215-5.

Clark, S. C. (2000), "Work/family border theory: A new theory of work/family balance", *Human Relations*, 53, 747–770.

Cho, E. (2020), "Examining boundaries to understand the impact of COVID-19 on vocational behaviors", *Journal of Vocational Behavior*, 119, 1–3.

Coates, B., Cowgill, M., Chen, T., and Mackey, W. (2020), *Shutdown: Estimating the COVID-19 employment shock*, Grattan Institute, 1–59.

Derks, D., Bakker, A. B., Peters, P., and Wingerden, P. V. (2016), "Work-related smartphone use, work-family conflict and family role performance: The role of segmentation preference", *Human Relations*, 69, 1045–1068. doi: 10.1177/0018726715601890.

Desilver, D. (2020), "Working from home was a luxury for the relatively affluent before coronavirus – not any more", https://www.weforum.org/agenda/2020/03/working-from-home-coronavirus-workers-future-of-work/ (Accessed 8 June 2020).

Financial Express (2020), "COVID-19 treatment: Kudos! How doctors and nurses work inside hospital wards without sleep or rest; details", https://www.financialexpress.com/lifestyle/covid-19-treatment-kudos-how-doctors-and-nurses-work-inside-hospital-wards-without-sleep-or-restdetails/1926068/ (Accessed 4 June 2020).

Firmin, M. W., and Bailey, M. (2008), "When caretaking competes with care giving: A qualitative study of full-time working mothers who are nurse managers", *Journal of Nursing Management*, 16, 858–867.

Flaherty, E. (2020), "Faculty home work", *Inside Highered*, https://www.insidehighered.com/news/2020/03/24/working-home-during-covid-19-proves-challenging-faculty-members (Accessed 7 June 2020).

Fuller, S. (2008), "Job mobility and wage trajectories for men and women in the United States", *American Sociological Review*, 73(1), 158–183.

Gallego Gomez, C., and Roca, M. (2020), "Work productivity and work-life balance, 2020", EAE Business School, http://marketing.eae.es/prensa/_SRC_Productividad-Conciliacion.pdf (Accessed 4 June 2020).

Greenhaus, J. H., and Beutell, N. J. (1985), "Sources and conflict between work and family roles", *The Academy of Management Review*, 10(1), 76–88. https://doi.org/10.2307/258214.

Gudeta, K. H., and van Engen, M. L. (2018), "Work-life boundary management styles of women entrepreneurs in Ethiopia – "choice" or imposition?", *Journal of Small Business and Enterprise Development*, 25(3), 368–386.

Harrington, B. (2007), *The Work-Life Evolution Study*, Boston College Center for Work and Family, Chestnut Hill, MA.

Harter, J. (2020), "How coronavirus will change the 'next normal' workplace", *Gallup*, https://www.gallup.com/workplace/309620/coronavirus-change-next-normal-workplace.aspx (Accessed 4 June 2020).

Hewlin, P. (2003), "And the award for best actor goes To . . .: Facades of conformity in organizational settings", *Academy of Management Review*, 28, 633–643.

International Council of Nurses (ICN) (2020), "High proportion of healthcare workers with COVID-19 in Italy is a stark warning to the world: Protecting nurses and their colleagues must be the number one priority", https://www.icn.ch/news/high-proportion-healthcare-workers-covid-19-italy-stark-warning-world-protecting-nurses-and (Accessed 2 June 2020).

ILO (2011), "Decent work for domestic workers", International Labour Conference, https://www.ilo.org/wcmsp5/groups/public/---ed_protect/---protrav/---travail/documents/publication/wcms_168266.pdf (Accessed 11 June 2020).

ILO (2018), *Care work and care jobs for the future of decent work*, ILO, Geneva.

ILO (2020a), "ILO Monitor: COVID-19 and the world of work. Third edition. Updated estimates and analysis", https://www.ilo.org/wcmsp5/groups/public/@dgreports/@dcomm/documents/briefingnote/wcms_743146.pdf (Accessed 30 May 2020).

ILO (2020b), "COVID-19 and the world of work: Impact and policy responses", ILO Monitor 1st ed., https://www.ilo.org/global/topics/coronavirus (Accessed 29 May 2020).

Institute for Women's Policy Research (2020), "Women lost more jobs than men in almost all sectors of the economy", *Quick Figures*, https://iwpr.org/wp-content/uploads/2020/04/QF-Jobs-Day-April-FINAL.pdf (Accessed 8 June 2020).

Kabeer, N. (2020). "Labour market inequalities are exacerbated by COVID-19." The London School of Economics and Political Science, https://blogs.lse.ac.uk/covid19/2020/05/18/naila-kabeer-labour-market-inequalities-are-exacerbated-by-covid-19/ (Accessed 10 June 2020).

Karaalp-Orhan, H. S. (2017), "What are the trends in women's labour force participation in Turkey?", *European Journal of Sustainable Development*, 6(3), 303–312.

Kossek, E.E., and Lautsch, B.A. (2007), *CEO of Me: Creating a life that works in the flexible job age*, Pearson Prentice Hall, Upper Saddle River, NJ.

Kossek, E. E., and Lautsch, B.A. (2012), "Work-family boundary management styles in organizations: a cross-level model", *Organizational Psychology Review*, 2(2), 157–171.

Moore, S. (2020), "Coronavirus is giving us a glimpse of the future of work – and it's a nightmare", *The Guardian*, https://www.theguardian.com/commentisfree/2020/may/04/coronavirus-is-giving-us-a-glimpse-of-the-future-of-work-and-its-a-nightmare (Accessed 8 June 2020).

Morehead, A. (2001), "Synchronizing time for work and family: Preliminary insights from qualitative research with mothers", *Journal of Sociology*, 37, 355–369.

Myrie, J., and Daly, K. (2009), "The use of boundaries by self-employed, home-based workers to manage work and family: A qualitative study in Canada", *Journal of Family & Economic Issues*, 30, 386–398.

Ninaus, K., Diehl, S., Terlutter, R., Chan, K., and Huang, A. (2015), "Benefits and stressors – perceived effects of ICT use on employee health and work stress: An exploratory study from Austria and Hong Kong", *International Journal of Qualitative Studies on Health and Well-being*, 10, 28838. doi: 10.3402/qhw.v10.28838.

Nippert-Eng, C. E. (1996). *Home and work: Negotiating boundaries through every-day life*,University of Chicago Press, Chicago, IL.

OECD (2020), "Women at the core of the fight against COVID-19 crisis", http://www.oecd.org/coronavirus/policy-responses/women-at-the-core-of-the-fight-against-covid-19-crisis-553a8269/ (Accessed 25 May 2020).

Restubog, S. L. D., Ocampo A. C. G., and Wang, L. (2020), "Taking control amidst the chaos: Emotion regulation during the COVID-19", *Journal of Vocational Behavior*, Editorial, 1–6.

Rothbard, N., and Edwards, J. (2003), "Investment in work and family roles: A test of identity and utilitarian motives", *Personnel Psychology*, 56, 699–730.

Schomer, S. (2020), "Male and female workers are experiencing COVID-19 very differently", https://www.entrepreneur.com/article/349534 (Accessed 8 June 2020).

Senior, J. (2020), "On losing offices – the last boundary between work and home – amid coronavirus outbreak", https://www.firstpost.com/living/on-losing-offices-the-last-boundary-between-work-and-home-amid-coronavirus-outbreak-8395471.html (Accessed 4 June 2020).

United Nations (UN) Women (2020a), "Policy brief: The impact of COVID-19 on women", https://www.unwomen.org/-/media/headquarters/attachments/sections/library/publications/2020/policy-brief-the-impact-of-covid-19-on-women-en.pdf?la=en&vs=1406 (Accessed 25 May 2020).

United Nations (UN) Women (2020b), "COVID-19 risks creating and exacerbating women's vulnerabilities and gender inequalities in Palestine, warns UN women – Press Release", https://www.un.org/unispal/document/covid-19-risks-creating-and-exacerbating-womens-vulnerabilities-and-gender-inequalities-in-palestine-warns-un-women-press-release/ (Accessed 9 June 2020).

United Nations Development Programme (UNDP) (2020), "Briefing note: The economic impacts of COVID-19 and gender inequality. Recommendations for policymaking", http://americalatinagenera.org/newsite/images/cdr-documents/2020/04/PNUD_GENERO_COVID19__ENG_FINAL_1.pdf (Accessed 9 June 2020)

Verbeemen, E., and Bujwid D'Amico, A. (2020). "Why remote working will be the new normal, even after COVID-19", https://www.ey.com/en_be/covid-19/why-remote-working-will-be-the-new-normal-even-after-covid-19 (Accessed 7 June 2020).

Yang, J., Zhang, Y., Shen, C., Liu, S., and Zhang, S. (2019), "Work-family segmentation preferences and work-family conflict: Mediating effect of work-related ICT use at home and the multilevel moderating effect of group segmentation norms", *Frontiers in Psychology*, 10, 834. https://doi.org/10.3389/fpsyg.2019.00834.

Zhou, M., Hertog, E., Kolpashnikova, K., and Kan M. (2020), "Gender inequalities: Changes in income, time use and well-being before and during the UK COVID-19 lockdown", SocArXiv. June 2. doi:10.31235/osf.io/u8ytc.

Betül Yılmaz

Female Managers in Academia: An Evaluation of the Universities in Turkey

1 Introduction

All around the world, the problems women face in their work lives and the obstacles on their career progression have not been completely eradicated. In Turkey, women employment in work life has been steadily increasing. Even though the male and female population in Turkey are roughly equal, the number of women in employment is not even half the number of men in employment (TURKSTAT, 2020). On the other hand, the number of women in academia is about the same as the number of men in academia. However, this balance becomes quite disproportionate as one goes up the career ladder, with women falling behind men. Furthermore, the ratio of female academics in management positions is almost non-existent compared to men academics in management positions. Knowing the problems women face in academia and determining the career obstacles they encounter should have a positive impact on the number of women within the rectorate, which is the highest academic stage of managerial positions.

Started as European Women Rectors Platform in 2008, European Women Rectors Association (EWORA) was founded in 2015 as an NGO that provides education and research to help women take up leading roles in academia both in Europe and worldwide as well as to advocate for gender equality in academia. Since 2008, there have been regular European Women Rectors Conferences (EWORA, 2020). With these conferences, they take part in international studies regarding ensuring gender equality in higher education. These conferences, where there is also Turkish participation, are a positive development in terms of determining and finding solutions to problems women face in academia.

This study reports on the problems female academics and women in managerial positions in academia face in pursuing their career, and analyses the current situation in academia.

2 Women in Turkish Academia

Women obtained the right to higher education on September 12, 1914, with the establishment of İnas Darülfünunu (İnas University), which consisted of

Tab. 4.1: The Percentage of Female Academic Staff across the Years

Year	Percentage of Female Academic Staff (%)
1944–1945	13.9
1950–1951	15.9
1959–1960	18.8
1973–1974	25.4
1981–1982	26
1990–1991	31
1993–1994	33
1997–1998	33.8
2001–2002	36.6
2004–2005	38.2
2007–2008	40.3
2010–2011	40.8
2013–2014	42.7
2014–2015	43

Source: Şentürk, 2015: 6; https://istatistik.yok.gov.tr/, 2020

departments on arts and sciences (İnas Darülfünunu ve Kadınlar Dünyası Dergisi, 2019). In the academic year of 1932–1933, the first female academic was employed by "Yüksek İktisat ve Ticaret Mektebi," and women started working as academics for the first time in Turkey under the Republic Period. In the academic year of 1934–1935, the number of female academics skyrocketed to 93 (Şentürk, 2015: 6). This increasing trend has followed on steadily until today. Tab. 4.1 shows the percentage of women working at universities between the years of 1944 and 2015.

As observed in Tab. 4.1, there has been an especially sharp increase in female academic staff percentage starting from the academic year 1973–1974. From 1973 onward, new universities were established, and the university count rose from 8 to 19, with 11 new universities established. This can be explained as the direct proportion between the increasing need for academic staff and increasing number of female academics (Yüksek Öğretimde Değişmeler, 1988: 29).

The fundamental laws governing the universities as a result of the higher education system that was established during the Republic period are as follows: Law No. 2252 of 1933, Universities Law No. 4936 of 1946, Law No. 115 and 116 of 1960, and the Universities Law No. 1750 of 1973 (Yüksek Öğretimde Değişmeler, 1988: 13).

Tab. 4.2: The Percentage of Female Academics in Years

Year	**Percentage of Female Academic Staff (%)**
2015–2016	43.2
2016–2017	44
2017–2018	44.4
2018–2019	44.7
2019–2020	44.9

Source: https://istatistik.yok.gov.tr/, 2020

The Council of Higher Education (CoHE), to which academicians are affiliated today in Turkey, came into existence after a university reform in 1981 with the Higher Education Law No. 2547, which restructured the academic, institutional and administrative aspects, bringing all higher education institutions in the country under one roof. Today, there are 202 universities in Turkey, with 129 of them being public universities and the other 73 foundation universities (Yükseköğretim Bilgi Yönetim Sistemi, 2020). The "Women's Studies and Problems in Academia Unit," established by the Council of Higher Education in 2015, aims to raise awareness in individuals with regards to gender equality awareness and in women with regards to the protection of women's human rights (CoHE, Women's Studies in Academia Unit, 2020). Tab. 4.2 shows the proportion of women in academia in Turkey from 2015 to the present day.

It is observed that, in Turkey, in terms of the percentage of academics, the number of female academics is half the number of male academics in terms of their rank. Tables 4.1 and 4.2 show that the proportion of female academics steadily increases with each year.

According to the 2018 report World Bank Tertiary Education Academic Staff (% Female), Kazakhstan and Kyrgyzstan take the lead in terms of female academic proportions with 64 %. On the other hand, this ratio is 50 % in the United States, 45 % in the United Kingdom (last announced value in 2017) and 42 % in the EU countries; hence, none of these countries has a sufficient proportion of female academic staff (The World Bank, 2020). Although the proportion of female academic staff in Turkey is not sufficient compared to these countries, it has a promising steady increase over the years.

In Turkey, the ratio of female academics in higher education institutions is close to the ratio of male academicians. However, when we compare the ratio between male and female academics' titles, we see that it has not yet reached the desired level. As one goes up in the ranks in academia, the proportion of women compared to men decreases, and this can be explained by the fact that the role distributions experienced by women become apparent. Taking the academic advancement conditions in Turkey into account, we see that young female academics who have completed their PhD are either delaying their academic careers or are late in reaching the desired steps because of the roles otherwise assigned to them. In order to rise up in the academic ranks, female academics who have completed their PhD either put off marriage or lag behind in obtaining certain academic titles for reasons such as family or child duties when married (Yıldız, 2018: 30–31).

Another issue is gender discrimination. Özkanlı and Korkmaz (2000a; 2000b) state that although female academics do not face gender-based discrimination, male academics have a more advantageous position in obtaining titles. Yenilmez (2016) emphasizes the importance of analyzing the situation in Turkish academia, where there is a low representation of women in decision-making and management positions, and the gap between female academics with the Professor title as opposed to those with lower academic ranks widens more and more over time. Reviewing the literature shows that even though there are numerous studies on discrimination against women in Turkish academia, the literature is still limited (Tepe, 2019: 201).

When we examine the distribution of the numbers of academics by titles in Turkey, we can see that the higher one goes up in the academic ranks, and the gap between male and female academics expands. This is even more evident in the Professorship rates, which is the highest academic title. Table 4.3 shows that the ratio of female Professors to the total number of professors is 31.9 %. This shows that the number of female Professors is lower than the number of male Professors. While 39.7 % of female academics have the title of Associate Professor, 44 % are Assistant Professors, 50.2 % are Lecturers, and the Research Assistant, which is the entrance-level academic position, has a ratio of 50.8 %. As can be seen from this table, the higher the title, the lower the proportion of female academics compared to male academics. When the number of women in higher education institutions is examined in terms of titles, it can be interpreted that it is unequal to the proportion of men.

In the distribution of the number of academics according to their titles in Turkey, the significant decrease in the number of women as the academic title increases can be explained by the examination of the concepts of sticky floor and sticky ladder. Sticky floor refers to the "barriers to the rise of women who are relatively low paid compared to other employees who work at lower levels in the public sector and do not have the possibility of promotion" (Öztürk, 2017: 209) and sticky ladder refers to "the efforts and difficulties in rising up

Tab. 4.3: Distribution of Academic Numbers in Turkey by Academic Titles

	Male	Female	Total
Professor	18,976	8,911	27,887
Associate Professor	9,897	6,528	16,425
Assistant Professor	22,549	17,733	40,282
Lecturer	18,394	18,613	37,007
Research Assistant	24,191	25,020	49,211
Grand Total	94,007	76,805	170,812

Source: https://istatistik.yok.gov.tr/, 2020

in ranks at organizations" (Gül & Oktay, 2009: 427). Also known as the leaky pipeline, this situation can be explained as a case of women leaving or having to leave their desired position for a number of reasons as they rise up to senior positions (Öztürk, 2017: 209). Since the concept of leaky pipeline does not constitute an academic concept in the literature, this process that female academics go through can be explained by the concept of Telegraphic Speech in children's language development. Similar to the fact that children continue their communication in periods of language development with interrupted sentences, it can be interpreted as female academics trying to continue their career progress with interrupted periods (Karakuş, 2016: 537).

In academia, women experience gender-based vertical segregation on the career ladder due to the influence of multiple sociocultural factors. Vertical segregation is defined as hierarchical segregation and is another example of gender-based segregation, like horizontal segregation, in academia. The difficulties women face when advancing on the career ladder is an example of vertical segregation (Adak, 2018: 29–30).

As shown in Tab. 4.3, the Research Assistant title, which is an entrance-level academic position that constitutes the Master's and PhD process, is 50 % of the female academic population. However, compared to the ratio of female academics with the Professor title, we see that the ratio goes much lower at 31.9 %. The Research Assistant position is a much more precarious position, and it is uncertain whether the people who are in this position will continue to work after their Master's and doctorate degrees. In academia, women do not appear as much as men as we go up in the ranks, and the places women hold are hierarchically more precarious and offer no possibility of promotion. The fact that women are not distributed proportionally in academic staff also affects their participation in decision-making mechanisms in their institutions (Şentürk, 2015: 9).

Another issue that should be taken into consideration when evaluating women's positions in academia is related to the female academics' field of graduation. In Turkey, health sciences, education, arts and social sciences are seen as more preferable by women, while natural sciences, mathematics and engineering are seen as more preferable by men. This situation is also present in sub-fields of science. Women's preference rate is high in areas such as architecture and food engineering, which are the sub-fields of technical sciences preferred by men. This means gender-based horizontal segregation of the sciences (Adak, 2018: 29). Previous studies show that the field of social sciences are more feminine and the field of natural sciences are more masculine in Turkey. As a result, it is possible to speak of a sexist discrimination in academia at the level of sciences as well (Yıldız, 2018: 34).

3 Female Managers in Turkish Academia

Women's participation in management-level decision-making in academia is very low in Turkey. Situations that prevent or limit women from becoming senior executives in any organization are present also in academia. Traditional and cultural approaches as well as sexist approaches affect societies, institutions and even interpersonal relationships. In academia, the obstacles to women getting to where they want in terms of their career are unveiled much more clearly, and women may face glass-ceiling situations (Göker, 2019: 2). The glass ceiling is defined as the sum of the factors that prevent women in executive positions from going up in the ladder after they reach a certain stage. It is also possible to refer to the glass ceiling as an invisible barrier (Örücü, Kılıç, & Kılıç, 2007: 118).

The proportion of women in university administration in Turkey is very low. The number of women in positions such as Rector, Vice Rector, Dean, Vice Dean and the Head of Department, which are considered as executive positions, is very low compared to men as well. As a condition determined by the (CoHE), the Professor title must be obtained in order to be a Rector at universities. Today, the proportion of women with the title of Professor in Turkey is 31.9 %. This rate is low compared to male academics with the title of Professor.

When we examine the proportion of female rectors in Turkish academia, 6 out of 129 state universities and 12 out of 73 foundation universities have female rectors. Among all rectors, the proportion of female rectors is 9 %. This ratio is quite below what is desired. As can be seen in Tab. 4.4, the ratio of female rectors to male rectors in public universities remains a very low level with 4.6 %. This rate is higher in foundation universities, where the proportion of female

Tab. 4.4: Ratio of Female Rectors in Universities of Turkey (%)

	Male	Female	Total	Female Ratio (%)
State University	123	6	129	4.6
Foundation University	61	12	73	16.4
Total	184	18	202	9

Source: Women's Studies in Academia Unit, 2020

Tab. 4.5: Number of Deans in Turkish Universities

	Male	Female	Total	Female Ratio (%)
State University	1,172	216	1,388	15.5
Foundation University	303	106	409	26
Total	1,475	322	1,797	18

Source. Women's Studies in Academia Unit, 2020

rectors is 16.4 %. It is quite remarkable that of all the rectors in 129 public universities, 123 are male and 6 are female. Moreover, the ratio of female rectors in European universities is 14.3 %. Both in Turkey and in other European countries, these rates do not meet the desired rate for women in executive rector positions.

When we examine the number of Deans, which is another executive position at universities, 216 of the 1,388 Deans at state universities are women, and 106 of the 409 Deans at foundation universities are women. While the proportion of female Deans employed at the State University is 15.5 %, this rate is 26 % at the foundation universities. Thus, a total of 322 female Deans are employed, and the proportion of women among all deans is 18 %.

When we examine the alma mater fields of female rectors who are in executive positions in universities, we see that they have mostly graduated from Social Sciences, Engineering and Medicine programs. Furthermore, they are mostly clustered around Social Sciences fields. The alma mater fields of male rectors are Medicine, Engineering and Natural Sciences.

Another area where women can take an executive position in academia is the presidential position at the Council of Higher Education, where all universities are gathered under one roof. Since its establishment in 1981, seven presidents have served in the Council of Higher Education, and there have been no female academics among these presidents. The situation does not change much when we look at the members of the Council of Higher Education. There are a total of 21 members, of which only one is a woman. The Women's Studies in Academia Unit was established in 2015 within the Council of Higher Education, specifically aiming to "strengthen the social and economic positions of women, increase their contribution to the national economy, support their presence in decision-making and leadership positions, and make efforts to pave the way for similar further studies in universities" (CoHE, Women's Studies in Academia Unit, 2020). Women's Studies in Academia Unit is an important unit in increasing the number of women in executive positions in Turkey and helping eliminate the obstacles women face in their academic careers.

Women have different experiences than men in pursuing the career path they desire. The lived experiences of the female academics outside the academia as well as the sexist approaches female academics face slows them from going up the career ladder, and this in turn affects their chances of becoming an administrator (Özkanlı & White, 2009: 326).

Studying gender as a societal construct makes it easier to understand the impact of women on decision-making processes in Turkey. Gender roles can be expressed as women and men embodying the roles they are expected to play within the societal norms and traditions. Society places different behavioral patterns and obligations on men and women, expecting them to behave differently than they are (Ünnü, Baybars, & Kesken, 2014: 121). This is also true within the institutions in the society, and the institutions are not independent of the thought structure, cultural values, gender systems and the roles imposed on the men and women who are raised within this system. Thus, these factors affect the functioning of institutions (Erzeybek & Çifci, 2019: 62).

In traditional societies, the role of woman is seen as being responsible for household tasks and the child rearing, and as a person who has obligations to the house and their spouse. With the transition to the modern society, there have been changes in women's social status. Women had more educational opportunities and obtained opportunities to work in professional, managerial and bureaucratic jobs alongside men in public spaces. With the active participation of women in working life, women have had equal opportunities with men (Suğur & Suğur, 1998: 23). Although women have equal opportunities with men, they may face sexist approaches as well as career challenges and obstacles by their co-workers or managers. This is also the same for female academics at universities.

Female academics at Turkish universities have expressed that they have a conflict of roles in terms of their time and expectations of them. Gender-based discrimination in Turkey compared to other countries can be explained by the large proportion of women with the title of Professor. However, the same does not apply to the managerial positions. The conflict between career and family roles experienced by female academics in Turkey especially during their associate professorship is an example of this situation. Although female academics have equal rights as men, they are forced to work harder because of their roles in and out of work. Their roles such as being a wife, mother or keeping the house orderly push female academics into a conflict of roles in terms of their working as well as non-working times. Because of their responsibilities outside the business, female academics may be unable to take up senior management positions or may refuse positions within senior management (Özkanlı, 2010: 6–7). Female academics who work as senior managers can be trapped between their responsibilities at home and their responsibilities at work because they work overtime. Except the role conflict they experience, women also have a number of negative factors waiting for them at the workplace such as "mobbing, glass ceiling, leaky pipe, sticky ladder, sticky floor," all of which can be interpreted as contributing to their low representation in higher education administration

Mobbing is a systematic and long-term behavior that can cause psychological and physiological damages directly against an employee in an organization (Browne & Smith, 2008: 132). Erdemir (2019) included 26 dissertations theses related to academics being exposed to mobbing published between 2006 and 2016 registered to the Turkish National Thesis Center of the Council of Higher Education (CoHE) According to the results of this study, there was a reported rate of victims between 4 % and 100 % in state and foundation universities. Young, single or female academics reported to have been victim to mobbing more in terms of expressing oneself, social relationships, and communication and preferred to remain silent. The study also found that there was a negative correlation between mobbing and seniority, title, organizational justice, trust, loyalty and job satisfaction, while the organizational reasons for mobbing were expressed as nepotism, poor leadership and lack of solidarity and communication (Erdemir, 2019: 213).

Another reason why female academics have low representation in higher education is glass ceiling syndrome. Defined as a barrier in the careers of qualified people and especially women, the glass ceiling syndrome can occur due to individual, organizational and social factors. Individual factors include taking on multiple roles or women's personal preferences and perceptions. Organizational factors include lack of organizational culture, organization policies and mentors.

Finally, social factors contributing to glass ceiling syndrome include occupational segregation and stereotypes regarding gender (Mizrahi & Aracı, 2010: 217).

The fact that there is a lower ratio of women compared to men in high university administration positions (such as Rector and Dean) in Turkey indicates the presence of a glass ceiling in academia. The increase in the number of female academics in senior executive positions in the years 1990–2000 is not very high. In social sciences, female Dean rates are higher than average. However, this ratio can be explained by examining the gendered structure of the scientific fields in terms of their historical and social development (Özkaplan, 2013: 17). Today, the proportion of female academics in senior management compared to men is not very different from the previous years. The fact that women take up lower positions in academia than men today, as well as the fact that interdisciplinary distribution of genders is disproportionate, can be listed among the reasons for examining the glass-ceiling phenomenon (Öztan & Doğan, 2015: 195).

In terms of the obstacles to women's careers, another well-used definition apart from the term "glass ceiling" is sticky floor. Identified as factors that keep women at lower levels in organizations, sticky ground is interpreted as women seeing the glass ceiling and not moving up from their position and being trapped in low-level jobs (Üstün & Gümüşeli, 2017: 124). Women in academia may have difficulties in taking up appointment in higher education institutions even though they have obtained the relevant title, and consequently fall behind male academics. This difficulty manifests itself more in the transition to a higher title. Thus, female academics may not prefer senior management positions during the difficult period they go through and may have the idea that they have no place in higher management positions.

4 Conclusion

There is a great amount of research on women's studies in literature. The prominent studies on gender-based discrimination often discuss the problems and obstacles in women's career extensively. Studies on the career advancement of women working in academia, however, remain limited. The ratio of women in academia today is not sufficient compared to men in academia. This is especially evident in the ratio of female academics in senior executive positions, and the ratio is far from the desired amount.

Although the proportion of women in academia in Turkey is close to the proportion of men in academia, the difference between them increases as their academic rank increases. The proportion of female academics is especially low among senior executive positions compared to men.

It has been demonstrated in the literature that the work expectations of today's younger generation differ. For this younger generation, work-life balance is quite important. They do not accept long working hours. They want to allocate time to their social life as well as their work life. They do not accept gender discrimination and defend equal rights for all.

If the individuals of this younger generation take part in the academia in the following years, it can be stated that the current situation in the academia will be different from today with their changing working values. It is also thought that the numbers of female academics in senior management positions in academia will increase. It is also possible to say that career barriers will be lifted in working life, and that the numbers of men and women in executive positions will be more fairly distributed.

References

Adak N.(2018), "Akademide Kadınlar: Yükseköğrenime Giriş ve Kariyerde İlerleme", Akdeniz Kadın Çalışmaları ve Toplumsal Cinsiyet Dergisi, I (1) 23–38.

Browne, M. N., & Smith, M. A. (2008). Mobbing in the workplace and individualism: Antibullying legislation in the United States, Europe and Canada. *Employee Rights and Employment Policy Journal*, *12*, 131.

Erdemir B.(2019), "Türkiye'de Akademide Mobbing ve Çözüm Önerileri: Lisansüstü Tezlerin İçerik Analizi", Yükseköğretim Dergisi, 9(2), 213–233.

Erzeybek B., Çifci G.E.(2019), "Akademisyen Kadınların Toplumsal Cinsiyet Rolleri ve Evlilik Uyumu", Sosyal Çalışma Dergisi, 3(1), 61–80.

Göker Zeynep G.(2019), Akademide Kadınlar ve Toplumsal Cinsiyet Eşitliği, Tesev Toplumsal Cinsiyet Eşitliği Raporu (TESEV).

Gül H., Oktay E.(2009), "Türkiye ve Dünya'da Kadınların Çalışma Hayatında Yaşadıkları Cam Tavan Algıları Üzerine Kavramsal Bir Çalışma", Sosyal ve Ekonomik Araştırmalar Dergisi, 1(18), 421–436.

Karakuş H. (2016), "Delik Boru: Türkiye'deki Akademisyen Kadınlar Üzerine Bir Analiz", The Journal of Academic Social Science Studies, 53, 533–556.

Mizrahi R., Aracı H.(2010), "Kadın Yöneticiler ve Cam Tavan Sendromu Üzerine Bir Araştırma", Organizasyon ve Yönetim Bilimleri Dergisi, 2(1), 216–223.

Örücü E., Kılıç R., Kılıç T.(2007), "Cam Tavan Sendromu ve Kadınların Üst Düzey Yönetici Pozisyonuna Yükselmelerindeki Engeller: Balıkesir İli Örneği", Yönetim ve Ekonomi, 14(2), 117–135.

Özkanlı Ö.(2010), Türkiye ve Avustralya'da Yükseköğretim Kurumlarında Üst Düzey Kadın Yöneticilerin Durumu, Ankara, Ankara Üniversitesi Bilimsel Araştırma Projesi Kesin Raporu.

Özkanlı Ö.,Korkmaz A.(2000a), "Turkish Women in Academic Life: Attitude Measurement towards Gender Discrimination in Academic Promotion and Administration", Emerging Economies: Academy of Business Administrative Sciences 2000, International Conference Proceedings Book, St. Bonaventure University Publication, Prague.

Özkanlı Ö., Korkmaz A.(2000b), Kadın Akademisyenler, Ankara Üniversitesi SBF Yayını, No. 586.

Özkanlı Ö., White K.(2009), "Gender and Leadership in Turkish and Australian Universities", Equal Opportunities International, 28(4), 324–335.

Özkaplan N.(2013), "Kadın Akademisyenler: Cam Tavanlar Hâlâ Çok Kalın!", Kadın Araştırmaları Dergisi, 1(12), 1–23.

Öztan E.,Doğan, S. N.(2015), "Akademinin Cinsiyeti: Yıldız Teknik Üniversitesi Örneği Üzerinde Üniversite ve Toplumsal Cinsiyet", Çalışma ve Toplum, 3, 191–222.

Öztürk Umut C.(2017), "Akademideki Topuk Sesleri: Cam Tavan Perspektifinde Göller Bölgesi Üniversitelerinin Betimsel Analizi", Pesa International Journal Of Social Studies, 3(4), 202–213.

Şentürk B.(2015), "Çokuz Ama Yokuz: Türkiye'deki Akademisyen Kadınlar Üzerine Bir Analiz", ViraVerita E-Dergi, 2, 1–22.

Suğur S.,Suğur N.(1998), Çağdaş Yaşam Çağdaş İnsan, Editör: Gürhan Can, Eskişehir, AÖF Yayınları.

Tepe Fatma F.(2019), "Women's Discrimination in Engineering Faculties: A View from Turkey", Anemon Muş Alparslan Üniversitesi Sosyal Bilimler Dergisi, 7(3), 199–209.

Ünnü, N, Baybars, M, Kesken, J. (2014) Türkiye'de Kadınların Üniversiteler Bağlamında Yetki Ve Karar Verme Mekanizmalarına Katılımı. *Dumlupınar Üniversitesi Sosyal Bilimler Dergisi,* (42), 121–134.

Üstün S., Gümüşeli A. İ.(2017), "Many Lives of Women Rectors at Turkish Universities", Journal of Education and Training Studies, 5(8), 123–131.

Yenilmez-İnce M.(2016), "Women in Academia in Turkey: Challenges and Opportunities", Journal of Administrative Sciences, 14(28), 289–311.

Yıldız S. (2018), "Türkiye'de Kadın Akademisyen Olmak", Yükseköğretim ve Bilim Dergisi, 8(1), 29–40.

Internet Resources

CoHE, Unit of Women Studies in Academia (Çevrimiçi):https://kadincalismalari.yok.gov.tr/Sayfalar/DuyuruDetay.aspx?did=13, Date of Access:01.01.2020.

EWORA (Çevrimiçi): https://www.ewora.org/, Date of Access:03.01.2020.

İnas Darülfünunu ve Kadınlar Dünyası Dergisi, (Çevrimiçi): https://bianet.org/system/uploads/1/files/attachments/000/001/264/original/UniversitedeIlkKadinlar__opt.pdf?1417525942, Date of Access: 22.12.2019.

The World Bank(2020): https://data.worldbank.org/indicator/SE.TER.TCHR.FE.ZS?end=2018&start=2018, Date of Access: 02.01.2020.

TURKSTAT, Labour Statistics(2020): http://tuik.gov.tr/PreTablo.do?alt_id=1007, Date of Access: 05.01.2020.

Yüksek Öğretimde Değişmeler(1988) Türk Eğitim Derneği, XII. Eğitim Toplantısı, 17–18 Kasım 1988, (Çevrimiçi): https://www.ted.org.tr/wp-content/uploads/2019/04/ted_yuksek_ogretimde_degismeler_ocr.pdf, 22.11.2019.

Yükseköğretim Bilgi Sistemi, (Çevrimiçi): https://istatistik.yok.gov.tr/, Date of Access: 12.01.2020.

Section 3 Parental Researches on Women in Labor Markets

Zeynep Elitaş

Parental Time Investment in Children: How Parents' Education Affects Time Allocation

1 Introduction

Early childhood is the crucial period to stimulate children's skill development and thus improve chances to do well in later schooling and the labor market. There is a well-deserved practical and scientific interest on this topic; there is also a recent literature showing that children's outcomes are, in turn, key determinants of future adulthood outcomes, including earnings (Danziger and Waldfogel, 2000) and health (Currie et al., 2008). The differences early in life determine differing levels of educational attainment and even differing levels of involvement in the criminal justice system and patterns of family formation (Duncan et al., 2015).

Parents invest both material resources and time in raising their children (Becker, 1964, 1981; Becker and Lewis, 1973). It is well known that there is a strong link between parental childcare time and well-being of children. This is one of the rare issues on which there is a broad consensus among sociologists, psychologists and economists. Time investment in children, particularly at early ages, has significant life-long consequences, as it affects the children human capital accumulation process, as well as their psychological well-being (Cunha et al., 2006; Cunha and Heckman, 2010; Shonkoff and Phillips, 2000). Moreover, the quantity and quality of childcare time is generally assumed to be decisive for children's well-being and skill development (Kalenkoski, Ribbar and Stratton et al., 2005; Sayer, Gauthier and Furstenberg, 2004; Stafford and Yeung, 2005). Since Leibowitz's distinctive work on parental childcare time and increased human capital of children (Leibowitz, 1974), researchers have analyzed the relationship between parental time investment and child outcomes (Blau and Grossberg, 1990; Brooks-Gunn et al., 2002; Han et al., 2001), with most of the existing research finding a positive relationship between them. Therefore, understanding parental time dedication to childcare and studying what factors (e.g., education, income, occupation and race) influencing the time parents devote to their children may be important for both parents and policymakers and deserves some attention.

Among the factors influencing the time parents devote to their children, parental education appears as a crucial determinant. Prior research has found a positive relationship between parents' education and parental time investment in the child (Guryan, Hurst and Kearney, 2008). There is substantial evidence that the ability of parents to invest in their children varies considerably by education (Sayer, Gauthier and Furstenberg, 2004). More specifically, parental care increases by level of education (Bianchi, Robinson and Milkie, 2006; Leibowitz, 1974; Sayer, Gauthier and Furstenberg, 2004). Well-educated parents devote more time to their children compared to their less-educated counterparts. Moreover, the former also focus more on their child-related time on activities designed to nurture their children's cognitive development (Bianchi and Robinson, 1997; Hofferth and Sandberg, 2001).

Moreover, the role of educational attainment on time spent differs between mothers and fathers. Research shows that mothers invest considerably more time than fathers in childcare tasks (Bittman, 1999; Sayer, Bianchi, and Robinson, 2004). There are different hypotheses on this. One is that educationally homogamous parents specialize less in childcare. That is to say there is greater similarity between mother and fathers in their time use and relative dedication to childcare (Andersen and Bonke, 2007). According to other one, the varying role of education on time spent may be influenced by the sex of the children. We know from empirical studies that fathers spend more time on, and are also more involved with, sons than daughters (Andersen and Bonke, 2007; Lundberg, 2005). The childcare tasks in which parents engage also differ, with mothers doing more physical or routine care of children than fathers. Additionally, although mothers spend more absolute time playing with children, fathers spend a proportionally larger amount of their time engaged in play (Pleck, 1997; Sayer, Gauthier and Furstenberg, 2004).

What are the factors that lead to the fact that highly educated parents spend more time and spend time differently with children is an important question. It requires attention whether well-educated parents have different norms of parenting compared to less-educated ones. It is also important to search the effects which leads to different time allocation of mothers' and fathers' in deriving related policy implications with respect to the childcare. This study aims to shed light on these questions by investigating the effects of parents' education status on time spent with their children and to observe the determinants causing different time allocation of mothers and fathers. To the authors' knowledge, there is no study that empirically tests the impact of educational attainment of parents on their devoted time on children using a micro level childcare time data in Turkey. In this respect, this work will add to previous knowledge on the effects of parental education on time with children by providing a picture of how Turkish parents with different education levels allocate time to childcare. For this purpose, individual and household level micro data and detailed time-diary information on daily activities of childcare from the 2014–2015 time-use survey data conducted by TurkStat is used. Physical care time, education activities and other childcare activities are analyzed. Ordinary least squares (OLS), logit and multinomial logit models are estimated as a function of educational status, employment status, demographic factors and other control variables for each of these childcare time variables.

Results imply that the emphasis on care time is correlated with mothers' education. Being a higher educated mother has a significant effect on time spent with children. Moreover, the important result emerging from estimations for fathers is that the presence of highly educated mother is an important condition for fathers' time dedication.

The rest of the study is as follows: Section 2 discusses the literature on the link between parental time investment on children and education level. Section 3 presents the data set and the methodology. Results are shown in section 4; and section 5 concludes, providing directions for future research.

2 Literature Review

As mentioned earlier, the quantity and quality of childcare time is generally assumed to be an important determinant for children's well-being and skill development (Kalenkoski, Ribbar and Stratton et al., 2005; Sayer, Gauthier and Furstenberg, 2004; Stafford and Yeung, 2005). Two recent longitudinal studies provide empirical support for this assumption (Hsin, 2008; Würtz, 2008). Time investment in children, particularly at early ages, has significant life-long consequences, as it affects the children human capital accumulation, as well as their psychological health (Altıntas et al., 2016). Parental time is shown to play an important role in producing children abilities (Cunha et al., 2006; Cunha and Heckman, 2010; Shonkoff and Phillips, 2000).

An emerging body of evidence from longitudinal studies consistently shows that educational activity with parents is the most productive input for a child's cognitive skill development (Altıntas et al., 2016; Kalb and Van Ours, 2014). Del Boca et al. (2012) points out that parental time is more important for the cognitive development of children than money spending and emphasizes that early maternal time inputs are prominent for later life outcomes (Becker, 1981, 1991; Heckman and Carneiro, 2003; Leibowitz, 1974). Bradley and Crowyn (2004) and Pleck and Masciadrelli (2004) support the importance of the role of time investment in skill development.

As Altıntas et al. (2016) documents, there is a large number of studies showing that average time spent in primary childcare activities has increased substantially between the 1980s and 1990s across the advanced industrialized countries, such as the United States (Altintas et al., 2016; Bianchi, Robinson and Milkie, 2006; Chalasani, 2007; Sayer, Bianchi and Robinson, 2004), the Netherlands (Bianchi, Robinson, and Milkie, 2006), Canada (Gauthier, Smeeding and Furstenberg, 2004; Zuzanek, 2001), the United Kingdom (Sayer, Bianchi and Robinson, 2004) and Australia (Bittman, 1999, 2004; Craig, Powell and Symth, 2014). They mention that the results from Gershuny's (2000) analysis of 20 countries, Gauthier, Smeeding and Furstenberg's (2004) analysis of 16 countries and Guryan, Hurst and Kearney's (2008) analysis of 13 countries confirmed the trends in increased childcare time, especially since the 1980s.

Moreover, there is a consensus in the literature that the childcare is far more pronounced among the highly educated (Bianchi, Robinson and Milkie, 2006). Among the factors influencing the time parents devote to their children, prior research has found a positive relationship between parents' education and parental childcare time (Guryan, Hurst and Kearney, 2008). High-educated parents spend more time in childcare than low-educated parents (Altintas et al., 2016; Craig and Mullan, 2010; Guryan, Hurst and Kearney, 2008; Kalenkoski, Ribbar and Stratton et al., 2005; Leibowitz, 1974; Monna and Gauthier, 2008; Sayer, Gauthier and Furstenberg, 2004) and devote a larger amount of time in developmentally remarkable activities (Altintas, 2015; Bianchi and Robinson, 1997; Craig, Powell and Smyth, 2014; Guryan, Hurst and Kearney, 2008; Hofferth and Sandberg, 2001; Monna and Gauthier, 2008) as opposed to basic care activities.

Regarding the issue how education impact the allocation of childcare time of individuals is somewhat complicated in the literature. The human capital perspective suggests that a higher education means a pull to the market. Human capital theory predicts that the greater the investment a person has made in their marketable skills, the higher the wage rate they will command, and consequently, the stronger will be their attachment to the paid workforce (Becker, 1994; Mincer and Polachek, 1974). Because the opportunity costs of foregoing wages will be higher, people who invest more in their own higher education will be drawn to allocate more time to paid than to unpaid labor (Becker, 1981). Therefore the theory predicts that educated women will spend less time doing household work and are likely to have fewer children because the opportunity costs of leaving the workforce are greater for the more highly educated (Becker, 1981). However, many point out that individual utility maximization is an inadequate framework for understanding decisions about caring for children (Craig, 2006; Nelson, 1996). In their words, literature states that education may also exercise a pull to the home or a pull to care. Parents who have invested in their own education may be the ones most concerned with their children's acquisition of human capital in the ways outlined above. With some exceptions, previous time-use investigation has found that highly educated parents spent more overall time with children. Highly educated parents have also been found to spend a greater proportion of their time with children in active care, and paternal education has been found to be associated with an increase in time fathers spend playing, reading or taking children out. From the human capital perspective, there are two explanations to this positive relationship between parents' education and parental childcare time. One is that parents may see investing in their child's education as a luxury good, and thus highly educated parents may decide to invest more in their children compared to their low-educated counterparts. Also, highly educated parents may feel that market-purchased childcare options are poor substitutes for parental time, and thus they trade off their time with market-purchased childcare services (Andersen and Bonke, 2007; Bonke and Andersen, 2009; Leibowitz, 1974). This leads us to hypothesize that childcare and, especially developmental care, increases with parents' education. Therefore, taken together, theory states that potentially the effects are contradictory.

Another point is that, contemporary research also displays that the time allocation experienced by mothers and fathers varies. Sayer, Gauthier and Furstenberg (2004) discuss that mothers and fathers perform household labor to the extent that they have available time, as determined by competing demands. Employment status and spouse employment status are typically used as measures of competing time demands (Twiggs, McQuillan and Ferree, 1999). Moreover, they discuss that mothers invest considerably more time than fathers in childcare tasks (Bianchi, Robinson and Milkie, 2006; Bittman, 1999; Guryan, Hurst and Kearney, 2008; Sayer, Gauthier and Furstenberg, 2004). Keizer et al. (2019) also mention about gender roles and shared parenting literature by investigating the role of parents' equally sharing childcare responsibilities as a mediator between educational attainment and child outcomes.

Literature also addresses the fact that the childcare tasks in which parents engage may differ, with mothers doing more physical or routine care of children than fathers. Sayer, Gauthier and Furstenberg (2004) mention that although mothers spend more absolute time playing with children, fathers spend a proportionally larger amount of their time engaged in play (Pleck, 1997). They discuss that, in the past, fathers with employed wives were also found not to spend more time in childcare activities as compared with fathers with nonemployed wives, but recent research indicates that fathers in two-earner families may now be spending more time caring for children than they have historically (Pleck, 1997). Moreover, the study reveals that the effect of paternal education on fathers' time is for children is more mixed than the effect for mothers, varying with the age of the child and type of activity engaged in with children. Some research indicates that fathers' education has no effect on direct physical care of young children (Aldous et al., 1998; Marsiglio, 1991), but does increase the time that fathers spend playing, reading or going on outings with their preschool-age children (Cooney et al., 1993). For school-age children, paternal education is positively related to more time talking with children and helping them with homework (Aldous et al., 1998; Marsiglio 1991).

There have been few studies investigating childcare in Turkey. However, none of them seeks to describe the parents' education as it influences the time devoted to childcare activities. There are two studies in childcare preferences. One estimates the factors that affect childcare preference of married working women having children being 5 years old and younger with multinomial logit model (Kakıcı et al., 2007). By using raw data of 1998 Turkish Population and Health Search survey of Hacettepe Institute of Population Studies, they find that mother's age and education level are important factors in childcare preferences. Second one focuses on childcare choices of working women. They determine the factors that affect childcare choices of working women that have child under age 5 in Turkey using pooled data for years 1993, 1998, 2003 and 2008 from Turkey Demographic and Health Survey data sets conducted by Hacettepe University, Institute of Population Studies. They analyze the changes of childcare choices over the years of working women using multinomial logit and multinomial probit models (Gunes et al., 2017). Furthermore, Kongar and Memis (2017) examine gender differences in time allocation among married couples over the life cycle using 2006 Turkish time-use survey. They find that there are large discrepancies in the gender division of both paid and unpaid work; the gender gap in paid and unpaid work is largest among parents of infants compared to parents of older children and couples without children. Married women's housework time remains relatively unchanged across their life cycle, while older men spend more time doing housework than their younger counterparts.

3 Data and Methodology

3.1 Data

Individual and household level data set from the 2014–2015 time-use survey conducted by TurkStat is used in the analysis. Besides collecting information on household characteristics and family composition as well as individual characteristics such as education, employment, earnings and demographic information, the survey has a detailed time-diary component on daily activities of childcare. A merged data set from individual-level data, the household-level data and time-diary information is utilized.

The sample of the study consists of family households having at least one children aged between 0 and 5 in the household.[1] Those type of households having children at home aged between 0 and 5 but if the children are coded as relatives, having two wives living in the household, containing more than one extended family in the same household are excluded from the analysis.[2]

Time-diary data provides a more detailed information than the data derived from responses to "usual activity" survey questions. These diaries contain the information about time spent in child's physical care and educational activities. The respondents are asked to complete a weekday and a weekend time diary identifying the daily activities of childcare for each 10-minute interval as well as whether they were together with when doing the different activities, i.e., his/her partner, children, other people or alone. Average activity time is average value in 24 hours of total time spent by individual for any activity. This period is average taken over all people aged 10 and older and all year (workdays

1 There are 4979 observations (individuals) and 1805 family households in the analysis (that we have 1805 mothers and fathers for observation).

2 By "extended family" the author means that there is one household head and spouse and for instance they have a son and daughter-in law and/or has a daughter and son-in law and grandchild in the same household. Because by the construction of the data, one cannot able to observe exactly who is the mother or father of these children. One cannot be able to differentiate between them. This is a rather small number of observations and our estimations are therefore likely to suffer from larger error terms. Surprisingly, there are households in the data in which there is one household head reporting that he has a spouse, and spouse reports herself as *married*. However, household head reports himself as *never married*. So most probably, they are not an officially married couple but with children aged 0–5. In those cases, they are assumed to be married and are included in the data set since it is known for sure that this female (wife) is the mother of the child in the household.

and weekends as well as period of the holiday). Since the data contains a direct diary information from both partners for the same day, the time use data in the analysis is likely to be substantially more reliable than in most time use surveys, such as for example the recent American Time Use Survey, where only one representative of the household was filling out a diary.

Respondents are asked separately for their time allocation in: (i) child's physical care activities such as feeding and dressing, medical care of children, (ii) educational activities: there are two groups of educational activities, one is directly asked as teaching the child and the other is talking or reading to them or playtime activities. These two are combined in one activity and named as "educational activities," (iii) other childcare activities: There are two activity group in the questionnaire asking as accompanying to a child (can be activities where the child was present such as listening to radio and/or looking at TV) and other childcare activities. They are again combined in one and classified as "other child care activities."

Therefore, three different childcare activity groups are constructed: "physical care activities," "educational activities," and "other child care activities." These are measured as the aggregate number of intervals where it was performed multiplied by 10 minutes and calculated in absolute numbers of minutes, in other words, how much time respondents spend time to those activities. The information refers to one weekday and one weekend day per respondent. In the analysis, they will also be distinguished between weekdays and weekends. So there will be "physical care activities" conducted at weekdays and physical care activities conducted at weekends. Similarly, "educational activities" are conducted at weekdays and weekends, and "other childcare activities" at weekdays and weekends.

In addition to time spent on childcare activities variables (with pre-school children aged between 0 and 5), demographic variables are also included in the estimations. Age is categorized into five groups: between 18 and 24, between 25 and 29, between 30 and 34, between 35 and 39 and 40 and above.[3] Parents' education level (mother's and father's education) – measured as completed

3 Age is assumed to correlate with time investments in children due to two possible effects: one, older parents may have less energy to devote to their children; two, age may capture cohort effects. One should expect that older men will spend less time with children than younger ones, while the opposite might be the case for older women, who are likely to be more home orientated than their younger sisters.

education is included in five categories: no degree, primary school and secondary school; high school degree and college degree). In order to control for time availability and the degree to which there are trade-offs between caring and market work, parents' employment status (employed or not employed) is also included. Household monthly average net income is included in five categories: 0–1080 TL, 1081–1550 TL, 1551–2170 TL, 2171–3180 TL and 3181+ TL. Household size is also controlled using number of individuals in the household. In order to identify the possible impact of child preferences, number of children aged between 0 and 5 and the number of children aged six and older are involved. Health condition of respondents are controlled and have constructed three categories out of five: individuals with very good health, with a good health and those having average or bad and worse health condition. Furthermore, a control variable for having a physical/mental problem, a chronic disease or disability condition is included. This question is asked to respondents who answered their health condition as average, bad or worse. We therefore assume those who reported that they have a very good or good health as they don't have a physical/mental problem, a chronic disease or disability condition. Tab. 5.1 shows descriptive statistics for all variables used in the estimations.

Table 5.1 shows that the largest group of individuals included in estimations is between the ages of 30–34. Almost 93 % of fathers are employed while the ratio for mothers is only 25 %. A majority of both mothers and fathers are primary school graduates with the ratio of 35 %. The highest share belongs to the very low-income category (0–1080 TL a month) around 26 %. Around 9 % of both mothers and fathers state that they have physical or mental problems or chronical disease or disability. Regarding the dependent variables, one can observe that the mean of weekday physical care activities is 177 minutes for mothers while it is much less for fathers. This group has the largest share in mothers' care activities followed by physical care activities conducted at weekends with 88 minutes at the mean. The mean educational care activities carried by mothers at weekdays are much higher (more than doubled) compared to those at weekends. On average, weekend activities of childcare performed by mothers are lower compared to their weekday counterparts. On the other hand, weekday educational activities have the largest share in fathers' time allocation. Moreover, physical care activities conducted by mothers are almost 12 fold higher than fathers. This picture tells us that fathers have not much to do with physical care activities of their children. It is still considered as mothers' job.

Tab. 5.1: Descriptive Statistics

	(%)					
Explanatory Variables	**Mother**	**Father**			**Mean**	**Std. Dev.**
Age categories				HH size	4.52	(1.48)
18≤Age≤24	10.14	1.50		Number of children aged 0–5	1.23	(0.49)
25≤Age≤29	25.82	13.63		Number of children aged 6+	0.98	(1.12)
30≤Age≤34	30.69	31.19		*HH income categories*		
35≤Age≤39	22.88	28.09		0–1080	26.48	(32.14)
Age≥40	10.47	25.60		1081–1550	24.76	(25.65)
Employed	25.48	92.91		1551–2170	17.29	(19.16)
Education categories				2171–3180	14.96	(20.11)
No degree	14.46	4.27		3181+	16.51	(26.12)
Primary school	34.24	34.13				
Secondary school	17.06	15.79				
High school	18.95	24.99				
College degree and higher	15.29	20.83				
Health Status						
Very good	14.63	15.18				
Good	69.03	68.03				
Average/Bad or worse	16.34	16.79				
Chronical disease	8.92	8.64				
Dependent Variables	Mother		Father			
	Mean	**Std. Dev.**	**Mean**	**Std. Dev.**		
Weekday Physical Care Actv.	177.81	(182.30)	14.83	(40.63)		
Weekday Education Actv.	78.78	(88.48)	55.08	(76.60)		
Weekday Other Childcare Actv.	22.50	(54.06)	5.00	(33.20)		
Weekend Physical Care Acvt.	87.30	(99.03)	9.77	(31.31)		
Weekend Education Actv.	35.45	(51.89)	30.85	(52.47)		
Weekend Other Childcare Actv.	9.57	(34.95)	2.70	(25.27)		

Notes: Number of observations are 4979 (individuals) and 1805 family households (1805 mothers and 1805 fathers) in the analysis.

3.2 Methodology

Parental childcare time with pre-school children aged between 0 and 5 are separately estimated for mothers and fathers' in the household with the following equation using ordinary least squares (OLS):

$$Y_i = \alpha + \beta X_i + \lambda Z_i + \varepsilon_i \quad (1)$$

where Y denotes parental time with one of those categories written above for individual i. X represents the vector of demographic variables and β is the corresponding vector of parameters. Z denotes the vector of education status variables and λ is the associated vector of parameters, and ε is i.i.d. error term.

4 Results

Tables 5.2 and 5.3 present ordinary least squares estimations. Time spent on child's physical and educational care in any day of the week or any day of the weekend by mothers having at least one child aged between 0 and 5 are estimated as a function of their demographic characteristics, education and employment condition and other control variables.[4] Separate regressions are estimated for mothers and fathers. Each column shows a separate estimation for each of the dependent variables.

Results estimated for mothers' document that the emphasis on care time is correlated with mothers' education. Being a higher educated mother has a significant effect in all estimations except time spent on physical care activities at weekends for high school graduates. Higher educated mothers spend more time both on physical or educational care compared to their low-educated counterparts. It is an evidence that maternal care increases by level of education confirming "education is a pull to care" hypothesis as mentioned in the descriptive part. This effect appears to be more distinctive for time spent on educational care activities compared to that on physical care activities. The effect of father's education level on mothers' time on child's physical and educational care is neglectable. There is no evidence of a significant effect that fathers' education level affects mothers' childcare time. However, this effect will reveal a different result in fathers' estimations. Being employed has a significant effect for all estimations for mothers except for the educational care

4 Average marginal effects of ordered logit models for the other care activities are not reported here but available upon the request.

Tab. 5.2: Ordinary Least Squares (OLS) Estimations for Physical and Educational Care Activities for Mothers

	Weekday Activities		**Weekend Activities**	
	Phy. Care	**Educ. Care**	**Phy. Care**	**Educ. Care**
Own-Educ. Level				
Primary	27.409*	13.006*	11.344	3.933
Secondary	(14.681)	(7.255)	(8.105)	(4.347)
High School	20.739	30.777***	7.612	12.698**
College and higher	(17.055)	(8.429)	(9.416)	(5.050)
	38.569**	43.243***	14.758	18.298***
	(17.893)	(8.843)	(9.879)	(5.298)
	74.727***	59.529***	30.473**	29.140***
	(21.586)	(10.668)	(11.918)	(6.391)
Father's Educ. Level	7.456	7.551	−4.832	−1.643
Primary	(22.383)	(11.062)	(12.358)	(6.627)
Secondary	11.719	12.953	−2.517	−2.418
	(24.104)	(11.913)	(13.308)	(7.137)
High School	22.900	14.161	5.393	−0.124
	(24.088)	(11.905)	(13.299)	(7.132)
College and higher	7.66	8.315	−5.470	−4.564
	(26.034)	(12.867)	(14.374)	(7.708)
Employed	−72.126***	−16.605***	−28.664***	−2.871
	(10.252)	(5.067)	(5.660)	(3.035)
Age Category				
25<=age>=29	−15.447	4.561	−6.308	−0.839
	(15.447)	(7.634)	(8.528)	(4.573)
30<=age>=34	−44.459***	0.231	−19.152**	−0.508
	(16.260)	(8.036)	(8.977)	(4.814)
35<=age>=39	−45.706***	−5.564	−20.142**	−4.198
	(17.488)	(8.643)	(9.655)	(5.178)
age>=40	−66.369***	9.582	−30.133**	−2.515
	(19.740)	(9.756)	(10.898)	(5.844)
HH size	−7.592	5.226*	−4.4141*	−3.248*
	(6.064)	(2.997)	(3.348)	(1.795)
Num. of child aged 0–5	87.268***	10.959**	45.301***	6.869*
	(10.607)	(5.242)	(5.856)	(3.140)
Num. of child >= aged 6	−10.931	−3.317	−4.920	−0.440
	(7.594)	(3.753)	(4.192)	(2.248)

Tab. 5.2: Continued

	Weekday Activities		Weekend Activities	
	Phy. Care	**Educ. Care**	**Phy. Care**	**Educ. Care**
HH average income				
1081–1550	19.361*	1.824	8.167	5.071
	(11.576)	(5.721)	(6.391)	(3.427)
1551–2170	19.479	−0.03	7.757	3.260
	(11.576)	(6.542)	(7.308)	(3.919)
2171–3180	16.136	−3.330	7.480	3.419
	(14.492)	(7.162)	(8.001)	(4.291)
3181+	13.319	5.295	5.073	4.658
	(16.907)	(8.356)	(9.334)	(5.006)
Health status				
Good	−16.829	0.317	−8.492	0.427
	(11.664)	(5.765)	(6.440)	(3.453)
Average/Bad or worse	−5.475	6.737	−8.622	9.954*
	(18.742)	(9.129)	(10.199)	(5.469)
Chr. Disease/Disability	20.158	−2.725	9.893	4.349
	(20.073)	(9.921)	(11.083)	(5.943)
Observations	1805	1805	1805	1805

Notes: * $p<0.10$, ** $p<0.05$*** $p<0.01$. Standard errors are in parentheses.

time conducted at weekends. Employed mothers spend less time in childcare as expected. However, it is the physical care activities which are worst affected compared to educational ones in magnitudes. The trade-off between time to care and employment is smaller in magnitude with regards to educational care. Findings for mothers' regressions also give prominence to the impact of age. Mothers spend less time to physical childcare as they age obviously. There is no evidence of significant effect on their time allocation to educational care activities, though. Once more, educational care seems least affected, which is very small in magnitudes. Household size negatively effects mothers' time allocation to care and is only significant for educational care. This result could be justified by the fact that as household size expands, the number of tasks and amount of responsibilities for mother increases. The number of children between the ages 0 and 5 in the household is an important condition for mothers' time dedication, not surprisingly. Number of children older than 5 in the household decreases amount of time to care although no significant effect is found. Health condition does not seem to have any significant effect except that having not a good health increases mothers' time allocation for educational care activities at

Tab. 5.3: Ordinary Least Squares (OLS) Estimations for Physical and Educational Care Activities for Fathers

	Weekday Activities		**Weekend Activities**	
	Phy. Care	**Educ. Care**	**Phy. Care**	**Educ. Care**
Own Educ. Level				
Primary	5.436	25.477**	2.592	14.658**
Secondary	(5.233)	(9.600)	(4.079)	(6.624)
High School	6.506	33.001***	4.191	19.290***
College and higher	(5.609)	(10.290)	(4.372)	(7.100)
	8.091	36.595***	3.508	20.699***
	(5.584)	(10.245)	(4.353)	(7.069)
	14.896*	38.652***	9.083*	22.700***
	(6.039)	(11.079)	(4.708)	(7.644)
Mother's Educ. Level				
Primary	−0.154	−6.228	−1.606	−2.711
Secondary	(3.355)	(6.155)	(2.615)	(4.247)
High School	−0.903	−4.917	−1.507	−1.978
College and higher	(3.911)	(7.175)	(3.049)	(4.950)
	2.626	−2.182	0.134	1.380
	(4.102)	(7.525)	(3.792)	(6.157)
	9.074*	29.534***	3.301	23.183***
	(4.864)	(8.924)	(2.782)	(6.157)
Employed	9.751**	33.533***	−3.227	11.417**
	(3.897)	(7.150)	(3.038)	(4.933)
Age Category	6.107	22.089	3.873	11.532
25<=age>=29	(8.073)	(14.810)	(6.293)	(10.218)
30<=age>=34	10.148	27.053*	7.894	12.334
	(7.969)	(14.620)	(6.212)	(10.087)
35<=age>=39	7.765	19.177	4.411	7.741
	(8.079)	(14.822)	(6.298)	(10.227)
age>=40	6.396	17.683	3.416	7.732
	(8.129)	(14.913)	(6.336)	(10.289)
HH size	−1.843	−8.195***	−1.150	−4.640***
	(1.399)	(2.567)	(1.090)	(1.771)
Num. of child aged 0–5	7.893***	21.410***	3.885	13.873
	(2.442)	(4.480)	(1.903)	(3.091)
Num. of child>=aged 6	−1.578	−0.912	−0.975	−0.368
	(1.735)	(3.183)	(1.352)	(2.196)
HH average income				
1081–1550	1.034	1.391	1.530	2.360
	(2.673)	(4.904)	(2.083)	(3.383)

Tab. 5.3: Continued

	Weekday Activities		Weekend Activities	
1551–2170	2.115	3.334	2.325	3.173
	(3.067)	(5.626)	(2.390)	(3.882)
2171–3180	1.562	7.702	3.031	3.579
	(3.359)	(6.163)	(2.619)	(4.252)
3181+	9.797**	9.817	7.642	8.743*
	(3.833)	(7.032)	(2.988)	(4.852)
Health status	−2.029	13.638*	−2.653	6.934
Good	(2.648)	(4.858)	(2.064)	(3.352)
Average/ Bad or worse	−4.133	1.090	−5.083	−2.138
	(4.082)	(7.488)	(3.182)	(5.167)
Chr. Disease/ Disability	2.802	−4.758	0.081	−1.809
	(4.571)	(8.386)	(3.563)	(5.786)
Observations	1805	1805	1805	1805

Notes: * p<0.10, ** p<0.05*** p<0.01. Standard errors are in parentheses.

weekends. Average income of the household has significant effect only for the low-income category for weekday physical care activities. Time spent on childcare decreases with the household's average income.

Turning now to fathers, Tab. 5.3 confirms that the emphasis on care time is correlated with fathers' education similar to mothers'. Higher educated fathers spend more time on educational childcare through educational distribution. However, time dedicated to physical care is not similar across educational distributions. Only in a college or higher degree category, the emphasis on physical care is found to be correlated with education, and it increases by level of education. The important result emerging from estimations for fathers is that the presence of highly educated mother is an important determinant for fathers' time dedication both on physical and educational care being the opposite of what is found for mothers' education. However, maternal education level in low education categories does not play a role in fathers' time allocation. Similar to what is observed in mothers' time allocation, being employed has a significant effect for almost all estimations except for the physical care at weekends. The effect is more distinctive for educational care since fathers do not engage that much in physical care activities. Age seems to be an important factor for mother's estimations. However, not found to be a significant determinant for fathers' marginal effects. Only in 30–34 age category, educational care time is correlated with fathers' age. Moreover, results suggest that the direction of the impact of age is not similar to those of mothers. Results reveal that fathers allocate more time to childcare both in this age category and in all other categories unlike what is observed for mothers. Household size negatively affects fathers' time allocation only in educational childcare. As the number of children between the ages 0 and 5 in the household increases, time dedication of fathers decreases similar to findings obtained for mothers. Health condition does not seem to have any significant effect except that having a good health increases fathers' time allocation for educational care at weekends. Average income of the household has significant effect only for the very high-income category for physical care activities. Even though no significant effect is found, time spent on childcare increases with the income for fathers being contrary to the observations for mothers.

5 Conclusion

Research on parental time investment in children associated with parents' education level has been relatively scarce in Turkey. The aim of this study is to describe the effect of parents' education on time spent with pre-school children aged between 0 and 5. For this purpose, parental childcare time is separately estimated for mothers and fathers on their education levels and other control variables. Since we analyze mothers' and fathers' childcare separately, we do not distinguish between joint parental and individual parental childcare. In the analysis, 2014–2015 time-use survey data and diaries of daily activities conducted by TurkStat for Turkey are used. These diaries contain the information about time spent in child's physical care and educational activities. I analyze the time that mothers and fathers devote to three types of childcare: physical childcare, educational childcare and other childcare.

Findings are consistent with previous studies to the extent that education is positively associated with parental investment in childcare. Both mothers and fathers with more education spend more time in childcare. At all education levels, I find that both mothers and fathers concentrate on their childcaring efforts during weekdays. Similar to other studies, such as Bittman (1999) and Sayer, Gauthier and Furstenberg (2004), I find that the effect of education is stronger among mothers than fathers. At all educational levels, mothers continue to invest more time in children than fathers. This suggests that care responsibilities are more centrally located within mothers' lives than fathers. Furthermore, physical care activities are still highly gendered in educated households. Broadly speaking, it is mothers who supply the higher allocation to physical childcare.

Highly educated fathers, as one would expect, are more likely than less educated fathers to involve in fatherhood. As a result, the gender gap in parental time investments in children may be smaller for the well educated than for the less educated. Fathers who are highly educated spend more time performing both physical and educational care than other fathers.

The effect of fathers' education level on mothers' time on child's physical and educational care is neglectable. However, father care with either a college or a higher degree is conducted alongside mother care. But still, while father care with higher degree of education is conducted alongside mother care, men with either a bachelor's or a postgraduate degree average slightly more time caring for their children independently than other fathers as mentioned above.

Research documents that both employed mothers and employed fathers spend less time in childcare, but employment effects are much stronger for mothers than fathers. This result is consistent with the question of whether educated women are particularly affected by the conflicting pull to work and care. As Craig (2006) suggests, at higher levels of education, education for women is associated with more time in childcare and more time in paid work. This suggests that highly educated mothers try to simultaneously access their market opportunities and maintain time in childcare. This is consistent both with economic theory that suggests those with more earning capacity will assign more time to the paid workforce and also with the idea that educated mothers particularly subscribe to the ideal of involved parenting.

References

Aldous, J., Mulligan, Y., and Bjarnason, T. (1998), "Fathering over Time: What Makes the Difference?", *Journal of Marriage and Family*, 60(4), 809–820.

Altintas, E., Casarico, A., and Sommacal, A. (2016), "Distributional Aspects of Parental Time with Children: Evidence from the Multinational Time Use Study (1961–2011)", mimeo.

Andersen, G. E., and Bonke, J. (2007), "Parental Investments in Children: How Bargaining and Educational Homogamy Affect Time Allocation", DemoSoc Working Paper, Paper No: 2007–20, 25–27.

Becker, G. S. (1964), *Human Capital: A Theoretical and Empirical Analysis, with Special Reference to Education*. Chicago, IL: University of Chicago Press.

Becker, G. S. (1981), "Altruism in the Family and Selfishness in the Market Place", *Economica*, 48(189), 1–15.

Becker, G. S. (1991), *Treatise on the Family*. Cambridge, MA: Harvard University Press.

Becker, G. S., and Lewis, H. G. (1973), "On the Interaction between the Quantity and Quality of Children", *Journal of Political Economy*, 81, 79–88.

Bianchi, S. M., and Robinson, J. P. (1997), "What Did You Do Today? Children's Use of Time, Family Composition, and the Acquisition of Social Capital", *Journal of Marriage and the Family*, 59(2), 332–344.

Bianchi, S. M., Robinson, J. P., and Milkie, M. A. (2006), "The Changing Rhythms of American Family Life", A volume in the American Sociological Association's Rose Series in Sociology.

Bittman, M. (1999), "Social Participation and Family Welfare: The Money and Time Costs of Leisure," Discussion Papers 0095, University of New South Wales, Social Policy Research Centre.

Bonke, J., and Andersen, G. E. (2011), "Family Investments in Children, Productivities, Preferences, and Parental Child Care", *European Sociological Review*, 27(1), 43–55.

Blau, F. D., and, Grossberg, A. (1990), "Maternal Labor Supply and Children's Cognitive Development", NBER Working Paper Series, Paper No: 3536.

Bradley, R. H., and Corwyn, R. F. (2004), "Family Process" Investments That Matter for Child Well-Being. In A. Kalil & T. DeLeire (Eds.), *Monographs in Parenting. Family Investments in Children's Potential: Resources and Parenting Behaviors that Promote Success* (pp. 1–32). Lawrence Erlbaum Associates.

Brooks-Gunn, J., Han, W-J., and Waldfogel, J. (2002), "Maternal Employment and Child Cognitive Outcomes in the First Three Years of Life: The NICHD Study of Early Child Care", *Child Development*, 73(4) 1052–1072.

Cooney, T. M., Pedersen F. A., Indelicato S., and Palkovitz R. (1993), "Timing of Fatherhood: Is "On-Time" Optimal?", *Journal of Marriage and Family*, 55(1), 205–215.

Cunha, F., and Heckman J. J. (2010), "Investing in Our Young People." NBER Working Paper Series, Paper No: 16201.

Cunha, F., Heckman J. J., Lochner J., and Masterov D. V. (2006), "Interpreting the Evidence on Life Cycle Skill Formation." In E.A. Hanushek and F. Welch (Eds.), *Handbook of the Economics Education* (pp. 697–812). Amsterdam: North-Holland.

Currie, C., Molcho, M., Boyce, W., and Holstein, B. E. (2008), "Searcing Health Inequalities in Adolescents: The Development of the Health Behaviour in School-Aged Children (HBSC) Family Affluence Scale", *Social Science and Medicine*, 66(6), 1429–1436.

Chalasani, S. (2007), "The Changing Relationship between Parents' Education and Their Time with Children", *International Journal of Time use Research*, 4(1), 93–117.

Craig, L. (2006), "Parental Education, Time in Paid Work and Time with Children: An Australian Time-Diary Analysis", *The British Journal of Sociology*, 57(4), 553–575.

Craig, L. and Mullan, K. (2010), "Parenthood, Gender and Work-Family in the United States, Australia, Italy, France and Denmark", *Journal of Marriage and Family*, 72, 1344–1361.

Craig, L., Powell, A., and Smyth, C. (2014), "Towards Intensive Parenting? Changes in the Composition and Determinants of Mothers and Fathers' Time with Children 1992–2006", *British Journal of Sociology*, 65(5), 555–579.

Dangizer, S., and Waldfogel, J. (2000), "Investing in Children: What Do We Know? What should We Do?", CASEpaper, 34.

Del Boca, D., Monfardini, C., and Nicoletti, C. (2012), "Children's and Parents' Time-Use Choices and Cognitive Development during Adolescence." Human Capital and Economic Opportunity: A Global Working Group Working Paper Series, 2012–006.

Duncan, G. J., Magnuson, K., and Votruba-Drzal, E. (2015), "Children and Socioeconomic Status." In M. H. Bornstein and T. Leventhal (Eds.) and R. M. Lerner (Ed.-in-Chief), *Handbook of Child Psychology and Development Science: Vol. 4. Ecological Settings and Processes* (7th ed.). Hoboken, NJ: Wiley.

Gauthier, A. H., Smeeding, T. M., and Furstenberg, Jr. F. F. (2004), "Are Parents Investing Less Time in Children? Trends in Selected Industrialized Countries", *Population and Development Review*, 30(4), 647–671.

Gershuny, J. (2003). *Changing times: Work and leisure in postindustrial society.* Oxford University Press on Demand.

Gunes, C., Birecikli, Ş., and Yıldırım, Z. (2017), "Childcare Choices of Working Women: Comparison of Discrete Choice Models with Pooled Data", *Sosyal Güvenlik Dergisi*, 7(1), 123–144.

Guryan, J., Hurst, E., and Kearney, M. (2008), "Parental Education and Parental Time with Children." *Journal of Economic Perspectives*, 22(3), 23–46.

Han, W. J., Waldfogel, J., & Brooks-Gunn, J. (2001). "The effects of early maternal employment on later cognitive and behavioral outcomes". *Journal of Marriage and Family*, 63(2), 336–354.

Heckman, J., and Carneiro, P. (2003), "Human Capital Policy," NBER Working Papers 9495, National Bureau of Economic Research.

Hofferth, S. L., and Sandberg, J. F. (2001), "How American Children Spend Their Time", *Journal of Marriage and the Family*, 63(2), 295–308.

Hsin, A. (2008), *Parenting, Investment in Children and the Social reproduction of Skills and Status*, Doctoral dissertation, Department of Sociology, University of California, Los Angeles.

Kakıcı, H., Emeç, H., and Üçdoğruk, Ş. (2007), "Türkiye'de Çalışan Kadınların Çocuk Bakım Tercihleri", *Ekonometri ve İstatistik*, 5, 20–41.

Kalb, G. and Van Ours, J.C. (2014), "Reading to Young Children: A Head-Start in Life?", *Economics of Education Review*, 40, 1–24.

Kalenkoski, C., Ribar, D., and Stratton, L. (2005), "Parental Childcare in Single Parent, Cohabiting, and Married Couple Families: Time Diary Evidence from the United Kingdom", *American Economic Review Papers and Proceedings*, 95(2), 194–198.

Keizer, A-G., Tiemeijer, W., and Mark, B. (2019), *Why Knowing What to Do Is Not Enough: A Realistic Perspective on Self-Reliance*. ISBN: 978-94-024-1725-8.

Kongar, E., and Memiş, E. (2017), "Gendered Patterns of Time Use over the Life Cycle: Evidence from Turkey", Levy Economics Institute Working Paper, No: 884.

Leibowitz, A. (1974), "Home Investments in Children", *The Journal of Political Economy*, 82/2, 111–131.

Lundberg, S. J. (2005), "Sons, Daughters, and Parental Behavior", *Oxford Review of Economic Policy*, 21(3), 340–356.

Marsiglio, W. (1991), "Paternal Engagement Activities with Minor Children", *Journal of Marriage and the Family*, 53(4), 973–986.

Mincer, J., and Polachek, S., (1974), "Family Investments in Human Capital: Earnings of Women", *Journal of Political Economy*, 82, 76–108.

Monna, B., and Gauthier, A. H. (2008), "A Review of the Literature on the Social and Economic Determinants of Parental Time", *Journal of Economic Issues*, 29, 634–653.

Nelson, J. A. (1996). *Feminism, Objectivity and Economics* (Vol. 7). Psychology Press.

Pleck, J. H. (1997), "Paternal Involvement: Levels, Sources, and Consequences". In M. E. Lamb (Ed.), *The Role of the Father in Child Development*, 66–103.

Pleck, J. H., and Masciadrelli, B. (2004), "Paternal involvement: Levels, Sources, and Consequences." In M. E. Lamb (Ed.), *The Role of the Father in Child Development* (4th ed., pp. 227–271). New York: Wiley.

Sayer, L. C., Bianchi, S. M., and Robinson, J. P. (2004a), "Are Parents Investing Less in Children? Trends in Mothers' and Fathers' Time with Children", *The American Journal of Sociology*, 110(1), 1–43.

Sayer, L. C., Gauthier, A. H., and Furstenberg, Jr., F. F. (2004b), "Educational Differences in Parents' Time with Children: Cross-National Variations", *Journal of Marriage and Family*, 66, 1152–1169.

Shonkoff, J. P., and Phillips, D. A. (2000), *From Neurons to Neighborhoods: The Science of Early Childhood Development*. Washington: National Academy Press.

Stafford, F., and Yeung, W-J. J. (2005), "The Distribution of Children's Developmental Resources". In D. Hamermesh (Ed.), *Economics of Time Use* (pp. 289–313). Elsevier.

Twiggs, L., McQuillan, J., and Ferree, M. M. (1999), "Meaning and Measurement: Reconceptualizing Measures of the Division of Household Labor", *Journal of Marriage and the Family*, 61, 712–724.

Würtz, A. (2008), Child Outcomes – Parental Time Investments and School Characteristics, PhD Thesis no. 2008: 3, Aarhus School of Business, University of Aarhus, Department of Economics.

Zuzanek, J. (2001), Parenting time: Enough or Too Little? *Isuma* 2, no. 2

Didem Pekkurnaz

Employment and Childcare Decisions of Women: An Empirical Analysis for Turkey

1 Introduction

Female labor force participation rate as well as female employment rate for Turkey have been lower than that for men (for those aged 15+ in 2019, labor force participation rate is 72 % for men vs. 34.4 % for women and employment rate is 63.1 % for men vs. 28.7 % for women). Although there has been a slight increase in these rates for women over time (e.g., for women aged 15+, labor force participation rate is 30.8 % in 2013 vs. 34.2 % in 2018 and employment rate is 27.1 % in 2013 vs. 29.4 % in 2018), these numbers are still quite lower than the OECD averages (for women, labor force participation rate is 64.6 % in 2018 and employment rate is 61 % in 2018). These lower rates for Turkish women have been noticed in many studies (see e.g., Dayıoğlu and Kırdar, 2010; Ilkkaracan, 2012; İnce Yenilmez, 2019; Karaalp-Orhan, 2017; Kılıç and Öztürk, 2014; Pekkurnaz, 2020). Those studies that also include an empirical analysis come up with a common result that an increase in the number of small children decreases the chance of being in the labor force or employed (see e.g., Dayıoğlu and Kırdar, 2010; Kılıç and Öztürk, 2014; Pekkurnaz 2020).

Childcare burden, as also discussed in the aforementioned studies, still constitutes an impediment to Turkish women's attachment to the labor market since they typically serve as primary care providers. According to the "2016 Family Structure Survey" conducted by the Turkish Statistical Institute, 86 % of households mothers are responsible for daycare of their small children who are aged between 0 and 5 (TSE, 2017). This statistic helps to explain why most women are not attached to the labor market in Turkey. Women with young children (especially younger than the compulsory primary school age) face work–family conflict when available childcare options are scarce. If their job allows they can take care of their children while working. Another option that is mostly utilized by Turkish women is getting help from relatives (specifically help from grandmothers). About 7.4 % of families use grandmother care (TSE, 2017). There are also paid childcare alternatives: babysitter or formal care (daycares and kindergartens) while only 2.8 % of families use nursery or kindergarten (TSE, 2017). This low rate of formal (institutional) childcare utilization results from the inadequate provision of childcare as well as higher childcare prices in Turkey (Hüseyinli and Hüseyinli, 2016; İnce Yenilmez, 2019). Turkey ranks the lowest among many OECD countries for the enrollment rate in early childhood education and care services for young children (see OECD, 2019 for further information).

The availability of high-quality and affordable childcare would mainly have three important effects on society. First of all, women will be more likely to be employed when publicly provided childcare increases (see e.g., Pekkurnaz, 2020) since they would have more time to spend for work if they can use formal childcare for their children. Secondly, there have been studies linked to the use of formal childcare and children's developmental outcomes. Studies show that high-quality formal care improves children's skills (see e.g., Abner, Gordon, Kaestner and Korenman, 2013; Felfe and Lalive, 2018). Finally, expanding childcare services would also enhance employment opportunities in the area of childcare for women (Hansen and Andersen, 2014). Therefore, we can expect that employment choices are interrelated with the childcare choices of women.

Given these childcare constraints, we may expect that women with small children would be looking for the best childcare alternative so that they can stay in the labor force. If a formal childcare option is available, it is expected that this option would be preferred as long as it is affordable since as mentioned above formal childcare has shown to have positive effects on child development. Moreover, childcare choices do not have to be set at the same time with the labor force participation decisions since women may also select among alternative childcare options while they are already attached to the labor market. Thus, social policies should be developed to help women struggling with balancing work and childcare. However, we need to understand the main determinants of childcare choices and labor force participation decisions of women beforehand to figure out the areas that are needed to be improved.

Considering these arguments above, this study aims to analyze the labor market and childcare choices of women with small children using the most recent available Turkey Demographic and Health Survey (TDHS) data (TDHS 2013). Firstly, women's labor force participation and formal (institutional) childcare use decisions are jointly estimated via the bivariate probit model to figure out the significant socioeconomic and demographic determinants for the full sample of women. To the author's knowledge, this is the first study that empirically estimates the determinants of the decision of formal childcare use jointly with the labor force participation decision for women with small children. Secondly, this study contributes to the literature by analyzing the most important factors on childcare choices of working women in Turkey by using the most recently available nationally representative data set. Those childcare choices include care by the mother, care by relatives and paid childcare options (babysitter or kindergarten). As discussed in the following section, the number of studies on this topic for Turkey is scarce. Although two studies investigate different childcare choices for the smallest child of working women in Turkey, their data sets are not the most recent one. In addition to this, this study makes another contribution by including the most relevant variables, which are omitted in their studies, consistent with the literature. Estimation results reveal that the mother's education level not only affects her labor force status but also determines the childcare choice made. Besides, women from high-wealth families, working with social security and working at regularly paid jobs are more likely to use formal care or paid care.

The rest of the study is as follows. Section 2 discusses the literature on childcare choices and employment of mothers. The data set used in the analysis is presented in Section 3. The methodology is shown in Section 4. Estimation results are shown in Section 5. Finally, section 6 concludes.

2 Literature Review

There is a broad literature on mothers' employment and childcare choices for different countries. The most relevant ones will be discussed in this section. Powell (1997) examines the impact of childcare costs on Canadian mothers' labor supply using a 1988 survey. Results of the bivariate probit model of labor force participation and paid childcare use imply that the number of children at different age groups, presence of older children and adults, partner's work hour flexibility and unearned income are the most important determinants of paid care use. Wetzels (2005) looks at the determinants of the joint decisions of labor market participation and paid childcare use for women in the Netherlands. The mother's education level, her age, nonlabor income and number of children are among the significant factors. Other studies for the Netherlands reveal that not only the earning capacity of mothers but also mothers' attitudes toward work and childcare use have significant effects on the joint decisions of the labor market and childcare use (Van Gameren, 2013; Van Gameren and Ooms, 2009). Bivariate probit model of Viitanen (2005) shows that age and presence/number of small kids have significant effects on labor force participation and paid childcare use decisions using a household survey in the United Kingdom. As shown in Borra (2010), age and number of children as well as the number of adults at home significantly affect labor force participation and childcare use decisions of Spanish mothers.

Mother's age, her educational attainment and family income are significant determinants of childcare options (center care, family homes and babysitter) for Swiss families as shown in Banfi, Farsi and Filippini (2009). Mothers with university degree are more likely to use childcare centers. Higher family income increases the likelihood of the use of childcare centers and babysitters. Borra and Palma (2009) examine childcare choices of Spanish families using Spanish time use and household budget surveys. Results show that families with a large number of adults and higher educated mothers are more likely to use daycare centers while they are less likely to get help from relatives. In addition, unearned income (family income less mother's earnings) has also a positive significant effect on daycare use. Older women are also more likely to use daycare centers or babysitters while they are less likely to take care of their children themselves. Another study for Spain by Suárez (2013) examines the childcare choices (home-based paid care, center-based paid care and unpaid childcare) of working mothers. Estimation results reveal that higher-income families are more likely to use paid childcare while mothers with university degrees are more likely to use only center-based paid care. Carlin, Davis, Kraft and Tout (2019) analyze the childcare selections of low-income families in Minnesota. Results show that the presence of adults at home decreases the use of center care while the availability of a family member or friend decreases both the use of center care and family care.

Although as discussed above empirical studies on childcare and employment decisions for women exist, there are only a few studies considering childcare choices of women in Turkey. Kakıcı, Emeç and Üçdoğruk (2007) analyze childcare choices of working women using TDHS-1998 survey data. Multinomial logit model results show that women working in the public or private sector have a higher probability of paid care use relative to women working as unpaid family workers. Those who work in public sector and are self-employed are less likely to use relative care. Older women and women with higher education are also highly likely to use paid care while low educated ones are more likely to use relative care. However, some important variables are missing in their study: presence and number of children at different age groups, presence of adults at home and wealth level of family and regional location. These variables have significant effects on childcare choices as shown in the results section (see Tab. 6.4). In addition, the main income source of the family is not a good proxy for family income or wealth as the main income source may not be enough to buy paid childcare.

Güneş, Üçdoğruk Birecekli ve Yıldırım (2017) investigate different childcare choices for working women in Turkey. They pool data from TDHS 1993, 1998,

2003 and 2008 surveys. Although this study includes the number of children, household size and regional location, two important variables – wealth and employment information – are not included. They use health insurance information of both women and their partners instead of employment conditions. Results show that working women whose partners have health insurance are more (less) likely to use paid care (relative care). However, health insurance influence the ability to buy health services not childcare services per se. Thus, the significant effect they found maybe capturing the effects of omitted variables. Hence, this study differs from those studies in two respects. Firstly, formal childcare use and labor force participation decisions are jointly estimated. Secondly, childcare choices of working women are analyzed using the most recent available data and with a different variable set.

3 Data

Data set is obtained from the THDS (2013). These nationally representative survey series have been conducted by Hacettepe University Institute of Population Studies once every five years since 1993. It is a cross-sectional survey, that is, it does not follow the same individuals. It has been designed to obtain information on fertility, family planning, child and maternal health, employment status, household characteristics of women at reproductive ages (from 15 to 49). TDHS-2013 data is the last publicly available one of TDHS series (THDS-2018 data set is not publicly available yet). There are 9,746 women surveyed. Among those 2,754 women whose children are less than 60 months old have complete information on the variables used in estimations. There are 683 working women whose children are 5 years old or smaller without missing information on the variables. Since a great majority of women are married at the time of the survey and there are not enough observations for single mothers in our sample, estimations are restricted to married women.

For women whose children are less than 60 months old are asked whether their children were attending formal childcare (daycare center, kindergarten or preschool) or not at the time of the survey. Given this information, the use of formal childcare is created as a binary variable (1 for users; 0 for nonusers). Besides, the person who is responsible for taking care of the smallest child (5 years old or smaller) of a working woman when she is at work is also asked. Answers include herself, relatives (such as female or male children and respondent's mother), babysitter and kindergarten. Childcare type is defined as three groups: herself, relatives and paid care (babysitter and kindergarten). Since convergence couldn't be achieved when four categories are used (because of lack of enough observations to run four categories), babysitter and kindergarten categories are merged.

Women's and their spouse's employment status, status at work and social security coverage are available in the data. The labor force participation variable takes the value of one for women who participate in the labor force at the time of the survey and zero for others. Work status for women has four categories: (1) employer, seasonal, self-employed or other, (2) waged worker, (3) government official and (4) unpaid family worker. Work status categories for spouses are (1) not working, (2) seasonal, unpaid family worker or other, (3) waged worker, (4) government official and (5) employer or self-employed. Information on social security coverage for workers is also available for both women and their spouses.

Other variables that can be obtained from the data set are the age of women, education level of women (no education/incomplete primary education, primary education, secondary education and high school and higher education level), presence of other adults (other than the spouse) at home, presence of children at the age group 6–13, presence of children at the age group 14–17, household size, households' wealth level (poorest, poorer, middle, richer and richest), area of living (urban or rural) and regional location (west, south, central, north and east). Tabs. 6.1 and 6.2 show descriptive statistics for all variables used in estimations.

4 Methodology

Firstly, equations (1) and (2) are estimated jointly via the Bivariate Probit Model to investigate the significant socioeconomic factors related to the joint decisions of labor force participation and formal care use. Y_1 refers to labor force participation decision, and Y_2 refers to the decision of formal care use. X denotes the vector of socio-demographic factors including age, education, number/presence of children, household size, spouse's employment information, wealth level, area of living and regional location. βs are the corresponding regression parameters. u_i and v_i are the error terms of equation (1) and equation (2), respectively. These error terms are assumed to have means equal to zero and variances equal to 1.

$$(1) Y_{1i} = \beta_0 + X_i\beta_1 + u_i$$
$$(2) Y_{2i} = \alpha_0 + X_i\alpha_1 + v_i$$

Tab. 6.1: Descriptive Statistics for Bivariate Probit Model

Dependent variables	(%)	***Explanatory variables***	(%)
Labor force participation	26.80	*Wealth level*	
Formal care use	10.34	Poorest	26.22
Explanatory variables		Poorer	23.71
Presence of children aged 6–13	48.08	Middle	19.75
Presence of children aged 14–17	12.85	Richer	16.09
Presence of other adult at home	21.64	Richest	14.23
Education level		*Region*	
No education/Primary incomplete	19.68	West	20.66
First level primary	36.02	South	14.31
Second level primary	17.97	Central	17.54
High school and higher	26.33	North	13.40
Household size	5.54[a]	East	34.10
Living in an urban area	72.59	*# of children aged <=5*	
Spouse employment information		# of children=1	65.72
Not working	5.48	# of children =2	29.67
Work with social security	70.30	# of children >=3	4.61
Work without social security	24.22	*Age groups*	
Seasonal, unpaid family worker, other	10.20	Age 18–29	49.67
Waged worker	46.11	Age 30–34	28.50
Government official	9.51	Age 35+	21.82
Employer or self-employed	28.69		

Notes: Number of observations are 2754.
[a]It is the mean of the variable.

Since the questionnaire design allows the investigation of different childcare choices only for the working mothers, Multinomial Probit Models are estimated to examine the impact of socioeconomic characteristics on different childcare choices of working women. In this case, the following model is estimated. Dependent variable Y_i has three categories: (1) herself, (2) relatives and (3) paid care (babysitter and kindergarten). X denotes the vector of sociodemographic factors including age, education, number/presence of children, household size, spouse's employment information, her work information, wealth level, area of living and regional location. γs are the corresponding regression parameters, and ε_i is the error term of equation (3).

$$Y_i = \gamma_0 + X_i\gamma_1 + \varepsilon_i \tag{3}$$

Tab. 6.2: Descriptive Statistics for Multinomial Probit Model

Dependent Variable ***Childcare type***	(%)	***Explanatory Variables***	(%)
(1) Herself	28.02	*Women employment information*	
(2) Other family members	52.36	Work with social security	42.77
(3) Paid care (babysitter or formal care)	19.62	Work without social security	57.23
Explanatory variables		Employer, seasonal, self-employed, other	28.17
Presence of children aged 6–13	47.79	Waged worker	24.04
Presence of children aged 14–17	15.49	Government official	17.85
Presence of other adult at home	17.40	Unpaid family worker	29.94
Education level		*Wealth level*	
No education/Primary incomplete	13.27	Poorest	24.48
First level primary	32.45	Poorer	17.55
Explanatory Variables	(%)	***Explanatory Variables***	(%)
Second level primary	12.54	Middle	14.60
High school and higher	41.74	Richer	15.63
# of children aged <=5		Richest	27.73
# of children=1	78.32	Living in an urban area	66.37
# of children >=2	21.68	*Region*	
Spouse employment information		West	24.34
Not working	4.42	South	11.80
Work with social security	70.94	Central	18.14
Work without social security	24.63	North	24.63
Seasonal, unpaid family worker, other	10.91	East	21.09
Waged worker	40.56	*Age groups*	
Government official	16.96	Age 18–29	35.10
Employer or self-employed	27.14	Age 30–34	34.96
Household size	5.14[a]	Age 35+	29.94

Notes: Number of observations are 678.
[a]It is the mean of the variable.

5 Results

5.1 Bivariate Probit Model

Two models are estimated regarding equations (1) and (2). Model 1 includes the information on the social security coverage of spouses while in model 2 job status of the spouse is used. If the error terms of equations (1) and (2) are correlated, the bivariate probit model is used. Otherwise, we can estimate them separately. Wald test is utilized to test if the correlation coefficient of error terms equals to zero or not. According to test results ($\chi^2 = 26.139$ with $p<0.01$ for model 1 and $\chi^2 = 26.113$ with $p<0.01$ for model 2) error terms for the labor force participation and use of formal care equations are correlated for both models, which means that those equations are needed to be jointly estimated. Table 6.3 shows the marginal effect of covariates on the joint decisions of labor force participation and formal care use for models 1 and 2.

Women in the age group 18–29 are less likely to join the labor force and use formal care than women who are at least 35 years old. This means young women may prefer to take care of their own children by withdrawing from the work and/or get help from relatives. Women with education levels lower than high school are statistically significantly less likely to join the labor force as well as to use formal childcare. Positive effects of higher education (or negative effect of lower education level) on labor force participation and paid care use are also available in other studies (Wetzels, 2005). Women refrain from work and tend to use formal childcare if they have more small children. This is also seen in Kimmel (1998), Powell (1997) and Viitanen (2005) (formal care can also be referred to as paid care).

While women are more likely to join the labor force when their spouses are not working or work without social security, the spouse's employment does not have a significant impact on the use of formal childcare. Women from the poorest families are more likely to join the labor force than women from middle wealth level families. Similarly, women from the highest wealth category are more likely to participate in the labor force than women from middle wealth families. Moreover, women from the richest families are also significantly more likely to use formal childcare than middle wealth level families. This result is also confirmed by other studies (Powell, 1997). On the other hand, women from poorer households are significantly less likely to use formal childcare than women from middle wealth level households.

Women located in urban areas are significantly less likely to be in the labor force than women located in rural areas. This result is also observed in a study by Kılıç and Öztürk (2014). The reason is that the labor force participation rate of women in rural areas in 2013 is higher than that of urban areas (36.7 % vs. 28 %, see Labor Force Statistics under Statistics by Theme in the web site of Turkish Statistical Institute). Women from the west, south, central or the east are significantly less likely to join the labor force than women from the north region.

5.2 Multinomial Probit Model

Table 6.4 shows multinomial probit results regarding equation (3). The average marginal effects of variables are estimated for the models 3 and 4. In model 3, social security coverage information is included while in model 4, job status information is used instead. According to model 3 results, women working under social security are statistically significantly more likely than women working without social security to use paid care (including babysitter and kindergarten) while they are less likely to take care of their children themselves.

Based on model 4, women who work in irregular jobs are more likely than women working as unpaid family workers to take care of their children themselves while they are less likely to get help from relatives. On the other hand, waged workers or women who work as government officials are statistically significantly less likely to take care of their children themselves but more likely to use paid childcare. Working women who are in the age groups 18–29 and 30–34 are statistically significantly more likely than older women to use relatives for childcare while they are less likely to use paid care. Similar to the bivariate probit result, working women with lower education levels are less likely to use paid care including kindergarten, and they tend to take care of their children themselves instead. This result is similar to the finding in Borra and Palma (2009) that higher education levels lead to a decrease in parental care while increasing paid care although they include both working and not working women. Similarly, more educated women are shown to be more likely to choose center-based care in Suárez (2013).

Results also reveal that when older children and other adults (except for spouse) are at home, working women are more likely to get help from them for childcare while they tend to decrease the use of paid care. This is similar to the result that the presence of older adults at home decreases the use of center-based care shown in Carlin et al. (2019). Working women whose spouses do not work are significantly less likely than those whose spouses work with social security to use paid childcare options. Moreover, working women whose spouses work as seasonal workers, unpaid family workers or other undefined job groups are

Tab. 6.3: Bivariate Probit Model Results

	Model 1		Model 2	
	Lfp	**Fc**	**Lfp**	**Fc**
Age groups (35+ ref.)				
Age 18–29	−0.068***	−0.077***	−0.067***	−0.075***
	(0.027)	(0.020)	(0.026)	(0.020)
Age 30–34	0.015	−0.030	0.013	−0.029
	(0.025)	(0.020)	(0.025)	(0.020)
Education level (High school and higher ref.)				
No education/Primary incomplete	−0.159***	−0.066***	−0.134***	−0.067***
	(0.034)	(0.024)	(0.034)	(0.024)
First level primary	−0.157***	−0.060***	−0.141***	−0.060***
	(0.027)	(0.019)	(0.027)	(0.019)
Second level primary	−0.176***	−0.044**	−0.162***	−0.044**
	(0.028)	(0.021)	(0.028)	(0.021)
# of children aged <=5 (=1 ref.)				
# of children=2	−0.080***	0.071***	−0.080***	0.070***
	(0.018)	(0.015)	(0.018)	(0.015)
# of children >=3	−0.086**	0.115***	−0.086**	0.113***
	(0.038)	(0.042)	(0.038)	(0.042)
Presence of children aged 6–13	−0.030	−0.016	−0.028	−0.017
	(0.019)	(0.014)	(0.019)	(0.014)
Presence of children aged 14–17	0.003	0.026	0.004	0.026
	(0.029)	(0.023)	(0.029)	(0.023)
Presence of other adults at home	−0.050*	−0.012	−0.049*	−0.013
	(0.027)	(0.021)	(0.027)	(0.021)
Household size	−0.000	−0.006	0.001	−0.006
	(0.005)	(0.004)	(0.005)	(0.004)
Spouse's employment (Work with social security ref.)				
Work without social security	0.070***	−0.011		
	(0.022)	(0.015)		
Not working	0.074*	0.014		
	(0.039)	(0.029)		

Tab. 6.3: Continued

	Model 1		Model 2	
Spouse's employment (Employer, self-employed ref.)				
Not working			0.061	0.005
			(0.039)	(0.030)
Seasonal worker, unpaid family worker, other			0.042	−0.037*
			(0.031)	(0.022)
Waged worker			0.012	−0.018
			(0.019)	(0.014)
Government official			0.106***	−0.003
			(0.034)	(0.021)
Living in an urban area	−0.095***	−0.019	−0.093***	−0.016
	(0.023)	(0.017)	(0.023)	(0.017)
Wealth level (Middle ref.)				
Poorest	*0.095****	−0.035*	0.119***	−0.032
	(0.030)	(0.020)	(0.030)	(0.020)
Poorer	*0.031*	−0.038**	0.040*	−0.036**
	(0.024)	(0.017)	(0.024)	(0.017)
Richer	0.021	0.019	0.011	0.018
	(0.025)	(0.020)	(0.025)	(0.020)
Richest	0.135***	0.087***	0.114***	0.081***
	(0.031)	(0.026)	(0.031)	(0.026)
Region (North ref.)				
West	−0.196***	−0.023	−0.173***	−0.022
	(0.031)	(0.019)	(0.032)	(0.020)
South	−0.262***	−0.026	−0.250***	−0.026
	(0.033)	(0.022)	(0.033)	(0.022)
Central	−0.225***	−0.033	−0.215***	−0.033
	(0.032)	(0.020)	(0.032)	(0.020)
East	−0.299***	−0.016	−0.293***	−0.019
	(0.030)	(0.020)	(0.030)	(0.020)

Notes: Table shows average marginal effects of covariates. Lfp refers to the labor force participation and Fc refers to the formal care use. Significance levels are * 10 %, ** 5 % and *** 1 %. Standard errors are in parentheses.

Tab. 6.4: Multinomial Probit Model Results

	Model 3			Model 4		
	(1) Herself	**(2) Other family members**	**(3) Paid care**	**(1) Herself**	**(2) Other family members**	**(3) Paid care**
Woman works with social security						
	−0.343***	0.089	0.254***			
	(0.047)	(0.055)	(0.040)			
Woman's job status (Unpaid family worker ref.)						
Employer, temporal, self-employed or other				0.149***	−0.212***	0.063
				(0.053)	(0.056)	(0.039)
Waged worker				−0.268***	0.066	0.202***
				(0.050)	(0.061)	(0.045)
Government official				−0.230***	0.038	0.192***
				(0.072)	(0.081)	(0.052)
Age groups (35+ ref.)						
Age 18–29						
	−0.031	0.186***	−0.155***	−0.012	0.164***	−0.152***
	(0.047)	(0.055)	(0.036)	(0.046)	(0.055)	(0.038)
Age 30–34						
	−0.031	0.151***	−0.120***	−0.020	0.140***	−0.119***
	(0.041)	(0.048)	(0.031)	(0.040)	(0.047)	(0.033)
Education level (High school and higher ref.)						
No education/Primary incomplete						
	−0.001	−0.062	0.063	0.069	−0.027	−0.042
	(0.064)	(0.102)	(0.093)	(0.067)	(0.097)	(0.088)
First level primary						
	0.079	−0.048	−0.031	0.145***	−0.062	−0.083*
	(0.055)	(0.067)	(0.048)	(0.055)	(0.065)	(0.047)
Second level primary						
	0.141**	−0.081	−0.060	0.192***	−0.096	−0.096**
	(0.062)	(0.071)	(0.046)	(0.063)	(0.070)	(0.048)
# of children aged <=5 (=1 ref.)						
# of children >=2						
	0.013	0.022	−0.035	0.012	0.033	−0.045
	(0.041)	(0.051)	(0.037)	(0.040)	(0.050)	(0.037)
Presence of children aged 6–13						
	−0.021	0.009	0.011	−0.010	0.023	−0.013
	(0.036)	(0.045)	(0.031)	(0.036)	(0.044)	(0.032)

(*continued on next page*)

Tab. 6.4: Continued

	Model 3			Model 4		
Presence of children aged 14–17						
	−0.051	0.147**	−0.096**	−0.025	0.125**	−0.100**
	(0.048)	(0.062)	(0.043)	(0.049)	(0.062)	(0.043)
Presence of other adults at home						
	−0.052	0.196***	−0.144***	−0.034	0.184***	−0.150***
	(0.054)	(0.067)	(0.046)	(0.054)	(0.066)	(0.043)
Household size						
	−0.010	0.020	−0.011	−0.015	0.015	0.000
	(0.010)	(0.015)	(0.014)	(0.011)	(0.015)	(0.014)
Spouse's employment (Work with social security ref.)						
Work without social security						
	0.070*	−0.023	−0.046			
	(0.042)	(0.058)	(0.051)			
Not working						
	0.015	0.131	−0.146***			
	(0.077)	(0.092)	(0.054)			
Spouse's employment (Employer, self-employed ref.)						
Not working				−0.011	0.146	−0.135**
				(0.070)	(0.095)	(0.068)
Seasonal worker, unpaid family worker[a]				0.069	0.146	−0.216***
				(0.296)	(0.637)	(0.030)
Waged Worker				0.007	0.003	−0.011
				(0.037)	(0.048)	(0.035)
Government official				0.097	−0.066	−0.031
				(0.069)	(0.076)	(0.041)
Living in an urban area						
	0.019	0.042	−0.061	0.012	0.054	−0.066
	(0.039)	(0.053)	(0.041)	(0.040)	(0.053)	(0.044)
Wealth level (Poorest ref.)						
Poorer						
	0.010	−0.046	0.036	−0.006	−0.019	0.025
	(0.053)	(0.075)	(0.063)	(0.054)	(0.068)	(0.050)
Middle						
	0.038	−0.123	0.085	0.026	−0.121	0.095*
	(0.063)	(0.081)	(0.058)	(0.064)	(0.076)	(0.050)

Tab. 6.4: Continued

	Model 3			Model 4		
Richer						
	0.117	−0.265***	0.148**	0.073	−0.240***	0.167***
	(0.073)	(0.089)	(0.061)	(0.076)	(0.086)	(0.055)
Richest						
	−0.015	−0.134	0.149**	−0.105	−0.099	0.204***
	(0.080)	(0.096)	(0.064)	(0.078)	(0.090)	(0.060)
Region (North ref.)						
West						
	0.144***	−0.204***	0.060*	0.163***	−0.207***	0.044
	(0.043)	(0.052)	(0.031)	(0.047)	(0.055)	(0.034)
South						
	0.129**	−0.166**	0.037	0.102*	−0.133**	0.031
	(0.054)	(0.065)	(0.041)	(0.053)	(0.065)	(0.044)
Central						
	0.064	−0.115**	0.050	0.052	−0.095*	0.043
	(0.044)	(0.055)	(0.035)	(0.045)	(0.056)	(0.037)
East						
	0.218***	−0.299***	0.081*	0.185***	−0.259***	0.073
	(0.048)	(0.058)	(0.043)	(0.048)	(0.059)	(0.045)

Notes: Table shows average marginal effects of covariates.
Significance levels are * 10 %, ** 5 % and *** %1. Standard errors are in parentheses.
[a]It also includes other category.

less likely than those whose spouses are employers or self-employed to use paid childcare.

The probability of the use of paid care increases for working women from richer and richest families than those from the poorest households, while those from high-wealth categories are less likely to get help from relatives. Similarly, a higher family income has been shown to increase the use of paid care in Borra and Palma (2009). The use of paid center-based care also increases with higher family income as shown in Suárez (2013). Compared to working women located in the north region, working women from all other regions are less likely to get help from relatives for childcare while those who are located at other regions except for the central region tend to take care of their children themselves.

However, significant regional differences do not exist for paid childcare options for working women.

6 Conclusion

Childcare remains an obstacle for many women with small children in Turkey. Even though positive developmental effects of using formal (or institutional) care have gained great attention in the literature, Turkish families traditionally rely on relatives (especially grandmothers) for childcare since formal childcare is not affordable for every family. In this study, firstly, mothers' decisions of labor force participation and formal childcare use are jointly estimated. Secondly, childcare choices of working women are investigated using the most recent available TDHS survey data.

Consistent with the literature, the education level of the mother is shown to be an important determinant of both labor force participation and formal/paid childcare use. The study results reveal that mothers with lower education are less likely to obtain formal/paid childcare options compared to higher educated women. Thus, in order to increase the use of formal care we need to focus on policies to improve the education levels of females. Results also point to inequalities in obtaining formal care/paid care by wealth levels of families. As indicated in other studies, women from wealthier households are more likely to use formal childcare or paid care. Moreover, women whose spouses are not working have a lower probability to use formal or paid childcare, and they tend to be in the labor force to financially support the family. These findings indicate that affordable childcare is not available to every working mother or every woman with small children who are considering to work. Therefore, financial childcare supports should be enhanced to every family in need. Estimation results also show that women working with social security and at regularly paid jobs as waged workers or government officials are more likely to use paid childcare options. This implies that the financial security of working mothers allows them to choose better childcare options for their children. Thus, secure and regularly paid employment opportunities for women are needed to be improved.

Among demographic indicators, the mother's age is a significant predictor of labor force participation and childcare use. Younger women are less likely to be in the labor force relative to older ones. They tend to get help from relatives for childcare and refrain from using formal care or paid care. This means that women try to stay attached to the labor force as they age and rely more on formal care. In addition, mothers decrease labor force participation when they have a higher number of small children and are more likely to use formal childcare in this case. However, if working women have older children at home or adults are present at home, then they get help from them for childcare and decrease the use of paid care. This shows that relative care, when available, is widely used. Therefore, high quality and affordable formal childcare opportunities should be enhanced.

This study has some limitations because of the lack of data on prices of paid childcare alternatives, wage earnings of mothers and household income level. In order to overcome these limitations, both mothers' and their spouses' job information as well as wealth levels of households are used to control for their ability to pay. Therefore, collecting information on childcare payments and individuals' income levels are needed to make a better comparison between the studies for other countries and Turkey.

References

Abner, K. S., Gordon, R. A., Kaestner, R., and Korenman, S. (2013), "*Does Child Care Quality Mediate Associations Between Type of Care and Development?*", *Journal of Marriage and Family*, 75(5), 1203–1217. doi:10.1111/jomf.12055.

Banfi, S., Farsi, M., and Filippini, M. (2009), "An Empirical Analysis of Child Care Demand in Switzerland", *Annals of Public and Cooperative Economics*, 80(1), 37–66. doi:10.1111/j.1467-8292.2008.00377.x.

Borra, C. (2010), "Childcare Costs and Spanish Mothers' Labour Force Participation", *Hacienda Pública Española/ Review of Public Economics*, 194(3), 9–40.

Borra, C., and Palma, L. (2009), "Child Care Choices in Spain", *Journal of Family and Economic Issues*, 30(4), 323–338. doi: 10.1007/s10834-009-9167-6.

Carlin, C., Davis, E. E., Kraft, C., and Tout, K. (2019), "Parental Preferences and Patterns of Child Care Use among Low-Income Families: A Bayesian Analysis", *Children and Youth Services Review*, 99, 172–185. doi:10.1016/j.childyouth.2019.02.006.

Dayıoğlu, M., and Kırdar, M. G. (2010), "Determinants of and Trends in Labor Force Participation of Women in Turkey", Working Paper Number 5, Welfare and Social Policy Analytical Work Program, Washington DC: World Bank. Retrieved from http://documents.worldbank.org/curated/en/466591468316462301/pdf/754670NWP0Box300Participation0Women.pdf. Date of Access: 20.12.2019.

Felfe, C., and Lalive, R. (2018), "Does Early Child Care Affect Children's Development?", *Journal of Public Economics*, 159, 33–53. doi:10.1016/j.jpubeco.2018.01.014.

Güneş, C., Üçdoğruk Birecikli, Ş., and Yıldırım, Z. (2017), "Çalışan Kadının Çocuk Bakım Tercihi: Havuzlanmış Verilerle Kesikli Tercih Modellerinin Karşılaştırılması", *SGD-Sosyal Güvenlik Dergisi*, 7(1), 123–144. Retrieved from https://dergipark.org.tr/en/pub/sgd/issue/29767/319939. Date of Access: 30.01.2020.

Hansen, S., and Andersen, L. (2014), "A Gendered Investment Plan", *Economic Policy* Brief No 2, Brussels: Foundation for European Progressive Studies and Economic Council of the Labour Movement. Retrieved from https://www.feps-europe.eu/Assets/Publications/PostFiles/549.pdf. Date of Access: 28.01.2020.

Hüseyinli, N., and Hüseyinli, T. (2016), "Çocuk Bakımının Kadın İşgücü Üzerinde Etkileri ve Hukuki Düzenlemeler", *Akdeniz İİBF Dergisi*, 16(34), 108–137. doi: 10.25294/auiibfd.308032.

Ilkkaracan, I. (2012), "Why So Few Women in the Labor Market in Turkey?", *Feminist Economics*, 18(1), 1–37. doi: 10.1080/13545701.2011.649358.

İnce Yenilmez, M. (2019), "Female Employment and Care Economy in Turkey", *Sosyoloji Araştırmaları Dergisi*, 22(1), 69–95. doi: 10.18490/sosars.559091.

Kakıcı, H., Emeç, H., and Üçdoğruk, Ş. (2007), "Türkiye'de Çalışan Kadınların Çocuk Bakım Tercihleri", *İstanbul Üniversitesi İktisat Fakültesi Ekonometri ve İstatistik Dergisi*, 5, 20–40.

Karaalp-Orhan, H. S. (2017), "What Are the Trends in Women's Labour Force Participation in Turkey?", *European Journal of Sustainable Development*, 6(3), 303–312. doi: 10.14207/ejsd.2017.v6n3p303.

Kılıç, D., and Öztürk, S. (2014), "Türkiye'de Kadınların İşgücüne Katılımı Önündeki Engeller ve Çözüm Yolları: Bir Ampirik Uygulama", *Amme İdaresi Dergisi*, 47(1), 107–130.

Kimmel, J. (1998), "Child Care Costs as a Barrier to Employment for Single and Married Mothers", *The Review of Economics and Statistics*, 80(2), 287–299.

OECD. (2019), "Enrolment in Childcare and Pre-school". Retrieved June 13, 2020, from https://www.oecd.org/els/soc/PF3_2_Enrolment_childcare_preschool.pdf.

Pekkurnaz, D. (2020), "Employment Status and Contraceptive Choices of Women with Young Children in Turkey", *Feminist Economics*, 26(1), 98–120. doi: 10.1080/13545701.2019.1642505.

Powell, L. M. (1997), "The Impact of Child Care Costs on the Labor Supply of Married Mothers: Evidence from Canada", *The Canadian Journal of Economics*, 30(3), 577–594.

Suárez, M. J. (2013), "Working Mothers' Decisions on Childcare: The Case of Spain", *Review of Economics of the Household*, 11, 545–561. doi: 10.1007/s11150-013-9189-6.

Turkish Statistical Institute (TSE). (2017), "Family Structure Survey, 2016", *Press Release* No 21869. Retrieved June, 13, 2020, from http://www.turkstat.gov.tr/PreHaberBultenleri.do?id=21869.

Van Gameren, E. (2013), "The Role of Economic Incentives and Attitudes in Participation and Childcare Decisions", *Journal of Family and Economic Issues*, 34, 296–313. doi: 10.1007/s10834-012-9332-1.

Van Gameren, E., and Ooms, I. (2009), "Childcare and Labor Force Participation in the Netherlands: The Importance of Attitudes and Opinions", *Review of Economics of the Household*, 7, 395–421. doi:10.1007/s11150-009-9062-9.

Viitanen, T. K. (2005), "Cost of Childcare and Female Employment in the UK", *Labour*, 19(s1), 149–170. doi: 10.1111/j.1467-9914.2005.00325.x.

Wetzels, C. (2005), "Supply and Price of Childcare and Female Labour Force Participation in the Netherlands", *Labour*, 19(s1), 171–209. doi: 10.1111/j.1467-9914.2005.00326.x.

Section 4 Entrepreneurship and Women

Berna Balcı İzgi

Women's Entrepreneurship and Youth Female Labor Force Participation in Turkey

1 Introduction

Entrepreneurship creates new companies and opens new markets. Entrepreneurs support economic development of countries. They are not only individuals who bring together and produce for profit, but also they play a key role in sociocultural, political and intellectual changes. This multifaceted change is constantly interacting with each other. Entrepreneurship is also very old in this context. At the beginning of the 20th century, as the founder of modern entrepreneurship described Joseph Schumpeter (1883–1950) defined entrepreneurship as the creation of new components and accepted it as the basis of economic development. It is considered to be a male-only area, but in time, it became a women area as well. It is widely accepted that female entrepreneurs have an important role in economic development. Strengthening the position of female labor force creates a multiplier effect and accelerate economic growth as well.

From 1900s, women do have a rapid change and transformation in all areas of economic life. Historically, there is the fact that women work intensively in the agricultural sector. In his book, Boserup (1970) observed that agriculture was a women's work in some parts of Asia and Latin America, starting from the African continent. Over time, with the establishment of large factories, household industries could not compete against this, while women were excluded from industrial employment. It can be said that this situation continues in trade and for this reason, women's entrepreneurship also lagged behind. According to the UNDP statistics, women labor force has increased from 35 % in 1990 to 41 % today in nonagricultural sector.

In Turkey, however, female labor force participation rates are not as much as high as in developed countries. Female entrepreneurship is an important issue to be considered in creating a waged employment for women. This paper aims to show a picture about the female labor force participation and women being an employer in developed countries. Then it analyzes the relationship between women's entrepreneurship and labor force participation rates in var environment for (1991–2019) Turkey.

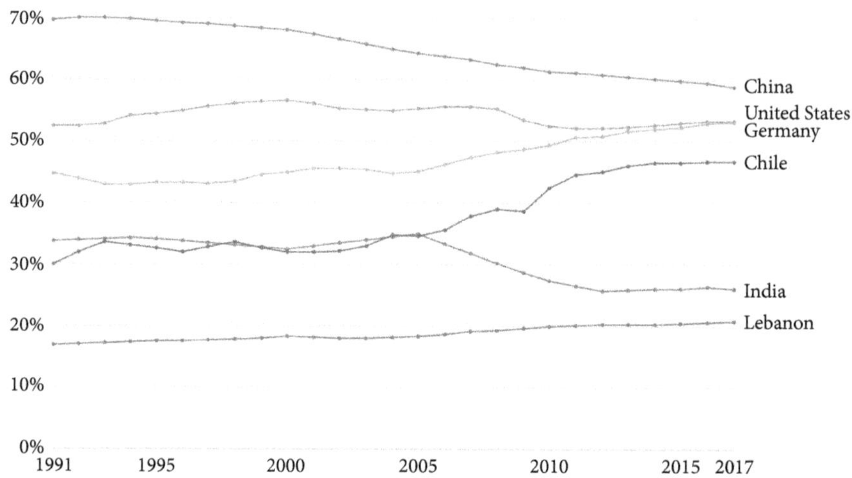

Graph 7.1: Female employment to population ratio (developed countries).
Source: World Bank (2020)

1.1 About Female Labor in the World

In last 50 years, the increase in women's labor force participation in many countries has led to an increase in labor supply and therefore, it has led to an increase in economic growth (Gilfillan and Andrews, 2010).Women's participation in the workforce is recognized as an important element of sustainable development.

Women entrepreneurs create jobs for themselves and for others, while they act as problem solvers in business life. However, they form a minority in entrepreneurial activity. GEM (Global Entrepreneurship Monitor) has provided evidence that mostly opportunity drives entrepreneurs in economies. In Graph 7.1, half of the countries women total early-stage entrepreneurial activity rates (TEA) are 5 % or less. Of 49 economies surveyed, six have equal TEA rates. These countries are Indonesia and Thailand, Panama in Latin America and Qatar, Madagascar and Angola in Middle East and Africa region.

Entrepreneurship is the ability of individuals to turn their ideas into action. Achieving goals requires creativity, innovation, risk-taking and the ability to plan and manage projects. The entrepreneurial activities of the European Commission are summarized in an Entrepreneurship Action Plan adopted in January 2013:

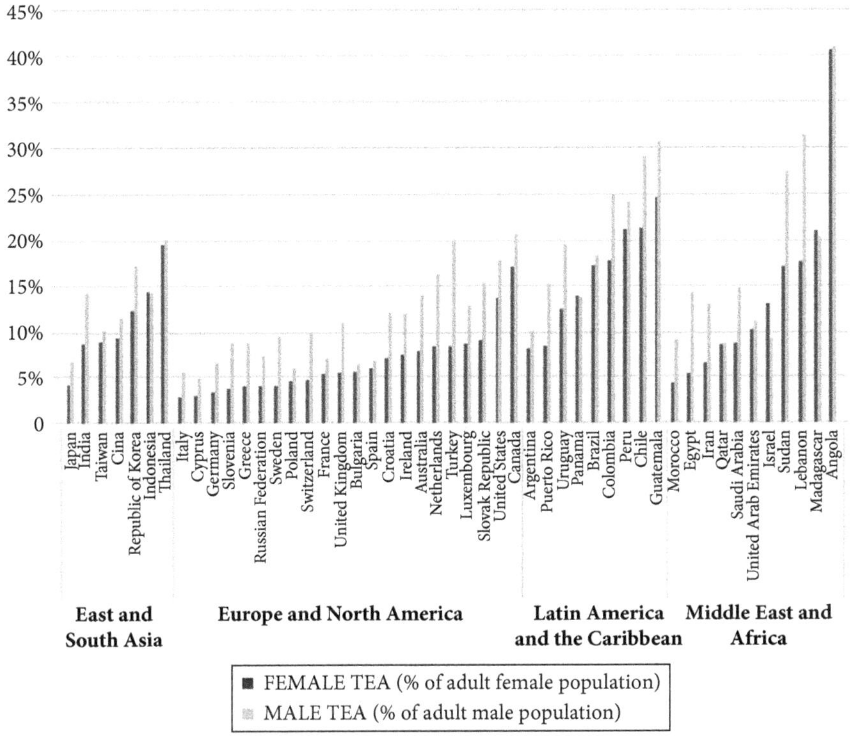

Graph 7.2: Total early-stage entrepreneurial activity (TEA) rates among adults (18–64) in 48 economies.

Source: Global Entrepreneurship Monitor Adult Population Survey, 2018

- educating young people about entrepreneurship,
- highlighting opportunities for women and other groups,
- easing administrative requirements and
- making it easier to attract investors

It is important that education in Europe should provide the right foundation for an entrepreneurial career. Problems such as access to finance and markets, fear of "criminal" sanctions in case of failure are some obstacles for entrepreneurs. The Commission aims to encourage more people to start their own business. Some groups are particularly targeted, such as women entrepreneurs, family businesses, self-employed, immigrants, seniors or social economy enterprises (https://ec.europa.eu/growth/smes/promoting-entrepreneurship_en).

1.2 Current Data for Turkey's Women Employment

It can be observed that public institutions increased their activities about women entrepreneurship in Turkey beginning in the 1990s. These developments can be considered improving the participation of women in economic activity and should be considered as the result of a growing interest in women's entrepreneurship. Increasingly, entrepreneurship among women is increasingly seen as a solution to women's unemployment and as a means for women to gain economic independence by earning their own earnings. Although policies, programs and activities in this field are rapidly becoming widespread, it is not possible to say that all these efforts have been documented in a comprehensive and systematic way to present the current situation of women entrepreneurship (Ecevit, 2008). What are the policies of the state toward women's entrepreneurship? What steps have been taken by the government and government agencies to encourage and support women entrepreneurs? Which nongovernmental organizations took part in activities to encourage women to be small entrepreneurs? Since there is no well-developed holistic policy for women's employment, entrepreneurship is embedded in several different policy frameworks. Moreover, there are also important differences between the approaches of these frameworks toward women entrepreneurship.

There is a project named "Employment and Training Project" signed by the World Bank and the Government of the Republic of Turkey. The project was signed on May 4, 1993, and it has a seven-year term protocol. The project was financed by the World Bank and supported by the Government of Turkey. In addition, the Directorate General for the Status of Women (KSGM) was organized by the Directorate General for the National Project for the participation of women in the development process between 1993 and 2000. In GAP region, vocational training given by different institutions or employing skill courses information on establishing business in these courses and trainings to develop hardware are not provided. The number of graduates and entrepreneurs of these courses are very limited (Özar, 2005: 27). Entrepreneurial women who complete the courses are unable to work due to lack of funding. Since most of the women attending these courses come from lower income groups, they also have limited courage to start their own businesses. Family and growing environment are effective in losing women's courage.

The ratios can show that urbanization has caused a migration from unpaid rural work to housework in cities for women. Female labor force participation rates are low in Turkey. Despite the egalitarian structure of the law, the qualitative development of women and the necessary mechanisms to enter the labor

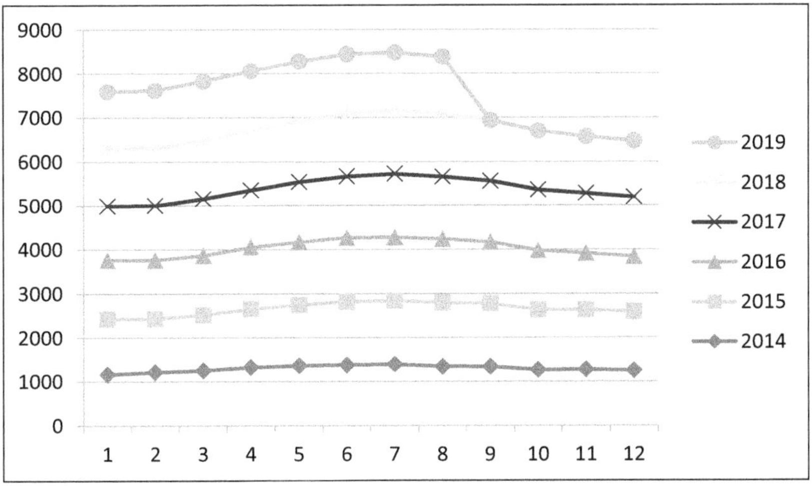

Graph 7.3: Turkey monthly women employment (thousand, ages 15–24).
Source: Turkstat, Laborforce statistics (2020)

market are missing. And it is one of the reasons women's unemployment is one of the main problems in Turkey (KSGM, 2010). The Labor Force participation rate (LFP) was 72 % in 1955; and in 2008, it was only 21.2 % (Yenilmez and Işıklı, 2010). In EU and OECD, the average LFP is 61 % approximately. Turkey is one of the lowest countries in this respect.

There is a declining trend from 2000s till now. Main reason is shown as migration to cities. The labor force participation rate of women was 42.4 % in year 2000 (Turkstat, Laborforce statistics). But it was 38.3 % in 2018. This ratio is for the 15, upper and graduates of high school.

2 Literature

While local, national and international researches in the field of women's studies continue with increasing diversity, the economic dimension of the issue comes to the forefront as a fundamental determinant. It is very important that the economic meaning of women's labor spent in reproduction of the labor force in a society should be expanded to include unrequited reproductive labor (Toksöz, 2011: 91). The socioeconomic determinants of female labor force participation rate in Turkey have been analyzed in the literature (Kasnakoglu and Dayioglu, 1997; Eryar and Tekgüç, 2012).

There are many studies about female labor force participation and economic growth and most of them have a u-shaped relation (Tansel, 2002; Gilfillan and Andrews, 2010; Verick, 2014). When it comes to women entrepreneurship, it is important to focus on different aspects of employment. Entrepreneurship is expected to increase as women's labor force participation increases, but creating employment in a sector should be not only focusing on that sector, but also taking into account inter-sectoral aspects of employment generation in Turkey (Şenesen and Şenesen, 2011: 250). Female entrepreneurship has been underestimated most of the time in social sciences (Yenilmez, 2012: 70). Among the reasons women are not included in the labor force, being busy with household chores stands out as an important reason. In Turkey, women who are in housework have the biggest percentage of women in labor force. In addition, it is an important reason for women on being out of labor force for İzgi (2012: 387). The fact that women have economic independence brings along the possibility of getting help in the housework. This makes it easier to get involved in the labor force and also on being an entrepreneur.

It is possible to make women a potential force in economic life that makes significant contributions to economic and social development. However, it can be stated that women face important obstacles in entrepreneurship activities and they are very difficult (Soysal, 2010). According to Minniti (2013), there are gender differences, and they are statistically significant about entrepreneurship. The most important problem faced by women entrepreneurs during starting, continuing and growing the business is the lack of capital and financial problems. Generally, male entrepreneurs and female entrepreneurs do not have equal opportunities in obtaining credit. Funding resources may vary for male and female entrepreneurs (Erdun, 2011 transferring from Sohl & Hill). As the financial source of entrepreneurs, family, close relatives and acquaintances, bank, joint business, government incentives, stock market and wealthy people called "business angels" can be shown (Çetindamar, 2002: 40). While male entrepreneurs can obtain loans from investors and banks as funding sources in addition to their core capital, women generally prefer to benefit only from their personal assets or savings in the initial stage of their venture.

Although there is a widespread opinion that entrepreneurs generally have low educational levels, research suggests that this view is not correct. The issue of education is important in this respect. The education level of the elderly parents is important in terms of female employment. The education level of the father and the mother increases the private education expenditures (Tansel and Bircan, 2006: 311). In addition, the wage gap is higher in those who have lower education (Addabbo and Favaro, 2011: 4589). In Alvarez-Noguera and Urban (2012) training has a positive effect on the probability of women undertake. In her study, Çatalbaş (2015) has used Panel data analysis with data from 12 regions at IBSS level 1 for Turkey (2008–2013). The study has shown that fertility rate, divorce rate, informal employment, economic crisis and the female labor force of education are important variables. Especially education of girls has a significant positive effect on female labor force participation.

As the risk-taking tendencies of women entrepreneurs increase, causes for being an entrepreneur were also increased. Because women tend to take risks within the framework of the reasons affecting them. In this context, it can be interpreted that the reasons for being an entrepreneur strengthens women's risk-taking tendencies (Erdun, 2011: 97).

Women start with a smaller amount of start-up capital than men for the year 1994 (Verheul and Thurik, 2001: 329). The lack of confidence of women entrepreneurs in their own business leads them to start with less financial capital. This is a discouraging effect in their business life activities. The lack of sustainable past business relationships of women entrepreneurs is cited as a reason for not having sufficient personal equity capital to finance their business. Women are borrowing less from banks and other financial institutions because of their lack of information about the financial system (D.A.I., Development Alternatives Inc., 1995).

As a last remark while working on women's entrepreneurship, it is argued that the acceptance of gender as a social structure rather than a variable is important for enriching the framework (Brush, Bruin and Welter, 2009: 19).

3 Methodology

An impulse response function measures the time profile of the effect of shocks at a given point in time on the (expected) future values of variables in a dynamical system (Pesaran and Shin, 1998: 18). It is a kind of hitting the economy at time t is compared with a base-line profile at time t+n, given the economy's history. Impulse response functions in linear multivariate models are used in forecasting generally. Unlike the orthogonaliztion of shocks, this study uses traditional impulse response analysis to see the variables in the var environment. Vector auto regression (VAR) analysis was applied to the series. VAR was first introduced by Sims (1980). It is the best representation of multi equation models. According to Gujarati (1995), var model has the advantage of treating all the variables like endogenous. Autoregressive model is presented with lagged values of the dependent variable in the right side of the equation. Since the variables are integrated of order one (I(1)), var model can be applied in this situation. The stochastic error terms are called as impulses or shocks in the system. According to Lutkepohl, the standard errors based on asymptotic theory are much more efficient computationally than those obtained with resampling methods (Luthkepol, 1990: 124).

Yearly data from 1991 to 2019 are collected from Worldbank Development Indicators. Two variables are LEMP: female employers as a percentage of female employment, LLFP: female labor force participation rates for ages (15–24). The series are in logarithmic forms. First the series are analyzed for stationarity condition with Augmented Dickey-Fuller test. Since the variables are integrated of order "1," then optimal lag selection and impulse response functions were used for var estimations.

The impulse response functions (irf) explain the reaction of an endogenous variable to one of the shocks in a moment. It shows the impact of the one variable on other variables in the system. It traces the effects on present and future values of the endogenous variable of one standard deviation shock to one of the shocks in signal processing the impulse response of a dynamic system. The μs are stochastic error terms called as impulses or shocks. The dependent variable is a function of its lagged values and the lagged values of other variables in the model.

The irf shows the response of the dependent variable in a var system to the shocks in the error terms such as μ_1 and μ_2. As an assumption μ_1 in dependent variable is considered to be increased by one standard deviation shock. This shock will increase the variable in current and future periods. The irf shows the impact of such shocks for several periods in the future. The data and its definition are shown below (Tab.7.1; Tab. 7.2; Tab 7.3). The model is as follows:

$$LEMP_t = \sigma_t + \sum_{i=1}^{k} LEMP_{t-i} + \sum_{j=1}^{k} LLFP_{t-j} + \mu_{1t}$$

Tab. 7.1: Descriptive Data

Variable	Obs	Mean	Std.Dev.	Min.	Max.
LEMP	28	−0.0320749	0.2973526	−0.4431669	0.3464226
LLFP	28	3.419677	0.124772	3.219476	3.625274

Tab. 7.2: Stationarity (Augmented Dickey-Fuller Test Statistic)

Variable	Level	First Difference
LEMP	−1.247363 (0.6385)	−7.336045 (0.0000)
LLFP	−1.238950 (0.6423)	−5.284340 (0.0002)

Note: t statistics and probability values in parentheses

Tab. 7.3: Vector Autoregression

Sample:1993–2018		AIC		−3.698876		
Log-Likelihood = 58.08538		HQIC		−3.559535		
		SBIC		−3.214992		
	Parms	**RMSE**		**R-sq**	**chi2**	**P>chi2**
LEMP	5	0.125607		0.8450	141.7502	0.0000
LLFP	5	0.063167		0.7755	89.80518	0.0000
LEMP	**Coefficient**	**Std. Error**	**t**	**P**	**95 % Confidence Interv**	
L1	0.448748	0.1789248	2.51	0.012	0.0980619	0.7994342
L2	0.4245783	0.1702506	2.49	0.013	0.0908933	0.7582632
LLFP						
L1	0.0261414	0.3829643	0.07	0.946	−0.7244547	0.7767376
L2	−0.5045981	0.4071958	−1.24	0.215	−1.302687	0.293491
Cons.	1.659902	0.7188659	2.31	0.021	0.2509504	3.068853
LLFP						
LEMP						
L1	0.0544396	0.0899806	0.61	0.545	−0.1219191	0.2307983
L2	0.0628637	0.0856183	0.73	0.463	−0.1049451	0.2306726
LLFP						
L1	0.6727527	0.1925912	3.49	0.000	0.2952809	1.050225
L2	0.2363487	0.2047772	1.15	0.248	−0.1650072	0.6377046
Cons.	0.318152	0.3615149	0.88	0.379	−0.3904041	1.026708

First and second lag of the variable LEMP has 1 % significant positive effect on variable LEMP ceteris paribus, while the LLFP variable does not have a significant effect on LEMP. In addition, LEMP variable does not have a significant effect on LLFP. The first lag of LLFP has a positive significant effect on LLFP ceteris paribus.

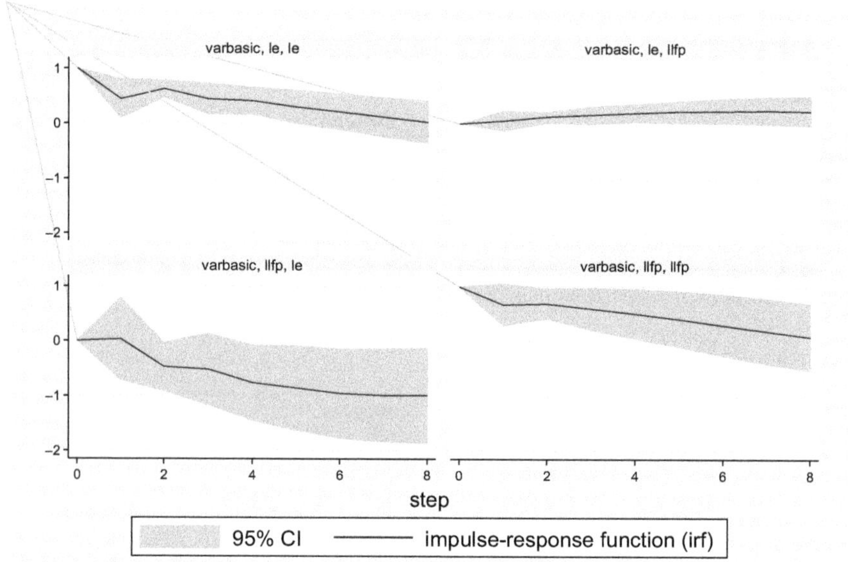

Graph 7.4: IRF graphs.

Tab. 7.4: Lagrange-Multiplier Test

Lag	Chi2	df	P>chi2
1	6.0382	4	0.19631
2	6.2979	4	0.17798

When we look at the irf multiple graphs, the response of being employer to the labor force participation rate is increasing from the second period. The other graphs are decreasing from the fifth period and so on. This means that in Turkey there is a tendency of decrease in the women labor force participation rate as well as female entrepreneurship. However, if the labor force participation rate can be increased, it will cause the ratio of women entrepreneurs.

The specification tests after regression are tests of normality and autocorrelation, and the stability conditions are valid according to the linear regression assumptions (Tab. 7.4; Tab. 7.5).

H_0: no autocorrelation at lag order.

All the eigenvalues lie within the circle (var satisfies the stability condition).

Tab. 7.5: Jarque-Bera Test

Equation	Chi2	df	P>chi2
Lemp	2.818	2	0.24436
Llfp	3.216	2	0.20031
All	6.034	4	0.19663
Eigenvalue			Modul
0.9384156+0.1783408i			0.955212
0.9384156−0.1783408i			0.955212
−0.3776652+0.0459764i			0.380453
−0.3776652−0.04597643i			0.380453

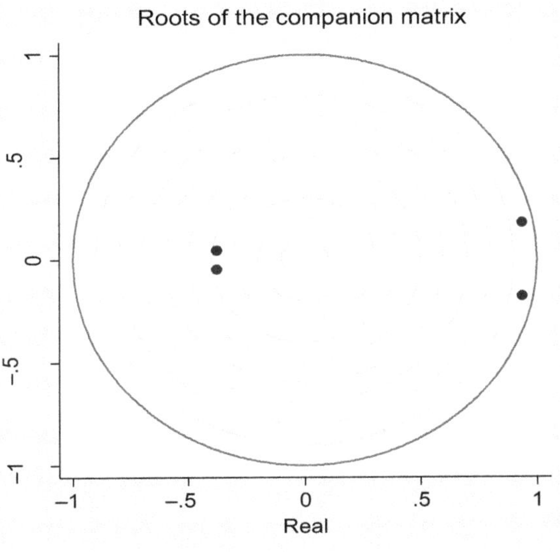

Graph 7.5: Roots of the companion matrix.

4 Results and Conclusion

Women's participation in the workforce is recognized as an important element of sustainable development. Women make a considerable contribution to wealth generation. Today, over ten million self-employed women are estimated for Europe. In researching women's entrepreneurship, it is more appropriate to look at wider contexts such as social structure.

In order for a permanent increase in employment and production, women entrepreneurs should be taken into account in creating world-class enterprises. It is important especially for our country that has a fragile economy.

According to the findings of my study, while female labor force participation did not have a significant effect on female employer status, it was seen that the female employer variable had a positive effect on female labor force participation. This result confirms the effect of supporting women's entrepreneurship on reducing unemployment. There is no general policy on women's employment. So far, a holistic approach to women's employment in Turkey is not in question.

The gender approach is a sine qua non for all projects that aim to empower women or improve their status. The lack of a gender approach may lead organizations involved in projects to subject women's empowerment to other objectives, such as increasing productivity and reducing poverty. It is not enough that women's empowerment is a project objective. In addition, it is important to address this understanding within a broad framework

References

Addabbo, F. & Davaro, F. (2011), "Gender wage differentials by education in Italy", Applied Economics, 2011, 43, 4589–4605.

Álvarez, C., Noguera, M., & Urbano, D. (2012), "Condicionantes del entorno y emprendimiento femenino: un estudio cuantitativo en Espana", Economía industrial, 383, 43–52.

Boserup, E. (1970), Women's role in economic development, St. Martin Press, New York.

Brush, C., Bruin, A., &Welter, F. (2009), "A gender-aware framework for women's entrepreneurship", International. Journal of Gender and Entrepreneurship, 1(1), 8–24, 1756–6266. DOI 10.1108/17566260910942318.

Çetindamar, D. (2002), Türkiye'de Girşimcilik, Lebib Yalkın Yayınları, İstanbul.

Çatalbaş, G. (2015), "Kadınların işgücüne katılımını belirleyen faktörlerin belirlenmesi: panel veri yaklaşımı", KAÜ İİBF Dergisi, Cilt:6, Sayı:10.

D.A.I. (Development Alternatives Inc.) (1995), "Supporting women-owned business in turkey:a discussion of needs, problems, opportunities and strategies", Discussion papers on Entrepreneurship, Growth and Public Policy, 0704.

Ecevit, Y. (2008), "Türkiye'de Kadın Girşimciliğine Eleştirel Bir Yaklaşım", Ankara Ilo, 72 s, ISBN: 9789228199239; 9789228199246 (web pdf).

Erdun, Ş. (2011), Kadın Girişimcilerin Risk Alma Eğilimi ve Kendine Güven Özellikleri Üzerine Bir Çalışma: Zonguldak Örneği, Zonguldak Karaelmas Üniversitesi Sosyal Bilimler Enstitüsü, Yüksek Lisans Tezi.

Eryar, D., & Tekgüç, H. (2012), "Gender role attitude and female labor force participation andattachment: A case study from Turkey", 3rd International Conference on Economics, TEA, İzmir, Çeşme.

Gilfillan, G., & Andrews, L. (2010), Labour Force Participation of Women Over 45, Australian Government Productivity Commission Staff Working Paper, 2–176.

Gujarati, D. (1995), Basic Econometrics, 3rd edn, McGraw-Hill, New York.

İzgi, B. B. (2012), "Kalkınma ve kadın işgücü: Eğitim eksikliği mi fırsat eşitsizliği mi", Farklı Boyutlarıyla Türkiye'de Kalkınma, Efil Yayınevi.

Kasnakoğlu, Z. & Dayıoğlu, M. (1997), "Female labor force participation and earnings differentials between genders in Turkey", in Economic dimension in gender inequality, Praeger, London.

KSGM (T.C. Başbakanlık Kadının Statüsü Genel Müdürlüğü), (2010), "Türkiye'de Kadının Durumu", Araştırma Raporu, Ankara.

Lütkepohl, H. (1990), "Asymptotic distributions of impulse response functions and forecast error variance decompositions of vector autoregressive models", The Review of Economics and Statistics, 72(1), 116–125, Published by: The MIT Press

Minniti, M. (2013), Entrepreneurial propensity of women, UN-NYC.

Özar, Ş., (2005), GAP Bölgesi'nde Kadın Girişimciliği, GAP-GİDEM Yayınları, Gap-Gidem-UNDP, Ankara.

Pesaran, H. H., & Shin,Y. (1998), "Generalized impulse response analysis in linear multivariate models", Economics Letters, 58, 17–29.

Şenesen, G. G., & Şenesen, Ü. (2011), "Decomposition of labour demand by employer sectors and gender: Findings for major exporting sectors in Turkey", Economic Systems Research, 23(2), 233–253.

Soysal, A. (2010), "Türkiye'de Kadın Girişimciler: Engeller ve Fırsatlar Bağlamında Bir Değerlendirme", Ankara Üniversitesi SBF Dergisi, 65(01), 83–114.

Tansel, A., & Bircan, F. (2006), "Demand for education in Turkey: A tobit analysis of private tutoring expenditures", Economics of Education Review 25, 303–313.

Tansel, A. (2002), "İktisadi Kalkınma ve Kadınların İşgücüne Katılımı: Türkiye'den Zaman-Serisi Kanıtları ve İllere Göre Yatay Kesit

Kestirimleri", ERC Working Papers in Economics, 01/05T, (http://erc.metu.edu.tr/menu/series01/0105T.pdf).

Toksöz, G. (2011), Kalkınmada Kadın Emeği, Varlık Yaynları, Say:1162.

Verheul, I., & Thurik, A. R. (2001), "Start-up capital: Does gender matter?", Small Business Economics, 16(4), 329–346..

Verick, S. (2014), "Female Labourforce Participatian in Developing Countries", ILO, India and IZA, Germany, http://wol.iza.org/articles/female-labor-force-participation-indeveloping-countries.pdf, Date of Access: 20.04.2015.

Yenilmez, M. İ. (2012), "Obstacles and future prospects of women entrepreneurs: The Turkish context", Economia Marche Journal of Applied Economics, XXXI(2).

Yenilmez, F., & Işıklı, B. (2010), "The comparison of labor force participation rate of women in Turkey with the World country groups", Anadolu University Journal of Social Sciences, 10(3), 77–92.

Internet Resources

Global Entrepreneurship Monitor Adult Population Survey, 2018.

https://ec.europa.eu/growth/smes/promoting-entrepreneurship_en.

https://ourworldindata.org/female-labor-supply.

Turkstat, Laborforce statistics.

Verda Özgüler and Fatma Kocabaş

The Outlook of Home-Based Female Entrepreneurship in Academia in Turkey

1 Introduction

The participation of women in all areas of society and the use of their productive capacity in labor markets can increase their individual well-being and are of great importance in the development of the country. However, due to different gender stereotypes in countries, factors hindering access to labor markets, and lack of education, women do not get what they deserve in the production process. Especially in developing countries, predominantly informal employment, unpaid family labor and low-wage jobs affect women more than men. As stated by Goldin, women's education increases the opportunity cost of free time, so women with higher educational attainment also have higher rates of paid work (1954: 2). Of course, there are also examples where women with low levels of education are in a relatively better position, as much as positive situations arising from high levels of education. However, in the broad sense, women are regarded a labor element that is either left out of the work force or that only enters as "secondary work force during times of need" due to their "invisible female labor" caused by the gender roles assigned to them by the society.

It is possible to take the history of developments related to women's paid work in labor markets back to the Industrial Revolution. In the process of industrialization, the role of women's labor in the production process has changed and transformed during the birth, maturation and shape shifting of wage labor and production relations with technological developments. It can be said that this change and transformation continue today. Women are increasingly struggling to exist in labor markets and to work and live on equal terms with men. In addition, women entrepreneurship is an important dimension in women's struggle to put herself in a productive position in social processes and labor markets.

Entrepreneurship is defined in many fields such as business and management, economics, sociology and psychology, and is dealt with in social, economic, institutional and behavioral dimensions. In this study, articles in academic journals and graduate theses written in Turkey from the perspective of gender roles and from the perspective of labor economics are presented with document analysis from qualitative research methods in which "home-based women entrepreneurship" is addressed.

2 Home-Based Work

Home-based work defines a wide range of areas ranging from beading at home to working at home in electronic media.[1] In general, home-based work is the production of goods and services for the market in people's homes. Working from home is defined by the International Labour Organization (ILO) with "Home Work Convention" dated 1996 and "The Recommendational Decree of Working at Home" No. 177, and 1996 No. 184, and "home workers" who do home-based work are also accepted as people who do not have autonomy and independence required within the scope of national laws, statutes and court decrees in accordance with the independent work. However, the distinction between "home-based employee" and "home-based employer" should also be made because the environment in *this type of work* is home. Home-based employees can also be divided into "home-based small goods producers" and "home-based low-wage workers" (Feldstead & Jewson, 2000: 16).

Home-based small goods manufacturers are the people who produce and sell the goods and services they produce in one-to-one relationship with the end user. Low-wage workers with household axes produce goods and services on behalf of third parties or intermediaries.

The determining element in home-based work is the place where the work is done. The person who works at home can make the production on their own account, on behalf of the agent, the employer, or the factory. If the person doing the home-based work also has the product made by others under them, they fall into the category of home-based employers (Kocabaş, Besler & Özgüler, 2017).

When taken to the "home" as the place where goods and services are produced, entrepreneurship falls under the scope of both "home-based employer" and "home-based small goods producers."

It is also necessary to analyze the aspects of home-based female entrepreneurship such as general types of entrepreneurship, characteristics, importance and sustainability. In other words, "people who deliver their own products to

---

1 Those who are in traditional production are described as "home-based workers," while those who are using new technologies in modern industries are described as "working from home." The history of home-based work dates back earlier than working from home. Working from home is a concept that includes partial work types such as remote work or tele-work.

buyers" by taking the house as the center and "people who have made the house as their base and who produce goods in their houses and market them" are not in the same entrepreneurship category.

According to the definition of the Turkish Statistical Institute (TurkStat), the entrepreneurs in the former category described above, in other words, people who supply their products to buyers could be described within the "self-employed" category. Conversely, the latter group, who in other words have their home as the work base and have production and marketing done at the house, fall under the home-based employer category. In terms of Turkey, there are no boundaries that can clearly draw the distinctions mentioned here, both in terms of definitions and previous literature. Home-based women's entrepreneurship refers to a type of entrepreneurship where "people who deliver their self-produced goods to buyers." This form of production is predominantly female-driven and is largely informal (David, 1996). The marketing of the handcraft produced on a small-scale household level, and the income obtained from it being seen as a "contribution to the family budget" is also closely related to the socioeconomic level and class of the women in charge of the production. Numerous existing studies with the term "micro-credit" include oriented measures to support women who fall under the small-scale production of goods and services.[2] This points to the economic and social efforts of women who take part in this production format, who are dealing with poverty and cannot enter the workforce for a variety of reasons, to become visible. For example, it is necessary to discuss whether a woman who tries to cover the cost of her child's stationery by selling the booties she knitted at home through her spouse and friends' connections should be considered as an "employee" or whether her activities should be considered as "work" in the social sense. Field research reveals that women who engage in this form of production consider themselves "employees" (Özgüler, 2012; Kocabaş, Besler & Özgüler, 2017).

3 Home-Based Female Entrepreneurship

Today, women can be found in almost every profession and in every aspect of working life. It can be argued that women in labor markets have been able to relatively improve their economic situation (Fatima and Sultana, 2009: 183). The relativity here refers to the link women establish or want to establish with

2 The survey on the web pages of CoHE National Thesis Center and DergiPark shows that there were 53 graduate thesis and 9,557 articles with the keyword "micro-credit."

the labor market is influenced by many factors other than their own wishes and desires, and income they earn differs depending on it. In the most general terms, the neo-classical working-leisure model's description of the labor supply is based on the premise that the individual's desire to work for how many hours depends on the market's wage rates. In the model, the individual decides to work as many hours as they wish by comparing their psychological assessment of the work with the wage rates of the market (McConnell, Brue & Macpherson, 2015: 19; Biçerli, 2016: 23–25). It treats labor supply as gender neutral. For women, however, deciding how many hours a week to work depends on the necessity to balance "psychological evaluation of work with the help of gap curves" and "market wage rates shown using budget constraints" as well as a number of factors in the family, bestowed upon her because of the traditional gender roles, such as persuading their father and/or spouse to work, taking care of their children and taking care of household tasks (or organizing the household work even when there is paid help in the house) (Johnstone, 1968: 103; Lisaniler & Bahatti, 2005: 2119; Yıldırım & Doğrul, 2008: 239).

There have been increases in the number of married women joining the workforce in recent years. The analysis of labor supply also addresses individual decision-making mechanisms as well as the household as an economic unit. The household can be treated as a unit who consumes, has choices for leisure time and uses his time on other non-market activities. In statistical definitions, household, which is defined by the criterion of "joint decision-making of living, earning and spending in the same household," is a concept different to family. When family is considered as a household, members have to relate to labor markets in different forms such as "full or part-time paid work," "home-based marketing and manufacturing" or "the use of invisible labor in the household." For example, women whose spouses earn higher wages may have a higher preference for not working. When the spouses are in a position to decide who should work within the workforce and who should work within the household by evaluating the "opportunity cost," the party that gets paid relatively less could prefer to stay out of the workforce (Greenstein, 1986: 560). The neo-classical labor/leisure model, which approaches the issue of work and labor supply predominantly from an economic perspective, leaves out the positive outcomes created by the participation of women in the workforce outside of home, albeit poorly paid, in regards to social participation.

In terms of trying to balance so many variables in order to take part in social life and labor markets, women see "having their own business" or, in other words, "being an entrepreneur" as an alternative way to reduce the barriers faced in a paid working relationship.

Women with concerns about fulfilling their household responsibilities as well as working and generating income are forced to choose between three options in the form of "being employed, being unemployed, doing home production" (Fraundorf, 1979: 405). There are new inequalities as well as improvements in women's roles, employment and professional status in working life. For example, definitions of paid employment outside of the home (working woman) do not include full-time domestic work (England & Brown, 1992: 18). However, women are free domestic labor providers outside the labor markets, and they also take part in the working life in a household-oriented manner, both dependently and independently.

Women's home-based entrepreneurship can be explained as being able to convert the value created by production at home into income by marketing it in some way. In this context, seemingly mutually inclusive terms such as "self-employment," "becoming an employer" and "becoming an entrepreneur" need to be clearly defined as they are different to each other.

An important part of the activities within the scope of self-employment is found within the informal economy. A self-employed person can be defined as an entrepreneur who develops products, production processes, distribution and marketing methods himself (Gündoğan, 1999: 76). The category of self-employment includes employers, self-employed workers and their assistants, as well as paid and unpaid family workers.

As shown in Tab. 8.1, in Turkey, 267,000 women were self-employed in the agricultural sector, while 1,995,000 men were employed with the same status in 2018. The number of women in free family labor in the agricultural sector is greater than that of men. In agriculture, there are 560,000 male unpaid family workers[3] and 1,880,000 female unpaid family workers. The number of women who are employers in the agricultural sector is very low. Although the number of women who are employers in nonagricultural sectors is higher than in the agricultural sector, the number is still considerably lower than the male employers. There are 109,000 female employers compared to the 1,121,000 male employers in the nonagricultural sectors. The number of male employers in the nonagricultural sectors is about 10 times the number of female employers. Furthermore, the number of men in the category of self-employment in these

---

3 The number of employed women should also take into account the unpaid family workers as well as wage workers. Women who work on family land or work in a family-owned workplace are considered economically active and are included in the labor force. In Turkish statistics, unpaid family workers are counted among those employed (Tansel, 2002).

Tab. 8.1: "Those Employed according to Work Status" in the Agricultural and Nonagricultural Sectors) as of 2018 in Turkey (per 1,000 people)

	In the Agricultural Sector					**Nonagricultural Sectors**				
	Total	**Wage worker / Paid Daily**	**Employer**	**For Their Own Account**	**Unpaid Family Worker**	**Total**	**Wage worker / Paid Daily**	**Employer**	**For Their Own Account**	**Unpaid Family Worker**
Total	5,297	544	51	2,262	2,440	23,441	18,991	1,230	2,674	572
Man	2,943	341	48	1,995	560	16,776	13,302	1,121	2,039	314
Woman	2,353	203	3	267	1,880	6,665	5,689	109	608	258

Source: http://www.tuik.gov.tr (Date accessed: 29.01.2020)

sectors is much higher than women. Compared to 608,000 self-employed women, 2,039,000 men work on their own account.

Women's position in the economic life is also closely related to her status in other fields. Equality should be instated in areas such as access to vocational and technical professional education at all levels, transition to economic life without discrimination, equal treatment in employment, equal pay and pregnancy protection (Gwartney & Stroup, 1973: 580). In many countries, there is a general equality in principle and in laws regarding employment and occupation. In fact, there are additional protections for the women's pregnancy and maternity. However, these areas, which are subject to regulation and additional protection, are also the reasons that drive women away from having close ties with labor markets. The level of participation in labor markets is not the same in every country. Empowerment of women in social life depends on effective participation in labor markets. For this reason, home-based female entrepreneurship is a type of employment that will make important contributions to the participation of women in the labor markets.

A small number of well-educated women in Turkey work in formal economics as high-status white-collar workers. Socioeconomic, cultural, demographic and geographical factors influence the professional and employment status of women in Turkey. Women can take part in the labor market as housewives, unpaid family workers in agriculture, manufacturing workers and low-level non-manufacturing workers (Hoşgör & Smits, 2006: 3).

Since women who do home-based work see themselves as participating in production, they also want to be able to produce outside the home if possible (Özgüler, 2012). This finding raises the question of whether home-based women entrepreneurship is done out of necessity or preference.

From this point of view, entrepreneurship support should be set up in a way that enables women to go into production in the field outside the home in line with their preferences, rather than being stuck with the necessity of domestic production. This approach obliges women to be supported in areas such as gender roles, education, household, children and elderly care labor, which require them to choose the home over the field. Entrepreneurship is shaped by the individual's entrepreneurial and innovative characteristics due to its nature and its emergence. In recent years, entrepreneurship has started to evolve into a state where it can contribute to production at a level that creates qualified added value through the concept of "entrepreneurial ecosystem," which develops individual capacities with institutional arrangements. Thus, it is very important to consider all aspects of home-based female entrepreneurship.

4 Academic Studies on Home-Based Female Entrepreneurship in Turkey

Within the scope of academic studies in Turkey, this study covers graduate theses and articles in peer-reviewed academic journals.

4.1 Methodology

As part of the study, a scan was carried out in DergiPark and the national CoHE database in October 2019 with the keywords "home-based female entrepreneurship." Studies containing the keywords in their abstract were transferred into Excel files. The study utilized a qualitative research method called document analysis. The research population consists of 9,855 studies comprising 9,388 articles and 467 graduate theses obtained with a keyword search of "home-based female entrepreneurship" among the articles in the DergiPark system and the graduate theses in the national CoHE database.

The studies in two Excel files, containing 9,388 articles and 467 graduate theses, were then converted into a single data file by parsing the titles suitable for the research topic. At this stage, an expert was consulted and the Excel database files were given their final shape accordingly.

4.2 Data Analysis and Discussion

The studies directly related to home-based female entrepreneurship, which is the main subject of this study, were saved to the computer with their full text and were then analyzed qualitatively. Table 8.2 contains the 9,388 articles and 467 graduate thesis studies that were considered to be directly related to the subject of the research.

The studies included in Tab. 8.2 were analyzed by the MAXQDA 2018 qualitative data analysis program. In this analysis, the most frequently repeated concepts were found with the word cloud[4] tool, and then the 10 most common concepts were examined in terms of the context in which they were used in each study.

Table 8.3 shows that the most emphasized concept is employment. Women who market their products even for small prices become productive and their conditions are researched within scope of productivity. The emphasis on

4 The picture, in which the word frequency is indicated by size (larger indicates more frequent) and color (darker indicates more frequent), is given in Appendix 1.

Tab. 8.2: Academic Studies on Home-Based Female Entrepreneurship

Code	Year	Thesis / Article Author	Title of Thesis / Article	Journal/Language/Volume/Issue/ Pages of the Published Article	University/Language/ Type/Area of the Thesis
tez_002	2005	Elif Sinanoğlu Koç	The Concept of Women Entrepreneurs and Self-Employed Women Entrepreneurs in Konya, an Applied Research		Selçuk University / Turkish / Master of Science / Economics, Education
eekg_001	2013	Gul Aktaş	I Produce Therefore I Am: The Unseen Labor of Women Working With a Home Axis in Buldan in Family and Social Life	*Journal of Social and Humanities Sciences*, 5 (1), 258–267	
eekg_002	2016	Hasan Aslan	A Field Research on Social and Economic Lives of Women Working With EV-Axis: The Case of Denizli Province	*Fe Magazine*, 8 (1), 68–90	
eekg_003	2017	Arzu Tay Bayramoğlu & Gökhan Dökmen	An Evaluation on the Relationship Between Female Employment and Micro Credit Applications in Turkey.	*Bartın University Journal of the Faculty of Economics and Administrative Sciences*, 8 (16), 41–64	
eekg_004	2016	Mehmet Kaya & Bahar Burtan Doğan	Flexible Working Model: Home Axis Working	*Journal of Electronic Social Science*, 15 (58), 1069–1099	
eekg_005	2012	Kuvvet Lordoglu	A Qualitative Comparison of Women Working at Home and Some Problems	*Journal of Women's Studies*, 0 (1),	

(*continued on next page*)

Tab. 8.2: Continued

Code	Year	Thesis / Article Author	Title of Thesis / Article	Journal/Language/Volume/Issue/ Pages of the Published Article	University/Language/ Type/Area of the Thesis
eekg_006	2017	Ibrahim Sani Mert	Entrepreneurship of Housewives: A Qualitative Research In Gaziantep Province	*Journal of the Institute of Social Sciences of Bingöl University*, 7, 63–78.	
eekg_007	2016	Fatma Özlem Tezcek &Özlem Polat	Workers of the factory inside the House	*Fe Journal*, 8 (1), 49–68.	
khç_001	2018	Nagihan Durusoy Öztepe & Sezgi Akbaş	Social Security of Those Who Work on Their Behalf and Account in Turkey	*SGD-Journal of Social Security*, 8 (1), 67–94.	
khç_002	2019	Ekrem Erdoğan & Serpil Çiğdem	Portfolio Working and Changing Career Behaviors: Evaluation of Freelance Employees ' Experiences	*PESA International Journal of Social Research*, 5 (2), 184–199	
khç_003	2019	Mevlüt Yılmaz	The Transforming Structure of Employment Relations In Neoliberal Capitalism: The Rise of Non-Standard Forms of Work	*Opus Journal of International Community Studies*, 14 (20), 1710–1734	
khç_004	2015	Burak Darici & Mehmet Taşçı	Self-Employed Works: An Econometric Application on Turkey	*Management and Economics: Celâl Bayar University Journal of the Faculty of Economics and Administrative Sciences*, 22 (1), 19–40	

Tab. 8.3: The Most Commonly Used Concepts in Research Studies

Concept	Frequency	Percent (%)
Employment	267	3.25
Production	258	3.14
Economic	205	2.49
Employees	202	2.46
Women	180	2.19
Employees	154	1.87
Labor Force	142	1.73
In Turkey	139	1.69
Entrepreneur	131	1.59
Independent	127	1.54
Entrepreneurship	124	1.51
Employer	118	1.43
Of the work	113	1.37
Work	113	1.37
Turkey	109	1.33
Credit	107	1.30
Income	104	1.26
Sum of those with more than 100 frequency	2,593	31.53
Sum of those with less than 100 frequency	5,630	68.47
Total	**8,223**	**100.00**

employment and productivity mainly takes place in studies with codes tez_002, eekg_003, eekg_004, eekg_007, khç_002, khç_003.

The concept of production emphasizes that entrepreneurship is a factor of production and considers home-based female entrepreneurship as one of the most flexible forms of work. These views are mainly included in the studies with the codes eekg_004, eekg_007, khç_001, khç_003.

Within the context of the concept scanned with the code "economic," it is observed that the role of home-based female entrepreneurs in the economic development of the country has come to the fore. In addition to the individual benefits of home-based women entrepreneurship, the idea that it is important for the development of the country is emphasized mainly in tez_002, eekg_004, khç_003 code studies.

When we evaluate the research included in this study in general, they can be summarized with their aspects of home-based women entrepreneurship that provide flexibility to women and that emphasize the fact that they employ themselves through their own efforts. The house offers an opportunity for a woman to create employment for herself by combining the roles of work and family (Loscocco & Smith-Hunter, 2004: 164).

The entrepreneurial motivations of men and women in general are not exactly the same. However, if the subject is compared in terms of "home-based female entrepreneurship" as opposed to other types of entrepreneurship rather than the distinction of male and female entrepreneurs, we obtain clearer results. Indeed, even among women who prefer "home-based" or "out-of-home" area as their field, there are significant differences in the way their entrepreneurship can be uncovered and maintained. The motivation of women who engage in entrepreneurial activity outside of the home is similar to that of men. While there are similarities between "home-based" and "out-of-home" categories in terms of earning money to be independent, accomplishing such aims and using their unique skills and talents to increase job satisfaction or requests, in the "home-based" entrepreneurship category, the desire to create a working model that is compatible with family responsibilities becomes prominent (Longstreth, Stafford & Mauldin, 1987: 35).

Entrepreneurship, which has been seen as a male activity throughout history, has been increasingly attractive for women as well (Bozat, 2017: 26). Since entrepreneurs have the potential to develop themselves firstly, and the society they live in by creating employment (Demirel & Tikici, 2004: 49), it is important for women to be entrepreneurs when it comes to their participation in labor markets, being productive, and taking part in the process of creating economic value. Societies perform differently when it comes to entrepreneurship. The differences in the social and economic positions of women in developed and developing countries are also prominent in the field of entrepreneurship.

New jobs created by women appear especially after the 1980s. The 1990s brought about a technological transformation that occurred in parallel with the transformation process. This in turn created an increase in female entrepreneurs who started to take part in nontraditional sectors such as communication and marketing as well as traditional sectors (Atalay & Varol, 2016: 183). Therefore, many women are increasingly participating in working life and starting their own businesses due to these social and technological changes. As women begin to take part in the working life as entrepreneurs, they are becoming increasingly independent in both social and economic terms by being stripped of the roles that society has imposed on them (Çabuk,Südaş & Araç, 2015: 425).

5 Conclusion

Generally speaking, entrepreneurship is a process that provides benefits for individuals and society, provides economic returns and converts these returns into innovations. There are many applications in this process that involve improving social, economic, individual, social and environmental conditions. Many new jobs and employment opportunities have emerged thanks to the enterprises established as a result of entrepreneurial activities. Therefore, the entrepreneurial individual can create economic and social benefits for herself by establishing a business while also creating additional employment. Entrepreneurship, which makes direct and indirect contributions to the employment process, reduces unemployment and raises the level of individual and social welfare.

The participation of women, who make up half of the population, in the production process is very important for the economic and social development of Turkey. Indeed, women can achieve success in every sector without heeding any social distinctions such as women's work and men's work. However, because of certain barriers such as education level and gender roles, it is difficult for them to find work and keep it. Thus, an important step will be taken in the field of female employment when the ability to create jobs in accordance with women's own qualifications and abilities is supported, and opportunities are provided for the longevity of the enterprises they establish. For example, an agro-tourism enterprise founded by a woman living in rural areas as an unpaid family worker will ensure that her work or labor is registered and visible, and will contribute to both the individual and the national economy. A highly educated woman living in the city becoming a "green entrepreneur" based on her concerns about the climate, environment and sustainability will also have important benefits on societal and economic grounds. A look at the literature shows that in fact, the rural, green, purple, social and technological entrepreneurship distinctions proposed for women are not very important. Any business that women establish, work in and create employment, regardless of its type, will potentially make significant contributions to women's employment. What is important here is that women establish a business and ensure the longevity of this business.

Women's entrepreneurship is also an important impetus for the country's growth and development. Especially in developing countries, women fall behind in labor markets in relation to paid employment compared to men. "Home-based female entrepreneurship," a form of employment participation where gender roles and lack of education are trivialized, is actually a very common type of work but one that is not fully reflected in the records.

Women strive to produce and market small household products in order to fulfill the obligations required by gender roles, such as caring for children and the elderly, as well as to contribute to the family budget.

As long as this form of work remains a solution that women find through their own efforts, they will be avoiding the potential to reveal positive aspects such as long-term and sustainable business development and social visibility that attract people to the working life, as seen in general entrepreneurship practices.

For this reason, it is necessary to support home-based female entrepreneurship, which is an option for women who want to work for a wage but cannot find a job in order to provide additional income to the household in Turkey. While female entrepreneurship plays an important role in development, it is also effective in preventing women's unemployment and combating poverty. The fact that women are entrepreneurs increases female employment by preventing unemployment. Despite the importance of female entrepreneurship in macro and micro dimensions, women face many obstacles both because they are women and because of legal and bureaucratic issues. The state plays an important role in overcoming these obstacles. It should encourage women to become entrepreneurs by supporting them with entrepreneurship courses and grants and loans, as well as regulations on overcoming bureaucratic and legal obstacles. Furthermore, nongovernmental organizations play an important role in promoting female entrepreneurs. There are many activities taking place in this area in Turkey as well.

It is necessary to ensure awareness in the individuals living in the community and in every part of the society, starting with the family, which is the smallest unit of the society.

References

Atalay, Y. & Varol, Ç. (2016). İleri Teknoloji Sektöründe Kadın Girişimciliği: "Ankara'daki Sektörel ve Mekânsal Farklılaşmalar", *Planlama*, *26*(3), 181–192, https://www.researchgate.net/publication/308998639_Woman_Entrepreneurship_in_High-Tech_Sector_Sectoral_and_Spatial_Differentiations_in_Ankara, (Date of Access: 20.11.2019).

Biçerli, M. K. (2011). *Çalışma Ekonomisi*, İstanbul: Beta Yayınları.

Bozat, Z. A. (2017). Kadın Girişimciler ve İnovasyon; Topluluktan Faydalanma Yönteminin Getirebileceği Çözümler: Şişli Bölgesindeki Kadın Girişimciler, *AÇU Uluslararası Sosyal Bilimler Dergisi*, *3*(1), 26–37, https://dergipark.org.tr/tr/download/article-file/328599, (Date of Access: 20.11.2019).

Çabuk, S., Südaş, D. H. & Araç, K. S. (2015). Kadın Girişimcilerin İş Yaşam Süreçlerinin İncelenmesi: Adana İlindeki Girişimciler Üzerine Bir Uygulama, *Mustafa Kemal Üniversitesi Sosyal Bilimler Dergisi, 12*(31), 423–441, https://dergipark.org.tr/en/download/article-file/183440, (Date of Access: 02.10.2019).

David, N. (1996). *Worlds Apart Women and the Global Economy.* Bruxelles. ICFTU.

Demirel, E. T. & Tikici, M. (2004). Kültürün Girişimciliğe Etkileri, *Fırat Üniversitesi Doğu Anadolu Bölgesi Araştırmaları Dergisi, 2*(3), 49–58, https://openaccess.firat.edu.tr/xmlui/bitstream/handle/11508/8377/F1.pdf?sequence=1&isAllowed=y, (Date of Access: 10.10.2019).

England, P. & Brown, I. (1992). Trends in Women's Economic Status, *Sociological Perpectives, 35*(1), 17–51, https://journals.sagepub.com/doi/abs/10.2307/1389367, (12.03.2019).

Fatima, A. & Sultana, H. (2009). Tracing Out The U-Shape Relationship Between Female Labor Force Participation Rate and Economic Development for Pakistan, *International Journal of Social Economics, 36*(1/2), 182–198, https://www.emerald.com/insight/content/doi/10.1108/03068290910921253/full/pdf?title=tracing-out-the-ushape-relationship-between-female-labor-force-participation-rate-and-economic-development-for-pakistan, (11.03.2019).

Feldstead, A. & Jewson, N. (2000). *In Work, At Home: Towards an Understanding of Homeworking*, London: Routledge.

Fraundorf, M. N. (1979). Labor Force Participation of Turn-of-the Century Married Women, *Economic History, 39*(2), 401–418, https://www.sciencedirect.com/science/article/abs/pii/0014498380900169, (16.04.2019).

Goldin, C. (1954). The U-Shaped Female Labor Force Function in Economic Development and Economic History, *NBER Working Paper WP. No. 4707*, 1–49, https://www.nber.org/papers/w4707.pdf, (02.03.2010).

Greenstein, T. N. (1986). Social-Psyhological Factors in Perinatal Labor Force Participation, *Journal of Marriage and Family, 48*(3), 565–571, https://www.jstor.org/stable/pdf/352042.pdf?refreqid=excelsior%3Acb680e1265e7af51f0cb4155a27432e7, (11.07.2019).

Gündoğan, N. (1999). Kendi Hesabına Çalışma: Kavram, Ölçüm ve Özellikleri, *Ekonomik Yaklaşım, 10*(34), 75–87, https://econpapers.repec.org/article/eydeyjrnl/v_3a10_3ay_3a1999_3ai_3a34_3ap_3a75-87.htm, (05.08.2018).

Gwartney, J. & Stroup, R. (1973). Measurement of Employment Discrimination According to Sex, *Southern Economic Journal, 39*(4), 575–587, http://eds.a.ebscohost.com/eds/pdfviewer/pdfviewer?vid=1&sid=6fed40f6-0850-4eca-8cad-b4969f5c01fb%40sdc-v-sessmgr01, (23.10.2011).

Hoşgör, A. G. & Smits, J. (2006). Variation in Labor market Participation of Married Women in Turkey, *Nice Working Paper, Radbaud University*, 1–14, http://www. home.planet.nl/~smit9354/.../Gunduz-Hosg, (12.11.2011).

Johnstone, E. (1968). Women in Economic Life: Rights and Opportunities, *Annals of the American Academy of Political and Social Science, 375*, 102–114, https://journals.sagepub.com/doi/10.1177/000271626837500116, (05.09.2011).

Kocabaş, F., Besler, S. & Özgüler, V. (2017). Ev Eksenli Çalışan Kadınlara Yönelik Niteliksel Bir Araştırma: Eskişehir El Sanatları Pazarı Örneği, *Mehmet Akif Ersoy Üniversitesi Sosyal Bilimler Enstitüsü Dergisi, 9*(18), 178–201, https://dergipark.org.tr/tr/download/article-file/289626, (12.11.2019).

Lisaniler, F. G. & Bhatti, F. (2005). Determinants of Female Labour Force Participation: A Study of North Cyprus, *Review of Social, Economic & Business Studies, 5/6*, 204–226, https://www.academia.edu/1863042/Determinants_of_Female_Labour_Force_Participation_A_Study_of_North_Cyprus, (26.08.2019).

Longstreth, M., Stafford, K. & Mauldin, T. (1987). Self-employed Women and Their Families: Time Use and Socioeconomic Characteristics, *Journal of Small Business Management, 25*, 30–37.

Loscocco, K. & Smith-Hunter, A. (2004). Women-home Based Business Owners: Insights from Comparative Analyses, *Women in Management Review, 19*(3), 164–173, https://www.researchgate.net/publication/228270860_Women_Home-Based_Business_Owners_Insights_from_Comparative_Analyses, (03.06.2019).

McConnell, C. R., Brue, S. L. & Macpherson, D. A. (2015). *Contemporary Labor Economics*, USA: McGraw-Hill Education.

Özgüler, V. (2012). Home-Based Women Workers: The Case of Turkey / Eskisehir, *International Journal of Business and Social Science, 3*(19), 261–271.

Tansel, A. (2002). İktisadi Kalkınma ve Kadınların İşgücüne Katılımı: Türkiye'den Zaman Serisi Kanıtları ve İllere Göre Yatay Kesit Kestirimleri, *ERC Working Papers in Economics*, 1–31, 01/057, http://www.erc.metu.edu.tr/menu/series01/0105T.pdf, (09.11.2009).

Yıldırım, K. & Doğrul, G. (2008). "Çalışmak ya da Çalışmamak" Türkiye'de Kentsel Alanlarda Yaşayan Kadınların İşgücüne Katılmama Kararlarının Olası Belirleyicileri, *Anadolu Üniversitesi Sosyal Bilimler Enstitüsü Dergisi, 8*(1), 239–262.

Internet Resources

https://wordart.com/create (29.01.2020).

http://www.tuik.gov.tr (29.01.2020).

Appendix 8.1: The Word Cloud Composed of the Most Frequently Repeated Words in Articles

Source: https://wordart.com/create

Section 5 Socioeconomic Issues and Women

Dilek Murat and Betül İnam

Effects of Public Spending on Poverty: An Empirical Application

1 Introduction

The concept of poverty in its most general form is expressed as the basic physical needs not being met of the individual, individuals or households, and the lack of adequate goods and services to sustain their lives and meet their needs does not have a source of income(Özgüler, 2014: 133). However, there is no objective and agreed-upon definition of poverty. The fact that poverty is closely linked to the social and political environment beyond its economic effects leads to the emergence of numerous approaches in the definitions and measurements of poverty. While the view that poverty can by definition include many criteria beyond income/consumption level is generally adopted, there are many different ideas on the number and nature of the criteria to be added (Şenses, 2014: 105). Among the definitions of poverty frequently used are absolute poverty, relative poverty and human poverty. While absolute poverty is defined as the minimum level of consumption and minimum income for the purpose of sustaining the physical life of the individual, relative poverty is concerned with whether people have a minimum level of living accepted by the society in which they reside. In the case of human poverty, the idea is that it is necessary to have economic, social and cultural opportunities as well as the financial means necessary to live humanly (Demirtürk et al., 2011: 34). As the definition and types of poverty expand, it becomes difficult to determine the causes of poverty. There are numerous causes that affect poverty. It is not possible to associate types of poverty in all countries and even in different settlements within the same country for the same reasons. The causes of poverty can also differ over time according to political and socioeconomic conditions (Şenses, 2014: 148). However, among the most common causes of poverty can be considered as, inequalities in income distribution; high interest rates; natural disasters; wars; economic crises; the tax system's unfair differences between individuals in ability; to be a monopoly in the market; informal economy; disabilities in education, health and social protection systems; demographics; unemployment; inflation; immigration; ethnicity or gender discrimination (Sarısoy and Koç, 2010: 330).

Access to education and health services, clean water, energy and critical services are still a major problem for many people today. Factors such as gender, ethnicity, geography, socioeconomic status and income injustice constitute important barriers in the fight against poverty. Poverty is a much broader and more fundamental problem when access to the abovementioned services and goods, besides income, is included in the calculations. In the broad sense, the number of those exposed to poverty is far greater than the number of the calculated poor indexed to income and consumption alone (World Bank, 2020).

Poverty is a fundamental problem for all mankind, but women experience poverty more severely. Women face higher levels of poverty than men due to negative discrimination against women in education, employment and low wages. The basis of the challenges women face in the labor market is that rates of health, education, nutrition and schooling are lower than those of women. This leads women to turn to sectors with low productivity and low earnings in the labor market. In addition, social and cultural norms are one of the major obstacles women face in the field of labor force participation and education (Şenses, 2014: 177–178). Women globally have 24 % less income than men. In developing countries, 75 % of women work informally. They don't have enough resources to get out of poverty. The value of free care jobs, such as childcare and housework, where women work, is estimated to be at least $10.8 trillion annually. This is more than three times that of the global technology industry (OXFAM, 2020).

The pandemic, which has been on the world agenda in the last six months, has come across as another cause that will profoundly affect poverty. With the impact of COVID-19 on the world, between 40 million and 60 million people will be dragged into extreme poverty (earning less than $1.9 a day) by 2020, according to World Bank estimates. At the global level, the extreme poverty rate could rise from 0.3 to 0.7 % in 2020, rising to 9 %. In addition, the proportion of people living on less than $3.20 a day could increase by 0.3 to 1.7 percentage points, which means that the number of people in this income group will increase from 40 million to 150 million (World Bank, 2020). It is estimated that the economic crisis caused by the virus could push more than half a billion people around the world into poverty if urgent and dramatic measures are not taken. As the disparities between rich–poor nations and men and women increase, the consequences of the virus will also be severe (OXFAM, 2020: 1).

The next part of the article is arranged as follows. Under the first chapter, the place of public expenditures in the fight against poverty has been evaluated in light of theoretical and empirical findings. Data and empirical findings are presented in the second title and the results of the research are given in the last title.

2 Public Spending and Fighting Poverty

Poverty is a problem that has existed from the past to the present. In today's sense, the emergence of poverty as a social problem in Europe begins with 16th century capitalism. During this period, the use of the poor as labor force was on the agenda. After this period, the perception of poverty has changed many times according to the conditions and times that have developed. At the end of the 18th century, the concept of the working poor with the Industrial Revolution was rejected; at the 19th century, liberal philosopher reintroduced alms and stated that there was no need for state intervention in the elimination of poverty (Buğra, 2011: 11–12). After the Great Depression of 1929, the idea that the state had to intervene in the economy in order for countries to overcome the economic crisis was accepted. In this way, it is aimed to eliminate unemployment and poverty, and to provide economic growth and development. After World War II, welfare state policies were implemented all over the world. It is possible to say that these policies, which can be summarized mainly in the form of full employment and the establishment of a comprehensive social safety net, have achieved significant successes in poverty reduction. However, these policies began to be abandoned from the 1980s onward. The reason for the abandonment of welfare state policies is the idea that social spending to prevent poverty increases poverty (Turkish State Planning Organization (DPT), 2007: 3). The rapid globalization since this period, the effectiveness of multinational corporations and the state being seen as an obstacle to the free market, has left the welfare state practices in second place. Economic policies implemented since the 1980s aim to reduce poverty indirectly. One of the major causes of poverty is the idea that poverty will decrease spontaneously by reducing unemployment and achieving economic growth (Solmaz and Avcı, 2017: 52). Since the 1990s, international organizations have put the issue of poverty back on their agenda and have emphasized that no purpose can be more important than this issue by linking poverty reduction with economic development (Şenses, 2014: 41). Until the 1990s, poverty-oriented policies consisted of puny practices devoted to the most socially vulnerable population; while at the end of the 1990s, with the Asian crisis and the rise in global poverty, dominant idea began to change (Merrien, 2013: 89).

The most effective means of combating poverty today are public spending. Although the absolute elimination of poverty through public spending is not possible, poverty can be reduced at a certain rate. The expenditures that have a significant impact on poverty reduction among public expenditures are education, health and social protection expenditures, which can be called social expenditures. These expenditures have a lot in common. For example, Positive externality spreads, complementary and reinforcing relationships between them, their ability to reflect social welfare at a global level, their ability to feed and enhance human capital and their effectiveness in reducing poverty and income inequalities can be counted among these (Haile and Zarazua, 2018: 371).

Education is one of the important factors in strengthening human capital. It is one of the most important tools for individuals to make effective choices and increase economic opportunities. Higher levels of education mean an improved financial ability, a better income level and better health for individuals beyond school success (World Bank, 2019: 27). So education is one of the keys to getting out of poverty. The goal in education is to prevent poor children from becoming poor and uneducated adults and to end generations of poverty (Klugman et al., 2002).

Health is an important source of well-being. Health affects the economy in a wide variety of ways. It is possible to say that there are lots of direct and indirect relationships between health and economy such as production losses, which develops due to illness of employees, increase in productivity as a result of better diet, learning more advanced skills in healthy individuals, routing the resources that will be spent for the improvement of the disease in healthy subjects to different destinations and the income potential healthy individuals being high (WHO, 2004: 15). Therefore, health is a candidate phenomenon to be both the cause and the result of poverty. Reforms with low costs in health have been key points in economic growth. Declining death rates and prolonged life expectancy increased the proportion of the active population of working age between 1960 and 2000 and increased production and income per capita. In addition, extended human life has led to a higher saving effort to secure retirement income, and is another reason for the jump in economic development for East Asian countries, which allocate 30 % of income to savings (Bloom et al., 2004: 11–12).

Social protection consists of a set of policies that are produced to ensure that women, men and children reach adequate living conditions throughout their lives. Reducing and preventing poverty plays an important role in eliminating social inequalities. In addition, countries invest in social protection for various reasons such as ensuring human development, increasing social cohesion, ensuring sustainable growth and supporting the workforce. Social protection is a vital tool in the 2030 Sustainable Development Goals, but it is fundamental to achieving some goals (United Nations, 2018). Social protection is extremely important for the improvement of services such as health and education, as well as its contributions to poverty, income injustice and inclusive growth. It is argued that social protection expenditures are necessary to reduce poverty in the first phase and injustice in income distribution in the second phase. It is emphasized that income inequalities are positively and strongly affected by cash benefits, which lead to a direct increase in the income of individuals and households. Cash supports are thought to provide continuous and regular income to protect against poverty shocks and provide an important financial support for services such as education, health care, job search, transportation and spending (Bhorat et al., 2017: 189).

As can be seen, public spending plays an important role in poverty reduction by affecting poverty in a wide variety of ways. The important part of the empirical studies that are carried out also supports the theory. A study for Indonesia investigated the effects of education and health spending on poverty. Significant effects of public spending on primary education and primary health-care services have been identified in this country on poverty. But it concluded that spending on tertiary education and secondary health care had less impact on poverty (Lanjouw et al., 2001). For many Eastern Bloc countries in a study, it is stated that because of the low expenditure on education and other public services, poverty will continue increasing and although education is important in the elimination of poverty, it was also emphasized that the elimination of income inequalities is extremely important for decreasing poverty (Klugman et al., 2002). A study for EU15 countries found that social spending has strong effects on poverty. Social spending has been shown to reduce poverty by an average of 7 % in both the EU15 countries and other member states (Caminada and Goudswaard, 2009: 25). A study in India drew attention to the relationship between education and poverty and found that educational attainment is critical in reducing the poverty rate (Sarkaria and Sharma, 2016). The study for 10 new EU member states analyzed the employment and education indicators and the results of poverty and social exclusion. It is estimated that if these countries meet their 2020 targets on education and employment, there could be a decrease of approximately 3.7 million in the population at risk of poverty (World Bank, 2013). In a different study for Nigeria, it was argued that improving health spending without addressing income inequalities in the poor will not be enough to improve the health and social status of the population. The study stated that health spending would be more effective on poverty once income inequality and education-related deficiencies were addressed (Riman et al., 2010). A study covering 25 European countries between 2005 and 2013 found that poverty declined as spending on social protection increased. This relationship is much stronger in individuals over 65 and unemployed (Solmaz and Avci, 2017: 46). Another study for Nigeria, using 1965–2014, found significant negative relationships between poverty and spending on education, health and agriculture. However, it has been stressed that obstacles such as population, inflation and corruption must be eliminated in order for the results of spending to be more efficient (Yahaya, 2019: 39).

In studies for Turkey, the decreasing effect of social expenditures on poverty was determined (Sarisoy and Koç, 2010; Karanfil and Özkaya, 2013; Çelikay and Gümüş, 2014).

3 Dataset and Empirical Findings

The aim of the study was to group OECD countries on the basis of poverty levels and to identify the factors that are effective in this grouping. The data to be used in the analysis was compiled from OECD and World Bank databases. In the study, the year 2015 data, which was the most recent data available, of thirty six countries comprised Finland, Belgium, Czech Republic, Ireland, Sweden, Germany, France, Estonia, Switzerland, Iceland, Portugal, Turkey, Poland, Austria, Australia, Denmark, Bulgaria, Canada, Chile, the Netherlands, Israel, Latvia, Lithuania, Mexico, Greece, Japan, Norway, England, Spain, Hungary, Luxembourg, Korea, USA, Romania, the Slovak Republic and Italy have been obtained. The countries analyzed were grouped according to whether the poverty rate levels were above or below 0.12; below 0.12 were considered to be low poverty rates, while 0.12 and above were considered to be high poverty rates groups. Variables included in the analysis for the purpose of grouping countries and their explanations can be followed from the following lines.

Poverty rate (%) (pov_rate): the poverty rate is the proportion of people whose income falls below the poverty line (in a given age group), taken as half of the average household income of the total population. It is also available by wide age group: child poverty (0–17 years), working-age poverty and elderly poverty (over 66 years). However, two countries with the same poverty rates may differ according to the relative income levels of the poor.

Gini coefficient (Gini_coeff): the Gini coefficient is based on the comparison of the cumulative ratios of the population with the cumulative income ratios they receive, and its value varies between 0 in the case of perfect equality and 1 in the case of perfect inequality.

Unemployment rate (%) (Unemp_rate): the unemployment rate is the number of unemployed people as a percentage of the workforce; it consists of unemployed people and paid workers or self-employed people.

GDP per capita (USD) (GDP_per_cap): GDP per capita relative to purchasing power parity (PPP). PPP GDP is gross domestic product converted into international dollars using purchasing power parity ratios. An international dollar has the purchasing power of the U.S. dollar over the same GDP as in the United States. The data are in fixed international dollars for 2011.

Inflation rate (%) (Inf_rate): inflation, as measured by the Consumer Price Index (CPI), is typically defined as the change in the prices of a basket of goods and services purchased by certain groups of households. Inflation is measured by a break in total excluding food, energy and food and energy in the 2015 base year as the annual growth rate and index.

Education expenditures (% GDP) (Edu_exp): the state's overall education expenditures (current, capital and transfers) are expressed as a percentage of GDP.

Health expenditures (% GDP) (Health_exp): the current level of health expenditures is expressed as a percentage of GDP. Estimates for current health spending include health-care products and services consumed during the year. These display buildings, machines, etc., do not include health-care spending.

Social protection expenditures (% GDP) (Soc_pro_exp): used as a percentage of GDP. Transfers to households and individuals to alleviate the burden of defined risks and needs include social benefits given in cash and in kind, administrative expenses and all expenditures under social protection programs.

The most important assumptions of discriminant analysis were checked before the interpretation of the analysis findings. For this purpose, Box's M Test was applied in order to test the equality of covariance matrices of variables in the first stage. According to the findings, the null hypothesis has been rejected (Box's M=92.408; F (Approx.=2.561; Sig.=0.000)). The null hypothesis refers to the homogeneity of covariance matrices of groups. In this case, it was understood that quadratic discriminant analysis should be applied. In the next phase, correlations between independent variables were examined to determine the absence of multicollinearity problem, which is another important assumption. As a result, all variables were included in the analysis because no significant coefficients greater than 0.70 were detected in the correlation matrix.

Canonical correlation, eigenvalue and Wilks' lambda statistics were calculated in order to evaluate the significance of discriminant function. According to the canonical correlation value calculated as 0.825, the model can explain about 69 % of the variance in the dependent variable. Since the dependent

Tab. 9.1: Standardized Canonical Discriminant Function Coefficients and Structure Matrix

Std. Can. Discr. Func. Coefficients		Structure Matrix	
	Function		Function
	1		1
Gini_coeff	0.940	Gini_coeff	0.846
Unemp_rate	0.371	GDP_per_cap	−0.400
GDP_per_cap	−0.321	Soc_pro_exp	−0.293
Inf_rate	−0.214	Health_exp	−0.238
Edu_exp	0.008	Edu_exp	−0.178
Health_exp	0.048	Unemp_rate	0.174
Soc_pro_exp	−0.156	Inf_rate	0.096

Source: Figure created by the authors.

variable has two categories, one discriminant function and eigenvalue have been obtained. The eigenvalue (2.131) calculated as greater than 0.40 shows that the function provides a good discrimination. Wilks' Lambda (0.319) and sig. (0.000) findings indicate that the distinguishing power of the discriminant function to be generated is statistically significant. The independent variables that should be included in the discriminant function reached by the analysis, the coefficient values for these variables and the structure matrix are presented in Tab. 9.1.

Gini_coeff, Unemp_rate, GDP_per_cap, Inf_rate, Edu_exp, Health_exp and Soc_pro_exp are important distinguishing variables in dividing countries into low and high poverty groups according to the values of standardized canonical discriminant function coefficients in Tab. 9.1. The coefficient marks for these variables are also in line with expectation. Gini_coeff, Unemp_rate, Edu_exp and Health_exp variables affect the numerical value of the poverty rate variable positively, while GDP_per_cap, Inf_rate and Soc_pro_exp variables affect it negatively. Structure matrix results show that the variables with the highest correlation with discriminant function are Gini_coeff, GDP per capita and Soc_pro_exp in order. The results of the correct classification rate used to evaluate the success of the analysis are as shown in Tab. 9.2.

When Tab. 9.2 is examined, 94.4 % of the countries in the low poverty group are correct, 5.6 % are misclassified, 88.9 % of the countries in the high poverty group are correct and 11.1 % are misclassified. In addition, the correct classification rate of the analysis is 91.7 %.

Tab. 9.2: Classification Results*

			Predicted Group Membership		
		Group	**1**	**2**	**Total**
Original	Count	1	17	1	18
		2	2	16	18
	%	1	94.4	5.6	100
		2	11.1	88.9	100

Source: Figure created by the authors.

* 91.7 % of original grouped cases correctly classified.

4 Conclusion

The phenomenon of poverty and poor people has always existed in the history of the world. However, with the rapid development of the world economy in the last 20–30 years, increasing income inequality and unemployment of the pandemic affected the global economic crisis and increasing poverty all around the world by 2020, and further the process is spread all over the world, without distinction of rich and poor countries. Today, about a billion people have to live on an income of less than a dollar for a day. The estimates suggest that poverty will increase in the coming period due to the pandemic process experienced by the world. According to World Bank estimates, between 40 million and 60 million people will drift into extreme poverty (below $1.9 a day) in 2020 by 2019 due to the economic shock experienced by the pandemic. It is also inevitable that disadvantaged groups of society will be affected extra. The benefits of human rights and opportunities for women, who make up half of humanity, are one of the key points for poverty reduction and sustainable development to be achieved. Women should therefore have equal opportunities in education, health care, income and political rights.

The most important constraint in the fight against poverty is state intervention. Because it is a concept that has many problems and negative externalities in poverty. One of the most important tools of state intervention is public spending and is often used in combating poverty. Public spending, which outweighs social characteristics in particular, keeps individuals away from the risk of poverty while also ensuring sustainable growth and development. Through public education expenditures, it is aimed to improve the personal abilities of individuals, to gain professional skills and thus to get out of poverty by generating income. The aim is to create a healthy society through public health expenditures and to raise the living standards of the poverty-stricken sectors by social protection expenditures.

In this study, 36 OECD member countries were grouped according to poverty levels, and the data compiled were evaluated by discriminant analysis. The results found that all variables included in the analysis were effective when the analyzed countries were divided into low or high poverty groups. Furthermore, the most effective variables in this grouping were the Gini coefficient, GDP per capita and social protection expenditures, which represent income injustice in order. Social protection expenditures, GDP per capita and inflation rates negatively affect poverty increases in these variables and have been found to be effective in reducing poverty. However, education spending and health spending have been found to increase poverty by positively affecting poverty. The result, which is out of the hold on education and health spending, can be explained by gender inequalities and inequalities in education in OECD countries. In addition, the fact that the outcomes of education expenditures are a long-term public expenditure may cause the results of the analysis to be realized outside the expectations. The fact that health expenditures increase poverty by positively affecting poverty can be explained as the fact that in most OECD countries, the financing of health systems is not entirely covered by tax revenues, that is, it is based on the premiums that individuals will pay. In this case, the benefits of health services for those who are unable to pay premiums remain limited, and health expenditures will benefit those in higher income groups than those in the poor. Finally, the negative impact of social protection expenditures on poverty reduction shows that the expenditures achieved their goals. It has been proven once again in our study that social protection expenditures, which will protect individuals from poverty shocks and support their spending on education and health, are important for poverty and are indispensable public expenditures for states today.

References

Bhorat, H., Cassim, A., Ewingu, A., and Steenkamp, F. (2017), "Social Protection and Inequality in Africa: Exploring the Interaction", *Income Inequality Trends in Sub Sahran Africa Divergence, Determinats and Consequences*, Chapter 8, Newyork: UNDP Publishing.

Bloom, D. E., Canning, D., and Jamison, D. T. (2004), *Health, Wealth and Welfare, Health and Development*, Washington, DC: IMF Publishing.

Buğra, A. (2011), *Kapitalizm, Yoksulluk ve Türkiye'de Sosyal Politika*, https://books.google.com.tr/books?id=UAOcDwAAQBAJ&pg=PT1&

dq=ay%C5%9Fe+bu%C4%9Fra&hl=tr&sa=X&ved=0ahUKEwjnr6Gnld_pAhXJysQBHfI_CJsQ6AEILzAB#v=onepage&q=ay%C5%9Fe%20bu%C4%9Fra&f=false Accessed: 01.05.2020.

Camiada, K., and Goudswaard, K. (2009), Social expenditure and poverty reduction in EU15 and other OECD countries, MPRA Papers No. 20138.

Çelikay, F., and Gümüş, E. (2014), "Sosyal Harcamaların Yoksulluk Üzerine Etkileri: Ampirik Bir İnceleme", *Anadolu Üniversitesi SBD*, 14(4), 127–138.

Demirtürk, R. B., Bozkuş, N., Cephe, A., Aktaş, B., Afşar, T. S., and Çıngı, H. (2011), "Yoksulluk Düzeyinin Modellenmesi Üzerine Bir Araştırma", *Sosyoloji Araştırmaları Dergisi*, 14(1), 30–67.

DPT, (2007), Gelir Dağılımı ve Yoksullukla Mücadele, Özel İhtisas Komisyonu Raporu, Yayın No: 2741.

Haile, F., and Zarazua, M. N., (2018), "Does Social Spending Improve Welfare in Low-Income and Middle Income Countries?", *Journal of International Development*, 30(3), 367–398.

Karanfil, F. and Özkaya, A. (2013), "Indirect Taxes, Social Expenditures and Poverty: What Linkage?", *Ege Akademik Bakış*, 13(3), 337–350.

Klugman, J., Micklewright, J., and Redmand, G. (2002), Poverty in transition: Social expenditures and the working-age poor, https://www.unicef-irc.org/publications/327-poverty-in-the-transition-social-expenditures-and-the-working-age-poor.html, Accessed: 01.05.2020.

Lanjouw, P., Pradhan, M., Saadah, F., Sayed, H., and Sparrow, R. (2001), Poverty, Education and Health in Indonesia: Who Benefit from Public Spending, http://documents.worldbank.org/curated/en/349171468771677180/Poverty-education-and-health-in-Indonesia-who-benefits-from-public-spending, Accessed: 01.05.2020.

Merrien, F. X., (2013), "Social Protection as Development Policy: A New International Agenda for Action", *International Development Policy*, 4(2), 89–106.

OXFAM, (2020), Why majority of the world's poor are woman, https://www.oxfam.org/en/why-majority-worlds-poor-are-women, Accessed: 11.05.2020.

Özgüler, V. (2014), *Gelir Servet ve Yoksulluk*, İstanbul: Cinius Yayınları.

Riman, H. B., Bassey, J. U., Ibi, E. E., and Edu, B. E. (2010), Poverty, Health Expenditure and Health Status: A Long Term Perspective with Evidence from Nigeria, https://papers.ssrn.com/sol3/papers.cfm?abstract_id=1540303, Accessed: 01.05.2020.

Sarısoy, İ., and Koç, S. (2010), "Türkiye'de Kamu Sosyal Transfer Harcamalarının Yoksulluğu Azaltmadaki Etkilerinin Ekonometrik Analizi", *Maliye Dergisi*, 158, 326–348.

Sarkaria, M., and Sharma, S. (2016), "Education and Poverty Relationship in Punjab", *International Journal of Management& Social Sciences*, 4(2), 394–416.

Solmaz, E., and Avcı, M. (2017), "Yoksullukla Mücadelede Sosyal Koruma Harcamaları: Avrupa Birliği Ülkeleri Üzerine Bir İnceleme", *Ekonomi ve Yönetim Araştırmaları Dergisi*, 6(1), 46–72.

Şenses, F. (2014), *Küreselleşmenin Öteki Yüzü Yoksulluk*. İstanbul: İletişim Yayınları.

United Nations (2018). The sustainable development goals report. *July*, 6, 2019.

WHO, (2004), *Investing in Health for Economic Development*, Puebla: Who Publishing.

World Bank. (2012). *The World Bank Annual Report 2012*. The World Bank.

World Bank. (2019). *Ending Learning Poverty*: What Will It Take?

World Bank. (2020). *Poverty and Shared Prosperity 2020*: Reversals of Fortune.

Yahaya, N. (2019), "Relationship between Government Expenditure and Poverty: A Study of Nigeria (1965–2014)", *Journal of Economics and Finance*, 10(6), 39–52.

Gülsüm Akarsu, Reyhan Cafri and Hanife Bıdırdı

Female Labor Force Participation and Poverty: Evidence from Regions of Turkey

1 Introduction

Poverty is defined as the lack of ability to meet the basic needs of people. Women are among the most affected by poverty. In many developed and developing countries, women constitute the majority of the poor. Because of this, women's participation in the labor force is one of the important factors that provide economic and social development by reducing poverty. Women are employed in the labor market, thus achieving their economic freedom and social dignity; they provide significant social gains for themselves, their families and their communities. There are quite a number of views on women's participation in the labor force, which thinks they have more obstacles than men. Women do not have access to the labor market at an equal rate, equal position and equal pay to men.

Women constitute a significant majority of the poor in the world. Globally, more women than men live in poverty. Women are disadvantaged compared to men in accessing health and education opportunities. Moreover, they have primary responsibility for raising children, and also transmit values to the next generation. Investing in women contributes to the country's growth, development and poverty reduction (Todaro & Smith, 2014). If women are educated more, child mortality and fertility are reduced, their labor force participation and earnings are increased and also education is extended to next generations. Women's labor force participation leads to the extra income and decline in women's dependency on their families and contributes to reducing poverty (WB, 2009; Klasen, 2000). Women have unequal access to economic opportunities in the world. In developed countries, increasing the female participation to labor force would reduce the number of people living in poverty (OECD, 2008). In developing countries, women are still facing significant obstacles in entering the labor market.

In Turkey, "women were mainly employed as unpaid family workers in the agricultural sector" (WB, 2009: xi); in the 1950s, as a result of rural to urban migration and a steady decline in the agricultural population, the majority of women who lost agricultural activity were not included in the labor force in urban areas.

With the acceleration of urbanization, this rapid decline in the agricultural population has pushed a significant portion of the women out of the labor force who are heavily employed in the agricultural sector and find it difficult to re-enter the labor force. At present in Turkey, women make up more than half of the total population of the country. However, Turkey suffers from the low labor force participation of women. In 2018, Turkey is the country with the lowest level of female labor force participation (34 %) among OECD and European countries (TURKSTAT, 2019; OECD, 2019). In fact, this rate is lower in some regions of the country.

The objectives of this study are to examine empirically impact on the poverty of women participating in the labor force at the regional level (NUTS-2) in Turkey using panel data method. Due to the availability of data, it was handled between 2014 and 2017. In the empirical model, poverty was explained as a function of GDP, income inequality, inflation, education, male labor force participation, urbanization, the share of agriculture in the GDP and trade openness as well as female labor force participation.

This study consists of five parts. In the first part, introductory information about the importance, scope and purpose of the study are presented. In the second part, studies on poverty and women are summarized. The third and fourth parts are devoted to empirical model, methodology and the data set, respectively. The fifth and last part includes empirical analysis results and conclusions.

2 Literature Review

In the literature, studies on poverty and female have generally focused on the impact of female-headed households or number of women in households on poverty (Buvinić & Gupta, 1997; Gangopadhyay & Wadhwa, 2004; Horrell & Krishnan, 2007; Klasen et al., 2015; Montoya & Teixeira, 2017; Liu, Esteve & Treviño, 2017; Adepoju, 2019). However, recently, attention has shifted toward the impact of women taking a more active role in working life, which has often been discussed in connection with female labor force participation and development.

In the literature, the connection between female labor force participation and development is considered to be U-shaped (Schultz, 1990; Luci, 2009; Choudhry, 2010). Mincer (1962) was one of the first to be a reference for many empirical studies linking women's labor force participation to economic growth. Similar to the debate in the early stages of the Kuznets hypothesis, it forms the basis of the "U curve hypothesis," in which women's participation in the labor force initially declined and then began to increase with economic development. Women's labor force participation rate in countries moving from agricultural economy to industrialization first decreases and then increases and follows a U-shaped curve. As a result, it is assumed that the countries on the left side of the U-shaped curve have low GDP and their economies are based on agriculture, while those on the right side are industrialized countries with high GDP. The study of Tansel (2001), one of the first and most important studies examining the relationship between economic growth and women's participation in the labor force in Turkey, supports the U curve. There are studies used in variables such as energy use (Pampel & Tanaka, 1986), fuel consumption (Fatima & Sultana, 2009) and education (Lincove, 2008) instead of GDP as indicators of economic development.

After researching the relationship between development and women's labor force, the relationship between the phenomenon of poverty, which is one of the most important problems related to development, and the participation of women in the labor force has begun to attract attention in the literature. These studies, in general, show that women's participation in the labor force is effective in reducing poverty. Evcim et al. (2019), as a result of their study with panel data analysis for eight MENA countries and Turkey, obtained the finding that women's participation in the labor force reduced poverty. In a report that explains the participation of women in the labor force as a coping mechanism in response to shocks and poverty in developing countries, it is emphasized that "women's supply of labor increases household incomes, which helps families to escape poverty and increase consumption of goods and services" (Verick, 2018: 3). In the study conducted by Haq and Amin (2017) in which the impact of women's working status on family income and poverty reduction was investigated through a questionnaire in Pakistan, 58 % of the total households reported that working women play a positive role in poverty reduction. Selim (2016) investigated the determinants of relative poverty in Turkey with a gender-specific emphasis using the panel logit regression model. The findings revealed that being a man would reduce the likelihood of poverty in Turkey. Blume et al. (2007), in their study of the determinants of relative poverty between immigrants and natives in Denmark and Sweden, concluded that "being a woman is associated with a significantly higher poverty risk" (Blume et al., 2007: 383). In the study of the impact of paid and unpaid women on poverty in India, the importance of education was emphasized, and the incidence of poverty decreased with the increase in the educational attainment of paid or unpaid women (Singh & Pattanaik, 2019).

Some studies emphasize that women's participation in the labor force will show different behaviors at different levels of poverty. For example, the findings of the study performed by El-Hamidi (2003), which examines the female labor behavior in different poverty levels in Egypt, support the reverse S-shaped labor supply. Accordingly, women at low-income levels must work to meet the very basic needs of their families. When economic conditions improve, women who are also responsible for housework and childcare are thought to be withdrawing from the labor market or working less. At a higher income level, women prefer to participate in the labor market while transferring some or all of their household chores to cleaners (El-Hamidi, 2003).

Studies on poverty and women have found that the number of women in households or households with female heads increases the poverty. However, Dalgıç et al. (2015), profiled the poverty according to the characteristics of the household and the head of the household in their study by using income and living conditions survey for Turkey and found that the fact that the head of the household was female decreased poverty contrary to expectations.

3 Empirical Model and Methodology

This study employs panel data methods to analyze the impact of female labor force participation on poverty. The analysis was based on the model given in equation (1) considering the multicollinearity problem among various variables and heterogeneity among regions and across time:

$$\begin{aligned} poverty_{it} = {} & \alpha_1 + \sum_{i=2}^{26} \alpha_i D_i + \sum_{t=2015}^{2017} \lambda_t D_t + \beta_1 lpcgdp_{it} + \beta_2 inf_{it} + \beta_3 gini_{it} \\ & + \beta_4 school_{it} + \beta_5 malel_{it} + \beta_6 femalel_{it} + \beta_7 (femalel \times lpcgdp)_{it} \\ & + \beta_8 urban_{it} + \beta_9 agri_{it} + \beta_{10} open_{it} + \varepsilon_{it} \end{aligned} \tag{1}$$

where, i=1,. . .,26 and t=2014, 2015, 2016, 2017 are the indices for regions and year, showing region-specific and time period fixed effects, respectively. In equation (1), poverty rate (poverty) was explained as a function of per capita income in natural logarithm (lpcgpd), inflation rate (inf), income inequality (gini), schooling ratio (school), male labor force participation (malel), female labor force participation (femalel), term showing the interaction between female labor force participation and income (femalel x lpcgdp), urbanization rate (urban), share of agricultural activities in total income (agri) and trade openness (open). A priori, poverty-reducing effects of the following variables are expected to increase with higher inf, gini, urban and agri. and Poverty is expected to increase with higher inf, gini, urban and agri.

As the panel data covers data on predefined regions over time, the model in equation (1) was estimated using within estimation method or Least Squares

Tab. 10.1: Variables and Definitions

Variables	Definitions
Poverty	Poverty ratio (%) according to 60 % of median income
Lpcgdp	Gross Domestic Product (GDP) per capita (2009 based) (TL) in logarithm
Inf	Consumer price index change rate (12-month averages as of year-end) (%), 2003 = 100: General
Gini	Gini coefficient according to equivalent household disposable income
School	Proportion of primary school graduates (15 years and over) in total population (15 years and over) (%)
Malel	Male labor force participation rate (%), (15 years and over)
Femalel	Female labor force participation rate (%), (15 years and over)
Urban	Proportion of population of provincial and district centers in total population (%)
Agri	Proportion of Agriculture in Gross Domestic Product (%)
Open	Ratio of imports and exports to Gross Domestic Product (%)

Source: Authors' own construction.

Dummy Variable (LSDV) regression technique and in order to check the presence of fixed effects (FE) and misspecification in the model, fixed effects tests for regions and time and tests for heteroscedasticity (LRH), autocorrelation (LMρ) and cross-sectional dependency (CD) are performed. If diagnostic tests indicate the presence of one of these misspecification errors in the models, the model was estimated again using Feasible Generalized Least Square Dummy Variable (FGLSDV) estimation in order to consider heteroscedasticity, autocorrelation and cross-sectional dependency along with the fixed effects (see Greene, 2003: 328; De Hoyos and Sarafidis, 2006; Baltagi, 2008: 15, for further information).

4 Data

The dataset includes the variables in Tab. 10.1. This panel dataset on these variables covers data on 26 regions (NUTS-2 Level)[1] over the period from 2014 to 2017. All the data was obtained from the TURKSTAT database. While investigating the impact of women in the workforce on poverty, variables that are thought to significantly affect poverty should not be neglected. In this

1 Region definitions can be found at https://ec.europa.eu/eurostat/documents/345175/7773495/TR.pdf.

context, the connection of the variables involved in the analysis with poverty is explained in the following paragraphs.

"Female participation in the workforce has become an important factor in household income, improving the living conditions of double-earning families and providing a barrier to economic instability and high levels of male unemployment" (El-Hamidi, 2003: 6). For this reason, it is important to take into account male participation in the labor force while investigating the effect of female participation in the labor force on poverty.

There is a strong relationship between growth and poverty. It has been suggested that economic growth reduces poverty only in theory without a fair distribution (Amadeo & Neri, 1997; Dollar & Kraay, 2000; Chang-Tsai, 2006). Poverty is claimed to be more susceptible to growth when inequality is lower. For these reasons, besides GDP, the Gini coefficient reflecting income distribution was included in the analysis.

The schooling ratio variable was included in the model to represent human capital because it is very obvious that human capital is very important for improving the plight of the poor (Ghazouani & Goaied, 2001; Chen & Wang, 2015).

Research shows that trade openness, a channel of globalization, plays an important role in the fight against poverty in the developing countries. There is no general conclusion that trade will increase or decrease poverty. The economy has many channels explaining the relationship between trade and poverty. It is argued that trade deficit will have a positive impact on poverty in the short run if it creates markets that demand more unskilled labor, but increasing the number of skilled labor by increasing education and information equipment in the regions for sustainable growth and low poverty rates is still important (Sönmez, 2018). According to Chang-Tsai (2006), it is thought that the increase in trade, especially exports and foreign investments, will increase employment due to job opportunities. Accordingly, the technology that comes with trade is expected to increase productivity and reduce poverty by achieving growth. In addition, there are empirical findings that trade liberalization helps to alleviate poverty, but is cheap and accessible, not the most powerful tool for poverty reduction (Pradhan & Mahesh, 2014).

Growth in the agricultural sector is thought to have led to greater reductions in poverty compared to other sectors (Ravallion & Datt, 1996). It is suggested that the agriculture sector could benefit poor people, considering that greater labor productivity in agriculture than in the rest of the economy, and that the poor are more likely to live in rural areas and earn their livelihood from agriculture (Dollar & Kraay, 2000). Also, since 1980, it is claimed that "Turkey has lost characteristics of an agricultural country; factors such as unemployment, seasonal work, and low wages have caused poverty to shift from rural to urban areas, and inadequate industrialization has caused poverty to be concentrated in urban areas" (Saatci & Akpinar, 2007: 631). Because of this assumption, it was thought that it would be good to include the "urban" variable in the analysis.

Inflation is thought to be an important factor for the poor. It is claimed that the poor are affected more in the inflationary period due to the lack of accession to the financial market and banking system in order to mitigate the negative effects of inflation. Therefore, macroeconomic stabilization programs, which have successfully lowered inflation, may have substantial favorable income effects on the poor (Fiess & Verner, 2004). According to Romer and Romer (1998), the effect of inflation on the poor should be considered as cyclical and long-term. Accordingly, in the short term, an increase in the unexpected inflation is believed to lead to a decline in unemployment and relatively benefit the poor. However, in the longer term, it is argued that higher inflation will not permanently reduce unemployment and may reverse the effects of inflation on the poor.

Figure 10.1 shows the map which classifies the regions based on the poverty ratio and female labor force participation rate. While darker colors show poorer regions, bigger circles indicate a higher level of female labor force participation. One can observe that there are regional differences with respect to both poverty ratios and female labor force participation rates. According to the data and as shown in Fig. 10.1, the poorest region is TRA1 (Erzurum, Erzincan, Bayburt) in 2014, TRA2 (Agri, Kars, Igdir, Ardahan) in 2015, TR21 (Tekirdag, Edirne, Kirklareli) in 2016 and TR62 (Adana, Mersin) in 2017. For the female labor force participation rate, the highest rate was realized in TR82 (Kastamonu, Çankiri, Sinop) and the lowest rate was recorded by the TRC3 (Mardin, Batman, Sirnak, Siirt) region throughout the whole period. Pairwise correlations[2] among the variables show that the correlations are low; there is not any significant multicollinearity problem among the explanatory variables of the model shown in equation (1).

5 Empirical Analysis and Results

The model in equation (1) was estimated by using pooled OLS and within estimation for fixed-effects models. The results are shown in Tab. 10.2. The tests for fixed effects show the statistical significance of regional fixed effects, only. However, as the diagnostic tests indicate the presence of heteroscedasticity problems within the estimation of the model with regional fixed effects given in column (3) of Tab. 10.2, the model was estimated by using the FGLSDV estimation method

2 In order to save space, the pairwise correlations are not presented but can be available upon request.

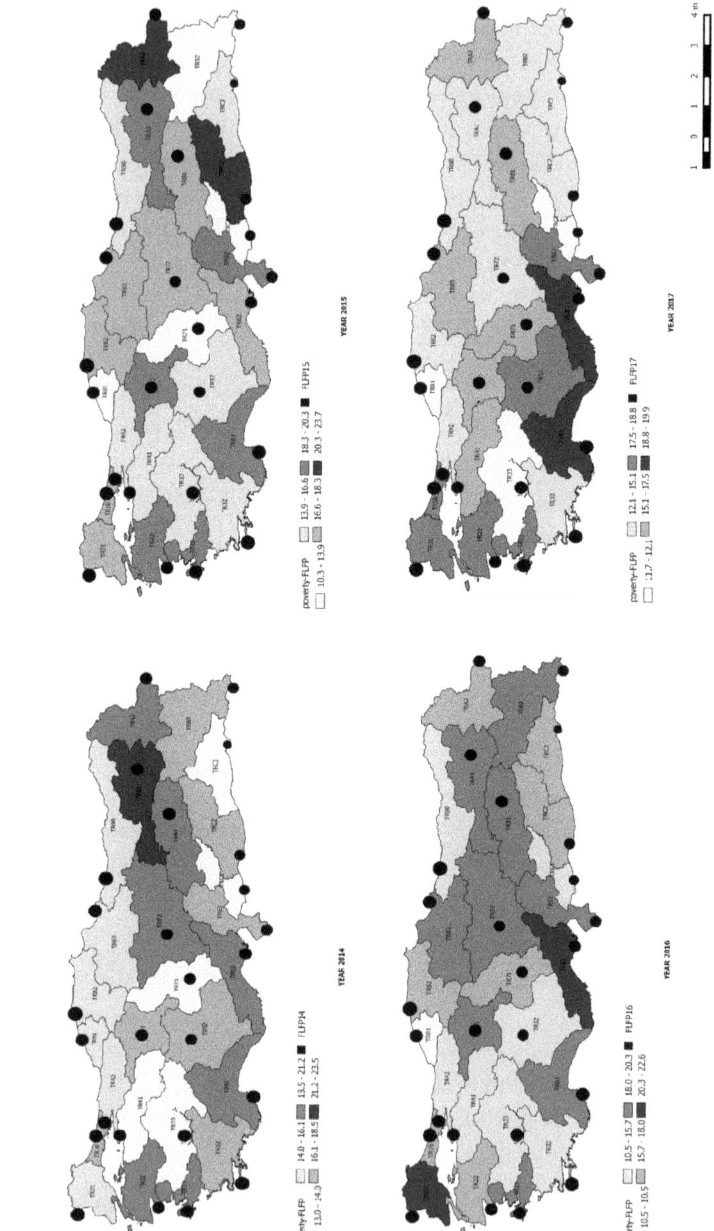

Fig. 10.1: Poverty ratio and female labor force participation rate across 26 regions of Turkey (2014–2017).
Source: Authors' own construction.

Tab. 10.2: Estimation Results

poverty	Pooled OLS	Regional FE	Regional and Time Period FE	FGLSDV with regional FE
lpcgdp	6.75**	5.92	13.50	2.77
	(4.48)	(1.25)	(1.45)	(1.05)
Inf	−0.17	−0.05	0.38	−0.15*
	(−1.62)	(−0.37)	(1.54)	(−1.87)
Gini	59.10***	59.23**	55.52**	50.37***
	(14.16)	(5.73)	(5.48)	(7.65)
school	0.003	−0.42	−0.43	−0.22
	(0.10)	(−1.13)	(−1.20)	(−1.10)
Malel	0.07	−0.09	−0.07	−0.22*
	(1.49)	(−0.27)	(−0.24)	(−2.54)
femalel	2.05**	3.21**	2.41**	2.42***
	(3.53)	(4.48)	(3.57)	(3.50)
femalel × *lpcgdp*	−0.20**	−0.32**	−0.23*	−0.22***
	(−3.58)	(−3.80)	(−2.99)	(−3.07)
urban	0.02**	0.24	0.19	0.47**
	(3.85)	(2.23)	(1.36)	(1.96)
Agri	−0.01	0.20	0.17	0.10
	(−0.20)	(0.64)	(0.49)	(0.71)
Open	−0.08***	0.03	0.05	0.08
	(−8.12)	(0.24)	(0.36)	(1.59)
constant	−77.36**	−70.93	−145.86	−61.25**
	(−6.26)	(−1.16)	(−1.44)	(−2.01)
R^2	0.5579	0.3687	0.3904	
LM_ρ	0.2204	0.4346	0.3907	
LR_H	18.7784	284.2791***	402.6489***	
Regional FE test		2.4473***	2.4089*,1	
Time-period FE test			0.7687[2]	
Joint FE test[3]			3.6469***	
CD test	−0.94	−1.20	−1.25	

Source: Authors' own calculation.

Notes: t-test statistics are shown in parentheses. These are based on Driscoll and Kraay (1998) standard errors corrected for possible cross-sectional dependence, heteroscedasticity, and autocorrelation.

*, **, *** indicate statistical significance of test statistic at 10 %, 5 %, 1 % significance level, respectively. Estimation results related to regional and time-period fixed effects are not shown due to space limitations. LM_ρ and LR_H are asymptotically distributed as χ_1^2 and χ_{25}^2 under null hypotheses of no autocorrelation and homoscedasticity, respectively.

[1] Test in the presence of Time-period FE, [2] Test in the presence of regional FE, [3] Joint Test for Regional and Time-period FE's. CD has an asymptotic standard normal distribution.

considering evidence of heteroscedasticity problem. The results are presented in column (5) of Tab. 10.2.

The findings show the statistical significance of inflation rate, income inequality, male labor force participation rate, female labor force participation rate and urbanization ratio. Higher urbanization and income inequality are associated with an increase in poverty ratio. There is no consensus in the literature on the impact of urbanization on poverty. This conclusion that urbanization increases poverty was consistent with the view that inadequate industrialization, unemployment and low wages cause poverty to be concentrated in urban areas (Saatci & Akpinar, 2007). Empirical studies have found that income inequality, such as the result of this study, adversely affects poverty. There is a widespread view that a fair distribution of income plays an effective role in reducing poverty (Wang et al. 2008; Chang-Tsai, 2006; Fosu, 2010; Apergis et al., 2011).

An increase in the male labor force participation rate reduces the poverty ratio. Male labor force participation partially reflects employment opportunities, in other words, unemployment. Therefore, the increase in male labor force participation gives positive signals about the economic stability of the country and it is expected to reduce poverty. The general belief is that the effect of inflation on the poor is negative. The result, however, is that inflation reduces poverty. This result is consistent with Romer and Romer's (1998) idea that unexpected inflation in the short term could benefit the poor by reducing unemployment.

Lastly, although the increase in female labor force participation rate worsens the poverty ratio, as per capita GDP increases after some level, female labor force participation contributes to poverty ratio reduction. This result can be related to the quality of the job that the female workers can acquire. Per capita GDP increase may show better job opportunities, especially for women. For example, the region which has the highest per capita GDP and lowest agriculture share (TR10-Istanbul) has the largest job opportunities, which may increase the chance of women to find well-paid jobs with better conditions. Although schooling ratio was found to be a statistically unimportant factor to reduce poverty, higher education, life-long learning and on the job training are very essential to gain the required qualification for these jobs.

6 Conclusion

In this study, the main aim is to understand the role of female labor force participation in poverty reduction and therefore, an analysis was performed using NUTS-2 regional-level data for Turkey over the period between 2014 and 2017. It is important to include other important variables affecting poverty in the analysis, which explores the effects of female's participation in the workforce on poverty. In this context, the analysis included the participation of females in the labor force, as well as GDP, income inequality, inflation, education, male labor force participation, urbanization, the share of agriculture in the GDP, and trade openness. In addition, the interaction variable was taken into account with the aim of uncovering how female's labor force participation and GDP together affect poverty. According to the results of the analysis, the effects of inflation, income inequality, male labor force participation, female labor force participation, urbanization and interaction variables are found to be statistically significant. Findings show that inflation and men's participation in the labor force positively affect poverty, while income inequality, women's participation in the labor force and urbanization increase poverty. Inflation is thought to benefit the poor by reducing unemployment in the short term. The participation of men in the labor force can be said to contribute to poverty reduction by pointing out that the overall state of the economy is good and that employment opportunities exist. Urbanization is thought to adversely affect poverty due to factors such as inadequate industrialization, unemployment, seasonal labor jobs and low wages. It is a common view that income inequality increases poverty, meaning that a fairer distribution of income is important in reducing poverty. On the contrary to expectations, it was found that the participation of females in the labor force negatively affects poverty. This result shows that women work in low-paid or unpaid family jobs in order to meet their family needs. However, it is concluded that the interaction variable consisting of GDP and the female's participation in the labor force reduces poverty. The results show the importance of female labor force participation to reduce overall poverty for high-income regions. It concludes that at higher income levels, women who have the opportunity to invest in education and training have reduced poverty by having better job opportunities. However, this conclusion needs further analysis, which is beyond the scope of this study. Therefore, as a policy recommendation, women should be supported to have better education and better job opportunities in order to cope with poverty effectively.

References

Adepoju, A. A. (2019). "Comparative Analysis of Determinants of Household Poverty among Rural Farming Households in Southwest Nigeria". Asian Journal of Agricultural Extension, Economics & Sociology, 1–12.

Amadeo, E. and Neri, M. (1997). "Macroeconomic Policy and Poverty in Brazil." Texto para Discussão N° 383, PUC-Rio, Rio de Janeiro, Dezembro De 1997.

Apergis, N., Dincer, O., & Payne, J. E. (2011). "On The Dynamics of Poverty and Income Inequality in US States". Journal of Economic Studies, 38(2), 132–143.

Baltagi, B. H. (2008). Econometric Analysis of Panel Data, Fourth Edition, John Wiley, West Sussex.

Blume, K., Gustafsson, B., Pedersen, P. J., & Verner, M. (2007). "At the Lower End of the Table: Determinants of Poverty among Immigrants to Denmark and Sweden". Journal of Ethnic and Migration Studies, 33(3), 373–396.

Buvinić, M., & Gupta, G. R. (1997). "Female-Headed Households and Female-Maintained Families: Are They Worth Targeting to Reduce Poverty in Developing Countries?". Economic Development and Cultural Change, 45(2), 259–280.

Chang-Tsai, M. (2006). "Economic and Non-Economic Determinants of Poverty in Developing Countries: Competing Theories and Empirical Evidence". Canadian Journal of Development Studies/Revue Canadienne D'études Du Développement, 27(3), 267–285.

Chen, K. M., & Wang, T. M. (2015). "Determinants of Poverty Status in Taiwan: A Multilevel Approach". Social Indicators Research, 123(2), 371–389.

Choudhry, M. T. (2010). Demographic Transition, Economic Growth and Labor Market Dynamics. Groningen: Groningen University Press.

Dalgıç, B., İyidoğan, P. V., & Güven, A. (2015). "Yoksulluk ve Yoksulluk Geçişlerinin Belirleyenleri: Türkiye Örneği". Sosyoekonomi, 23(24), 51–70.

De Hoyos, R., & Sarafidis, V. (2006). "Testing for Cross-sectional Dependence in Panel Data Models", The Stata Journal, 6(4), 482–496.

Dollar, D. & Kraay, A. (2000). "Growth Is Good for the Poor". International Monetary Fund Seminar Series, 35, 1–44.

El-Hamidi, F. (2003). "Poverty and Labor Supply of Women: Evidence from Egypt". In Tenth Annual Conference of the Economic Research Forum (ERF) (16–18 December 2003).

Evcim, N., Güneş, S., & Karaalp Orhan, H. S. (2019). "Yoksulluk ve Ekonomik Göstergeler Arasındaki İlişki: MENA Bölgesi Analizi", Pamukkale Üniversitesi Sosyal Bilimler Enstitüsü Dergisi, Sayı 36, Denizli. s. 291–310.

Fatima, A., & Sultana, H. (2009). "Tracing Out the U-shape Relationship between Female Labor force Participation Rate and Economic Development for Pakistan". International Journal of Social Economics, 36, 182–198.

Fiess, N. M., & Verner, D. (2004). "The Dynamics of Poverty and Its Determinants: The Case of the Northeast of Brazil and its States". World Bank Policy Research Working Paper 3259, April 2004.

Fosu, A. K. (2010). “Inequality, Income, and Poverty: Comparative Global Evidence”. Social Science Quarterly, 91(5), 1432–1446

Gangopadhyay, S., & Wadhwa, W. (2004). Are Indian Female-Headed Households More Vulnerable to Poverty. New Delhi: Bazaar Chintan.

Ghazouani, S., & Goaied, M. (2001). “The Determinants of Urban and Rural Poverty in Tunisia”. Economic Research Forum for the Arab Countries, Iran & Turkey.

Greene, W. H. (2003) Econometric Analysis, Fifth Edition. Upper Saddle River, NJ: Prentice-Hall.

Haq, U., & Amin, A. (2017). “The Role of Working Women in Poverty Reduction (A Case Study of District Peshawar)”. Dialogue (Pakistan), 12(2), 109–134.

Horrell, S., & Krishnan, P. (2007). “Poverty and Productivity in Female-Headed Households in Zimbabwe”. The Journal of Development Studies, 43(8), 1351–1380.

Klasen, S. (2000), “Does Gender Inequality Reduce Growth and Development? Evidence from Cross-Country Regressions”, World Bank Policy Research Report Working Paper No.7.,

Klasen, S., Lechtenfeld, T., & Povel, F. (2015). “A Feminization of Vulnerability? Female Headship, Poverty, and Vulnerability in Thailand and Vietnam”. World Development, 71, 36–53.

Lincove J. A. (2008). “Growth, Girl’s Education, and Female Labor: A Longitudinal Analysis”. The Journal of Developing Areas, 41(2), 45–68.

Liu, C., Esteve, A., & Treviño, R. (2017). “Female-Headed Households and Living Conditions in Latin America”. World Development, 90, 311–328.

Luci, A. (2009). The Impact of Macroeconomic Growth on Women’s Labor Force Participation: Does Panel Data Confirm the “Feminisation U” Hypothesis? Paris: Institut National d’Etudes Démographiques.

Mincer, J. (1962). “Labor Force Participation of Married Women: A Study of Labor Supply”, in Aspects of Labor Economics. Princeton, NJ: National Bureau of Economic Research, Princeton University Press.

Montoya, Á. J. A., & Teixeira, K. M. D. (2017). “Multidimensional Poverty in Nicaragua: Are Female-Headed Households Better Off?” Social Indicators Research, 132(3), 1037–1063.

OECD/Organisation for Economic Co-operation and Development (2008). Gender and Sustainable Development, https://www.oecd.org/social/40881538.pdf (10.01.2020).

OECD/Organisation for Economic Co-operation and Development (2019), Labour Force Statistic, https://stats.oecd.org (10.01.2020).

Pampel F. C., & Tanaka, K. (1986). "Economic Development and Female Labor Force Participation: A Reconsideration". Social Forces, 64(3), 599–619.

Pradhan, B. K., & Mahesh, M. (2014). "Impact of Trade Openness on Poverty: A Panel Data Analysis of a Set of Developing Countries". Economics Bulletin, 34(4), 2208–2219.

Ravallion, M., and Datt, G. (1996). "How Important to India's Poor Is the Sectoral Composition of Growth in India". World Bank Economic Review, 10, 1–25.

Romer, C. D., & Romer, D. H. (1998). "Monetary Policy and the Well-Being of the Poor", (No. w6793). National Bureau of Economic Research.

Saatci, E., & Akpinar, E. (2007). "Assessing Poverty and Related Factors in Turkey". Croatian Medical Journal, 48(5), 628–635.

Schultz, T. P. (1990). "Women's Changing Participation in the Labor Force: A World Perspective". Economic Development and Cultural Change, 38(2), 457–488.

Selim, S. (2016). "Socio-Economic Determinants of Poverty in Turkey: Panel Logit Approach". International Journal of Statistics & Economics, 17(3), 71–84.

Singh, P., & Pattanaik, F. (2019). "Economic Status of Women in India: Paradox of Paid–Unpaid Work and Poverty". International Journal of Social Economics, 46(3), 410–428.

Sönmez, F. D. (2018). "Ticaretin Yoksulluk Üzerine Etkisi; Türkiye için Temel Bulgular". Öneri Dergisi, 13(50), 35–51.

Tansel, A. (2001). "Economic Development and Female Labor Force Participation in Turkey: Time-Series Evidence and Cross-Province Estimates." Working Paper 0124, Economic Research Forum, Cairo, Egypt.

Todaro, M. P., & Smith, S.C. (2014). Economic Development, 2014, 12th edition. New York: Pearson.

TURKSTAT /Turkish Statistical Institution (2019). Social Structure and Gender Statistics, http://www.tuik.gov.tr/PreTablo.do?alt_id=1068 (10.01.2020).

Verick, S. (2018). "Female Labor Force Participation and Development". IZA World of Labor, doi: 10.15185/izawol.87.v2.

Wang, T. M., Ho, H. C., & Liu, Y. L. (2008). "The Effects of Income Growth, Economic Inequality and Changing Family Structure on Poverty Rates: A Case Study from 1990 to 2004". Taiwanese Journal of Social Welfare, 7(1), 29–63.

WB (2009). Female Labor force Participation in Turkey: Trends, Determinants and Policy Framework. Washington, DC: The World Bank.

Hasan Bakır

Financialization and Labor

1 Introduction

The relationship between precarious work and financialization that arises with the implementation of neoliberal policies is the main subject of this study. While secure employment was one of the main characteristics of capitalist society between 1945 and 80, the crisis in the 1970s and the policies that followed caused this social form to be turned upside down. Therefore, in this period, when liberalization policies were on the rise again, while the gains of labor were eliminated, capital was again in a strong position in class relations. Labor, who were employed precariously and sentenced to low wages, found the remedy to be indebted. With financial innovations, the ease of borrowing has relieved labor even a little bit.

Households' borrowing from financial institutions has risen very rapidly in recent years. Although consumer loans were initially used as an alternative means of payment by middle- and upper-income groups, it was later observed that consumer loans were used by low-income households and paid workers to meet their daily needs. The developments in the financial sector that mediate the developments mentioned at this point are also very important. In this context, this study will focus on the borrowing of laborers who are the central proponents of this process. So far, many studies have addressed households' relationship with finance and the evolving level of indebtedness. However, these analyses generally take into account the reasons and consequences of raising the level of indebtedness of households in developed countries. Developing countries, on the other hand, have received less attention. Although it remains lower compared to developed countries, the level of household indebtedness has also increased in developing countries. It is possible to evaluate the increase in consumer loans in this context (Karaçimen, 2015b: 751–752).

In this respect, the concept of financialization will be discussed in the second part of the study. In the third part of the study, how the financialization of labor happened will be evaluated. In the fourth part of the study, the experiences in the banking sector, which is one of the actors of this process, will be discussed. In the fifth part of the study, the process of financing and borrowing of labor in Turkey, one of the developing countries, will be examined in the context of consumer loans. The evaluations will be discussed in the results section.

2 Financialization and the Concept of Financialization from a Historical Perspective

Although it is possible to take the formation of the concept of financialization up to Hilferding (1910), Lenin (1916), Bukharin and Tobin (1965) in the recent past, as Tunali and Özdemir (2017) said in this study, the concept of financialization matured after 1980 will be mentioned (Tunali and Özdemir, 2017: 61). As a matter of fact, the concept of financialization has developed over time like the concept of globalization. Therefore, there is an ambiguity in the use of the concept and there is no agreed definition (Orhangazi, 2008: 3). Perhaps the only point agreed upon in this sense is that, as Krippner (2005: 173) said, the world we live in is the world of finance, and it would be quite difficult for us to escape its influence. Epstein, on the other hand, defined financialization as the increasing role of financial motives, financial markets, financial actors and financial institutions in the functioning of local and international economies (Epstein, 2005: 3). Palley similarly also stated that financialization is a process in which the impact of financial markets, financial institutions and financial elites on economic policy and economic outcomes have increased (Palley, 2008). Lapavistas (2011) has defined financialization from a broad perspective as the structural transformation of the capitalist economy, although he acknowledges that there is no agreed definition (Lapavistas, 2011: 611).

Indeed, significant transformations were witnessed in the world economy in recent years. While the roles of governments have declined in these transformations, the effectiveness of the market has increased. While economic transactions between countries increased, there was also a large increase in local and international financial transactions. These transformations are expressed as neoliberalism, globalization and financialization, respectively (Epstein, 2005: 3). Foster (2007) stated that although all the things about neoliberalism and globalization have been written and drawn, interest in financialization remains at a more limited level. However, it has been stated that the discussions about this concept have also taken place on the agenda (Foster, 2007: 1).

It is stated that the financialization of capitalism began from the late 1970s and 1980s, with reference to various transformations (Sema, 2017: 146). At this point, Sweezy (1997) highlighted three very important developments in capitalism's recent history, which began with the 1974–1975 recession: the first of which was the decline in growth rates. The second is the worldwide expansion of monopolistic multinational companies. The third is financialization. Foster (2011) interpreted financialization as the shift of the center of gravity of capitalism from production to finance (Foster, 2011: 17). Lapavistas stated that these stages, which he described as the views of the monthly review school, were related to the acquisition of surplus value by mature capitalism. In this context, Lapavistas (2011) stated financialization as the systemic transformation of mature capitalist economies and underlined that there are three main factors of transformation. The first is that non-financial institutions reduce their dependence on bank loans and have financial capacities. In this way, non-financial institutions have become less dependent on banks. The second is that banks improve their brokerage activities in the financial markets by lending to households. This is defined as the transformation of banks. It can also be stated that this process is a reaction to the initial situation. Finally, households are included in the finance field both as debtors and as assets holders. What is striking about this process is that a significant proportion of households entering the finance field are low-income and wage earners. Therefore, it is stated that a significant amount of the profits of the banks are obtained from low-income earners, i.e., financial expropriation (Lapavistas, 2011: 612, 623). Palley also referred to financialization as the transformation of the economic system at macro and micro levels. This transformation has also been associated with the increasing importance of the financial sector relative to the real sector, with the transfer of income from the real sector to the financial sector, and with wage stagnation and the injustice of rising income distribution (Palley, 2008: 2).

Therefore, financialization must be understood through considering a background shaped by low productivity growth, changing working relationships and global shifts in production. On the other hand, while there has been a non-bright and unreliable increase in real accumulation since the late 1970s, the financial sector has grown unusually in terms of profit, employment and the size of markets (Lapavistas, 2017: 41). Deriving financial profits from employees' personal income has also been referred to as financial expropriation in this context (Lapavistas, 2009a: 115).

In the post-World War II period, there was a significant increase in consumer credit, especially for the purchase of household and durable goods in the United States. Since the late 1970s, it has been noted that the working class has increasingly used credit in the United States and Europe. In the late capitalizing countries, consumer loans started to be given primarily to upper and middle-income groups and started to be given to the lower income segment of the society since the 2000s. As a matter of fact, this has become such that these loans have become an important part of the lives of the low-income groups. It is possible to evaluate the increase in consumer loans and household indebtedness in this context (Karachimen, 2015: 72). Another reason for the credit expansion in this process is that the risks on the financial sector have decreased with the financial innovations experienced. Because of these innovations, it is possible to reduce these risks by commodification them. As a matter of fact, thanks to securitization, which is one of the most popular issues of today, loans with varying degrees of reliability, maturity and purpose of use are collected into a single pool and then divided into new products. In this way, the risks on these products are divided into the areas of the products. The risk to the financial system is that borrowers cannot pay their debts. Although the transfer of risks is in question, it was observed with the global financial crisis that started in the USA that this would not be possible in the global financial system (Akçay, 2015).

Therefore, the concept of financialization is associated with concepts such as low growth and increasing inequality of income distribution on the macroeconomics, and another concept is financial fragility. The concept of financialization is associated with financial fragility as well as macroeconomic concepts such as low growth and inequality of income distribution. It is financial crises expressed by financial fragility. With financialization, the incidence of financial crises remains expressed. Indeed, it is possible to evaluate the crises seen in the 1990s and 2000s in this context. The global financial crisis seen in the United States and its impact spread to Europe is also the result of the financialization experienced (Palley, 2008: 2).

In this context, the global financial crisis in the United States is quite remarkable. The rise in mortgage lending has been assessed as the answer to the demand of certain income groups to buy homes. As a matter of fact, it is those in the lower income group working in the United States who want to borrow. Therefore, it can be stated that the personal income of the employees in this lower income group is financialized. Although this process is referred to as democratization of finance, if things go wrong it will lead to millions of people in the lower income group facing the risk of becoming homeless. So as long as house prices continued to rise and interest rates stay low, there was no problem. But rising interest rates and falling home prices have led to everything being turned upside down (Lapavistas, 2009a: 116–121). Therefore, the literature on financialization has created an important theoretical ground for the analysis of this crisis (Lapavistas, 2011: 611).

Today, finance has a strong influence in developing countries (Lapavistas, 2017: 41). One of the leading factors in this process is the deregulation of financial markets (Painceira, 2009: 4). Akyüz (1993) stated that financial freedom in developing countries covers the freedom of capital inflows and outflows along with the convertibility of money. The pressure for these transformations has been expressed by institutions such as the IMF and the World Bank (Painceira,

2009: 4). As a matter of fact, similar developments have been observed in Turkey, which is one of the developing countries. When we look at the developments after 1980, it is stated that Turkey has adopted neoliberal policies, adapted to international economic order and finally has become financialized, that is, the effectiveness of the Finance has increased (Tunali and Özdemir, 2017: 67). While financialization introduces itself as increased capital inflows, it also affects all areas of the economy. Therefore, the Turkish economy, which is integrated into the global system, has become open to the full impact of financialization. In this context, as is often emphasized in the recent period, Turkey turned the 2001 crisis into an opportunity and then grew rapidly. However, it is clear that this growth is based on further weakening of the working class (Ergunesh, 2009: 5–6). As a result, similar to developed countries, Turkey has faced an economic situation in which finance has gained prominence over the years, workers have lost their bargaining power, and trade and capital accounts have a deficit. Thus, as Painceira (2009) emphasized, the deregulation of labor markets contributed to the financial discipline of employees (Painceira, 2009: 4). In this context, the work will be continued by evaluating the relationship between labor and finance

3 Precarity and Financial Inclusion

In the 1970s, an attempt to overcome the clogging of capital accumulation and the predicament in which capitalism was present with a new paradigm was made. Hence, the last quarter of the 20th century marked the beginning of a period of fundamental restructuring in the political economy of contemporary capitalism. During this period, a transformation based on neoliberalism, globalization and finally finance took place. Liberalization, deregulation and technological innovations have a very important role in accelerating and increasing the impact of this transformation (Üzar, 2019: 76). The economic policies introduced in this process were based on the elimination of rigidity in the labor market. As a matter of fact, the policies implemented in both developed and developing countries have been realized in this direction in the ongoing process. Together with the neoliberal policies implemented since the 1980s, the aim was to make the labor markets more flexible. In this way, the organizational capacity of employees has been weakened and precarious forms of employment have become widespread. Indeed, these years are largely referred to as the years of public debt cycle and high inflation for emerging markets. The only way to deal with these problems is to implement the austerity policies proposed by the IMF. In particular, the translation of public debt and the debt instruments created for it have been the catalyst for the financialization experienced in the rising market. It can be stated that these countries have completed their financialization by ensuring integration into global financial markets. In addition to integration into global financial markets, practices such as privatization of public enterprises and flexible labor markets are emerging in these late capitalizing countries (Akçay, 2015).)

Again, commercial banks have undergone a major transformation during the development of financialization. One of the main reasons for this transformation is the declining commitment of large companies to bank financing. Companies in developed countries meet their financing needs by borrowing from undistributed profits and external financing needs from the open market. If expressed in Marxist terminology, monopolies are now less likely to resort to banks for the need for financing. In other words, they have become more familiar with the financial system. In short, companies have become financialized while relying less on banks. The deregulation process introduced after 1960 has a great impact on this process. With deregulation, banks lost the deposits that people were forced to deposit into banks, which had played a vital role in sustaining their activities. Therefore, the field of traditional banking narrowed further. At this point, banks reacted against declining profit levels. One of the most prominent of these reactions is the fact that banks are turning to the wages of workers and household income as a source of profit. Another one is that the banks are forced into financial market brokerage, which means they assume a kind of investment banking function (Lapavistas, 2017: 42–44).

Therefore, developments in the financial sector have come to the aid of a large audience who want to maintain their living standards. Private pension systems, life insurance, health insurance, equities, consumer credit or other derivatives have gradually become the financial instruments used by the middle- and lower-income groups. The most common use of these financial instruments is consumer credit. Today, lending activity in the form of consumer credit is one of the main activities of banks. The expansion of consumer credit compared to commercial loans is a new development. Considering that banks are a mechanism to convert idle resources into investment in the economy, commercial loans are also the main tools in the operation of this mechanism. Indeed, deposits deposited in banks are used as financing of the productive capital through commercial loans. It also takes its share of the profit generated by productive capital at the end of the production process as interest. Consumer credit differs from commercial credit at this point. Consumer credit is used directly to meet the needs of individuals, not productive capital (Akçay, 2015).

To understand the orientation of banks' towards consumer loans as a profit area, the labor force's attainment of a place within the market during the neoliberal period, the state's role in the changes during this process and the transformations on the reproduction of labor power of workers need to be considered. Considering that the world economy was shaped by neoliberal policies after 1980, regulations against wageworkers took place in the labor markets after this process. Indeed, factors such as wage growth falling below productivity gains, the creation of new needs of the consumer society, uncertainties in the labor market and the privatization of public services have increased the borrowing needs of wageworkers. Therefore, at this point, consumer loans have come to the aid of wage earners. In this context, consumer loans have increasingly become a means of enabling the reproduction of labor power (Karachimen, 2015: 79–80). At this point, increases in consumer credit are generally associated with wages failing to cover living costs and precarious work. The financialization process after the 2000s also ensured the survival of precarious and flexible labor through consumer loans. This means deepening financial inclusion (Akçay, 2015).

In this context, financialization and flexibility and precarity in labor markets were interpreted as different results of the same process. As a matter of fact, if risk transfer is possible in derivative products in financial markets, business contracts also shift the risks arising from working with subcontracting and subcontracting system from the main firm onto subcontractors. This is a brief summary of what happened after the 1970s. In other words, there is a close link between changes in working relationships and the financialization of everyday life. Just as precarious work provides the financing of labor, financialization brings with it precarious work arrangements (Akçay, 2015).

In the past forty years, when financial activities have become increasingly common, every segment of society has become acquainted with consumer credit, regardless of the reason, and there have been significant increases in household indebtedness. Therefore, it can be stated that this expropriation has become systematic, especially when financial institutions have expropriated the income of wage earners. Banks on one side of this relationship aim to maximize their profits, while wage earners on the other side of the relationship aim to reproduce their labor power. In other words, there is no balance of power in this relationship as in the relationship of money capital and industrial capital of the past. There is an imbalance rather than a balance between money capital and wage earners, and the extent of this imbalance is gradually increasing (Karaçimen, 2015a: 78–79).

In this context, borrowing has become a means of increasing the control of capital over labor, while on the other hand it has emerged as a solution to the increasing insecurity in the labor market. In other words, developments in the labor market and the capital market have led to a complete vicious cycle through increasing the commitment of labor to capital by feeding each other mutually (Karaçimen, 2015a: 80; Federici, 2016). As a matter of fact, the precarious and flexible forms of employment that have become widespread with the deregulation in the labor markets, together with unemployment, causes credit to be used as a substitute for wages in cases such as stagnation or decline of real wages. But these conditions also make it difficult for wage earners to pay their loans. Under these conditions, wage earners are forced to accept precarious jobs, longer hours and heavier working conditions to turn around their debts. On the other hand, the increase in borrowing levels makes employees more dependent on capital. Moreover, this indebtedness limits the power of employees to influence decision-making mechanisms socially, economically and politically. It is therefore stated that borrowing creates an opportunity to control society, hides class conflict, and personalizes workers' relations with capitalists (Karachimen, 2015: 81). As Güngen stated, it should be taken into consideration that the process is as much a political side as it is an economic one (Güngen, 2010: 91).

As a matter of fact, both the economic insecurity experienced and the lack of income of large sections of society reveal that these people are compelled to enter financial markets and consume new financial products in order to survive. In other words, the problems experienced in return for borrowing have been covered even though there is a slight increase (Akçay, 2015). In this respect, it is understood from the above explanations how important borrowing is for the workers to continue their lives during the financing process. In this context, it was aimed to evaluate the increasing borrowing of workers in the age of financialization in the context of consumer loans.

4 The Increasing Importance of Borrowing Dynamics and Consumer Loans in Turkey

Güngen (2010) stated that the efforts toward financialization experienced in the late capitalizing countries are quite limited. In this context, Painceira (2009) analyzed the reason for the increase in public domestic borrowing through treasury bonds in developing countries such as Brazil, Lebanon and Turkey. The result was that this increase was realized in order to overcome foreign debt problems. He also underlined that the reserves accumulated to prevent the financial independence created by financialization also strengthened the hegemonic position of the United States. Similar discussion in developing countries was also made by Lapavistas (2009b). Lapavistas revealed the costs of the integration of developing countries into world capital markets and the experienced reserve accumulation process to developed countries. Again, Lapavistas (2009a, 2009b, 2017) also cited the increase in consumer loans in developing countries and the financial expropriation process in their analysis. In Hardie (2007), his study of the functioning of the public bond market in late-capitalizing countries revealed the extent to which financialization is based on the sophistication of secondary markets and the depth of financial markets. In this context, the effective functioning of liquidity and its market encourages financial investment and determines the degree of financialization (Güngen, 2010: 92–93). It is possible to follow similar discussions in Turkey.

Considering the aftermath of 2001, the Turkish economy has been integrated into the global system, but still dependent on imports, with growing public and private sector debts, where unemployment problem reached to the peak level and precarious work is common, with households that have not gone beyond being indebted. Again, many problems such as unemployment, pressure on wages, unfairness of income distribution and loss of social welfare have arisen due to fiscal discipline and growth target. Therefore, the competitive strategy of countries like Turkey that want to compete internationally has been cheap labor. Another way to support this process is to increase labor market flexibility and insecurity by the government. In this context, the new labor regulations have increased the fragility of the economy by introducing low-wage and precarious employment on the one hand and borrowing of wageworkers on the other (Sema, 2017: 151–152).

Sema (2017) noted that consumption, which rose to prominence in the neoliberal era as never before in the history of capitalism, was closely related to the process of borrowing of the wage earners and the expansion of consumer loans to include the low-income group. Of course, the process here is not only unique to Turkey. In fact, compared to developed countries, the financing of labor remains more important in Turkey. However, the developments in the Turkish economy after 2002 are quite remarkable in terms of the financing of labor. As a matter of fact, borrowing in Turkey until the 2000s was mostly carried out on informal routes, while consumer loans increased in the later period. This increase in consumer loans has been associated with the borrowing of wageworkers, that is, the remanufacturing process of labor (Sema, 2017: 153).

It is possible to observe through Tab. 11.1 that the Turkish society, which was very careful about individual borrowing prior to the 2000s, changed its

Tab. 11.1: Ratio of Household Debt to GDP (%)

Date	Household Loans	GDP	Household loans/GDP
1998	1.484.124,60	**71 892 898**	2.064354943
1999	2.222.896,00	**107 164 345**	2.074286926
2000	6.855.284,00	**170 666 715**	4.016766835
2001	4.939.445,00	**245 428 760**	2.012577910
2002	6.638.109,00	**359 358 871**	1.847208884
2003	12.994.916,00	**468 015 146**	2.776601591
2004	26.433.935,00	**577 023 497**	4.581084674
2005	45.497.474,00	**673 702 943**	6.753343516
2006	67.116.845,00	**789 227 555**	8.504118307
2007	92.287.258,00	**880 460 879**	10.481698870
2008	114.342.351,00	**994 782 858**	11.494201980
2009	126.318.028,00	**999 191 848**	12.642019470
2010	167.876.337,00	**1 160 013 978**	14.471923630
2011	216.562.598,00	**1 394 477 166**	15.530021100
2012	256.285.277,00	**1 569 672 115**	16.327312860
2013	318.096.923,00	**1 809 713 087**	17.577201900
2014	341.305.729,00	**2 044 465 876**	16.694126960
2015	368.246.642,00	**2 338 647 494**	15.746137160
2016	404.363.312,00	**2 608 525 749**	15.501603240
2017	471.307.676,00	**3 110 650 155**	15.151420200
2018	487.509.605,00	**3 724 387 936**	13.089656970
2019	562.995.210,00	**4 280 381 145**	13.152922390

Source: CBRT, 2020;TurkStat, 2020

attitude after 2000. Especially between 2003 and 2013, there was a very significant increase in household borrowing in Turkey (Karachimen, 2015: 81). The ratio of household loans to GDP increased from 2.7 % in 2003 to 17.5 % in 2013 and declined slightly to 13.1 % in 2019. Rising loan interest rates have also had an impact in this decline.

To understand this rapid increase in consumer credit usage, it is necessary to understand the transformation of capital accumulation in Turkey and how the relations between banks, industrial capitalists and wage earners are realized with this transformation. In this way, it will be possible to explain how banks increase their profits by diversifying their activities and how the debts of wage earners rise (Karachimen, 2015: 82).

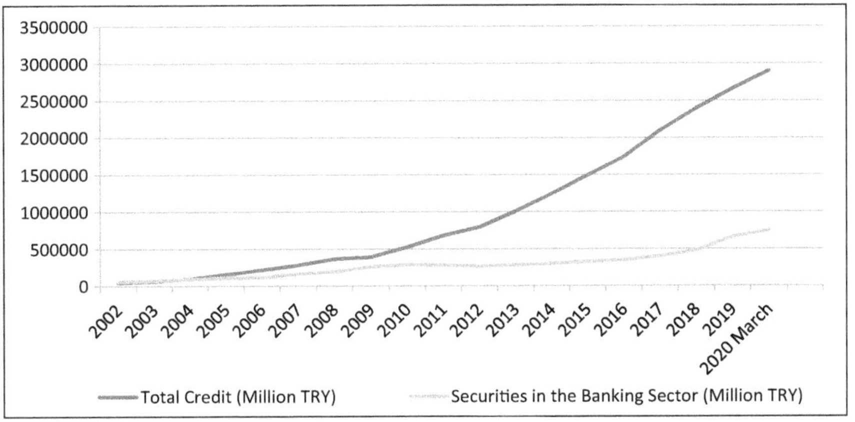

Fig. 11.1: Total credit volume and securities in the banking sector (Million TRY).
Source: BRSA, 2020a

As a matter of fact, it has been stated that the Turkish economy's connection to the global economic order has increased with the 2001 crisis. In this process, banks have kept pace with the changing process by changing their assets and liabilities. During the 1990s, banks provided a significant portion of their profits from high-yield, risk-free and tax-free government debt securities. However, falling interest rates and declining budget deficits due to the tight monetary and fiscal policies implemented after 2001 have reduced the high profits of banks in the past. For this reason, while the share of securities in the assets of banks gradually decreased, the share of loans increased. As can be seen from Fig. 11.1, the share of securities in the assets of banks fell from 2002 to 2013, while the share of loans rose (Karaçimen, 2015a: 82–83). Although it is observed that the total number of securities increased compared to the previous period as of March 2020 (BRSA, 2020b: 16), the increase in consumer loans continues.

In this increase in the share of loans, the bank's orientation towards consumer loans, which it sees as an alternative source of profit, played an important role. As a matter of fact, the increasing share of consumer loans in total loans (Fig. 11.2) is the most important indicator of this. The shift of banking activities from public finance to retail banking has been observed in Turkey as has been seen in many countries. As Karaçimen (2014) points out, the banking sector was deeply affected by the 2001 crisis and a series of transformations in the activities of the banking sector ensued in its aftermath. As a matter of

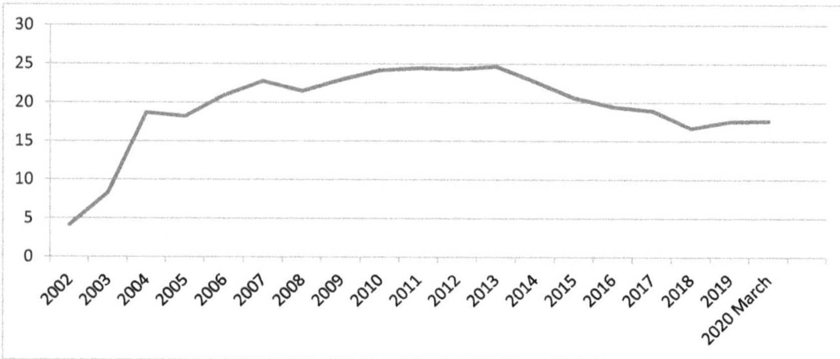

Fig. 11.2: Share of consumer loans in total loans.
Source: BRSA, 2020a

fact, the tight monetary and fiscal policies that have been implemented have led to the transformation of banking activities that have generated revenue from financing the public deficits of the past. In light of these developments, the banking sector, which holds most of the financial assets in Turkey, has turned to consumer loans in search of alternative sources of profit (Karaçimen, 2014: 162).

Again, with advertising and aggressive marketing strategy, a segment previously unfamiliar with borrowing from financial institutions has been encouraged. Indeed, the increase in the use of consumer loans by low-income households and wage earners is significant in this context. Of course, developments in the production and trade structure of the Turkish economy after the 2001 crisis have also been effective in this direction. It is also possible to evaluate deregulated labor markets and policies aimed at reducing labor costs in this context. As a matter of fact, factors such as unemployment in the Turkish labor market, recession in real wages, spread of low wages and precarious jobs have increased household borrowing (Karaçimen, 2014: 162).

As can be seen from Fig. 11.3, a significant increase in household borrowing from the financial sector has been observed since 2003. This is also important in terms of showing how household incomes are transferred to the financial sector (Karaçimen, 2014: 163). It is possible to observe the transfer made from the increase in the share of both the consumer loans themselves and the total loans.

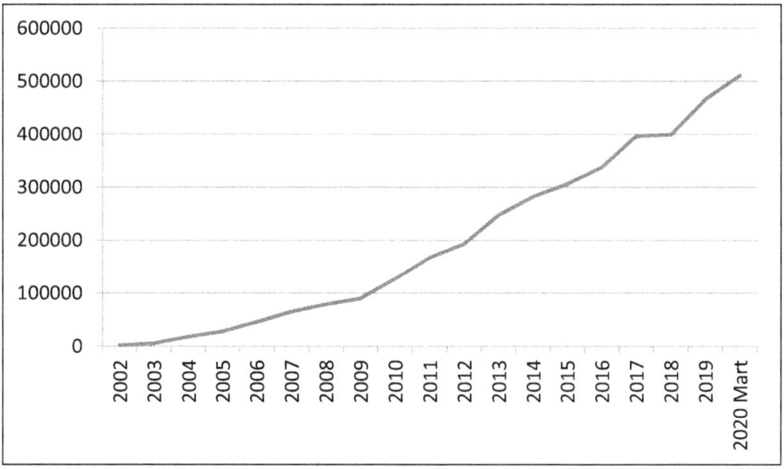

Fig. 11.3: Consumer loans.
Source: BRSA, 2020a

5 Financialization and Laborers: An Evaluation in the Context of Consumer Loans

To understand the increase in household borrowing, it is necessary to understand the transformation in the economy. What has happened in the past years in global terms is important in this context. The deregulation of labor markets and the privatization of basic services such as public education and health have profoundly affected society. As a matter of fact, income and work insecurities led to the borrowing of those who obtained income from wage in particular, which led to an increase in consumer loans (Karaçimen, 2014: 168). This increase in employee indebtedness forces workers to accept long hours of work, adopt a spiral of low wages and precarious work, and submit to work in poor working conditions. In other words, the increase in the debt level of employees increased the commitment of labor to capital (Karaçimen, 2015b: 764).

In his analysis, Karaçimen (2015b) found that credit and debt practices vary according to the employment status of employees. As a matter of fact, flexibility and insecurity in labor markets increase sensitivity to debt. In this environment, employees use consumer loans to substitute their wages, which are insufficient. In this way, employees' income is transferred to financial institutions (Karaçimen, 2015b: 764). As can be seen from Fig. 11.4, workers receive a wage

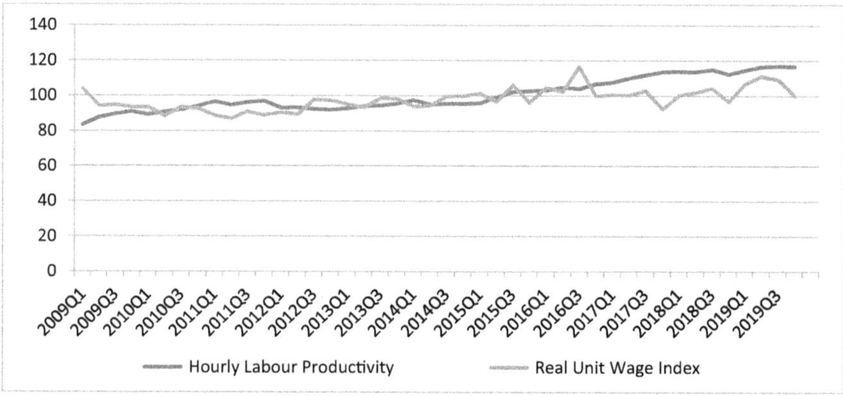

Fig. 11.4: The relationship between real unit wage index and hourly labor productivity (2015 = 100).

Source: TurkStat, 2020; TMMOB, 2019; Ministry of Technology and Industry, 2020

below the yield they put forth. In other words, they do not receive the reward of their efforts. At this point, consumer loans closed the resulting shortfall. However, as stated above, these increases in consumer loans reach the point where they cannot be paid over time and bring about a number of new problems.

After it is stated that the share of household income going to interest has increased, it will be useful to look at which income groups the borrowing is intensive. Indeed, the analysis showed that borrowing is usually done by low-income groups and wage earners. When the distributions of consumer loans by income groups were examined through Tab. 11.2, it was observed that the vast majority of consumer loans were used by low-income groups (Karaçimen, 2015a: 86–87).

According to Tab. 11.2, approximately 40 % of total consumer credit is used by those with incomes below TRY 2000 per month. This rate, which stood above 40 % between 2009 and 2013, has fallen below 40 % between 2015 and 2018. Again, it is understood from Tab. 10.2 that approximately 30 % of the total consumer credit is used by those with incomes between TRY 2000 and TRY 5000. Therefore, it can be stated that the high demand for consumer loans comes from the lower income group, which contributes to the reproduction of labor at the point of meeting the daily needs mentioned above.

In Tab. 11.3 above, more than half of those using consumer loans are wage earners. This shows the lack of wages earners receive, for this reason they tend

Tab. 11.2: Percentage Distribution of Total Consumer Credit Used by Income Groups

	2009	2010	2011	2012	2013	2014	2015	2016	2017	2018
TRY 0–1000	23	23	27	25	21	18	22	21	22	25
TRY 1001–2000	25	25	23	21	22	21	19	16	12	10
TRY 2001–3000	14	16	16	17	19	16	15	14	10	9
TRY 3001–5000	12	12	11	12	13	13	14	18	14	13
TRY 5001 +	19	17	15	15	16	22	20	21	30	30
Unclassified	7	7	8	10	8	11	9	10	12	14

Source: Banks Association of Turkey, 2020

Tab. 11.3: Percentage Distribution of Consumer Credit Users by Profession

	2009	2010	2011	2012	2013	2014	2015	2016	2017	2018
Paid Employees	56	58	52	55	48	52	61	64	63	61
Self-Employed	13	11	12	12	12	12	15	12	12	10
Other	26	26	30	28	34	31	15	15	15	17
Unclassified	5	5	6	6	6	5	9	8	10	11

Source: Banks Association Of Turkey, 2020

Tab. 11.4: Percentage Distribution of Credits Used by Goods and Services Groups

	2009	2010	2011	2012	2013	2014	2015	2016	2017	2018
Transport	5	4	4	4	3	2	2	2	2	2
House	48	47	44	44	44	44	47	49	49	48
Need-Based	46	37	39	37	37	37	51	49	49	50
Other	1	11	13	15	16	17	--	--	--	--

Source: Banks Association Of Turkey, 2020

to borrow. Therefore, this determination supports the statement that labor wages are below its productivity and workers become indebted to close this income gap.

When we look at the percentage distribution of loans made according to goods and services groups, it is seen from Tab. 11.4 that the highest share of consumer loans made available is in need-based loans. The contribution of these developments in consumer loans to economic growth is also evident. The political powers, unwilling to renounce growth, have implemented a number of policies that support this process at this point.

6 Conclusions and Recommendations

One of the major problems of our time is the indebtedness of precarious work and low wages. In this context, the increase in consumer loans for employees is related to employee insecurity. Because in an environment where unemployment is increasing and real wages are decreasing, the only way labor can sustain its life is by borrowing. At this point, consumer loans have a very important function. It is clear that the laborers are not the winners of this process, in which the laborers are indebted, are willing to work for low wages and where precarious employment becomes widespread. Therefore, while borrowing is now easy for the workers, it is very difficult to find a secure and high paying job. As a matter of fact, it has been observed that while a precarious and low-wage employment environment has been created on one side, borrowing of lower income groups has increased on the other.

In this context, it is impossible to separate Turkey, which has achieved its international integration, from these developments. As a result of the wage policy pursued under productivity and the changing consumption patterns, the orientation of the workers in Turkey towards consumer credits has accelerated. In this process, while low wages and precarious employment emerged, on the other hand, consumer loans were introduced to the workers in order to cover the income-expense imbalance.

However, wage policies that are navigating below the value created by labor, make it impossible to pay the resulting debt. As a matter of fact, it has been seen that the measures introduced in the event of debt failure are also the ones that support financialization. Measures such as transfer, structuring or postponing the debt do not solve the problem but simply delay it. Instead, it can be stated that an economic structure, where workers ‘ wages are increased and secure employment environments are re-created, can play a more effective role in solving this problem.

References

Akçay, Ü. (2015) “Güvencesizlik ve Finansal İçerilme”, Research Instiute on Turkey, http://riturkey.org/2015/11/guvencesizlik-ve-finansal-icerilme-umit-akcay/. Date of Access: 11.04.2020.

Akyüz, Y. (1993) "Financial Liberalization: The Key Issues", United Nations Conference on Trade and Development (UNCTAD) Discussion Papers, 56.

Banks Association of Turkey (2020) https://www.tbb.org.tr/tr/bankacilik/banka-ve-sektor-bilgileri/istatistiki-raporlar/59. Date of Access: 12.03.2020.

BRSA (2020a) Aylık Bankacılık Sektör Verileri, https://www.bddk.org.tr/BultenAylik (16.05.2020).

BRSA (2020b) "Türk Bankacılık Sektörü Temel Göstergeleri", https://www.bddk.org.tr/ContentBddk/dokuman/duyuru_0816_01.pdf (16.05.2020).

CBRT (2020), Aylık Krediler Mevduat Bankaları EVDS Sistemi https://evds2.tcmb.gov.tr/index.php?/evds/serieMarket#collapse_4. Date of Access: 11.03.2020.

Epstein, G. A. (2005) "Introduction: Financialization and the World Economy", Epstein G. A. (Ed.) Financialization and the World Economy, Cheltenham: Edward Elgar, 3–16.

Ergüneş, N. (2009) "Global Integration of the Turkish Economy in the Era of Financialisation", Research on Money and Finance, Discussion Paper No. 8.

Federici, S. (2016) "From Commoning to Debt: Financialization, Micro-redit and the Changing Architecture", Commitee for the Abolition of Illegitimate Debt, http://www.cadtm.org/From-Commoning-to-Debt (12.05.2020).

Foster, J. B. (2007) "The Financialization of Capitalism", Monthly Review, 58(11), 1–12.

Foster, J. B. (2011) Tekelci Finans Sermayesi, (der.) Hakan Tanıttıran, çev. Barış Baysal-Onur Gayretli-Selim Sezer, Kalkedon Yayınları,

Güngen, A. R. (2010) "Finansallaşma: Sorunlu bir Kavram ve Verimli bir Araştırma Gündemi", Praksis, 20, 85–108.

Hardie, I. (2007) "Trading the Risk: Financialisation, Loyalty and Emerging Market Government Policy Autonomy", PhD Thesisis University of Edinburg.

Karaçimen, E. (2014) "Financialization in Turkey: The Case of Consumer Debt", Journal of Balkan and Near Eastern Studies, 16(2), 161–180.

Karaçimen, E. (2015a) "Tüketici Kredisinin Ekonomi Politiği: Türkiye Üzerine Bir Değerlendirme", Praksis, 38, 71–97.

Karaçimen, E. (2015b) "Interlinkages between Credit, Debt and the Labour Market: Evidence from Turkey", Cambridge Journal of Economics, 39, 751–767.

Krippner, G. R. (2005) "The Financialization of the American Economy", Socio-Economic Review, 3, 1173–208.

Lapavistas, C. (2009a) "Financialised Capitalism: Crisis and Financial Expropriation", Historical Materialism, 17, 114–148.

Lapavistas, C. (2009b) "Financialisation Embroils Developing Countries", Research on Money and Finance Discussion Paper No. 14.

Lapavistas, C. (2011) "Theorizing Financialization", Work, Employent and Society, 25(4), 611–626.

Lapavistas, C. (2017) "Finansallaşma ve Kapitalizmin Krizi", İstanbul: Yordam Kitap.

Ministry of Technology and Industry (2020) https://www.sanayi.gov.tr/istatistikler/verimlilik-istatistikleri Date of Access: 11.03.2020.

Orhangazi, Ö. (2008) Financialization and the US Economy, Massachusetts: Edward Elgar.

Painceira, J. P. (2009) "Developing Countries in the Era of Financialisation: From Deficit Accumulation to Reserve Accumulation", Research on Money and Finance, Discussion Paper No. 4.

Palley, T. I. (2008) "Financialization: What It Is and Why It Matters", IMK Working Paper, No. 04/2008.

Sema, G. (2017) "Financialization of State and Household Indebtedness: The Case of Turkey", Orta Doğu Teknik Üniversitesi, Sosyal Bilimler Enstitüsü Yayınlanmamış Yüksek Lisans Tezi.

Sönmez, M. (2019) "Sanayide Emek: Ücretler aşağı, işsizlik yukarı", Sanayinin Sorunları ve Analizleri (48), TMMOB Makine Mühendisleri Odası, Nisan 2019, 250.

Sweezy, P. M. (1997). More (or less) on globalization. *Monthly Review*, 49(4), 1–5.

Tunalı, H. & Özdemir, O. (2017) "Türkiye'de Finansallaşmanın Emek Payı Üzerindeki Etkisi Üstüne Bir Deneme", İktisat Fakültesi Mecmuası, 67(1), 57–116.

TurkStat (2020), http://www.tuik.gov.tr/UstMenu.do?metod=temelist.Date of Access: 09.03.2020.

Üzar, U. (2019) "Kapitalizmin Finansallaşma Sürecinde Önemli Bir Sorun Olarak İşsizlik: Tartışma ve Analiz", Siyasal: Journal of Political Sciences, 28(1), 73–97.

Hakan Ulucan

Employment and Intimate Partner Violence against Women: An Analysis of the Effectiveness of the Violence Prevention Centers (SONIMs) in Turkey

1 Introduction

The female labor force participation rate is 49.6 percent, which is 26.5 percent lower than that of men in the world. When they search for a job, women are more likely to be unemployed than men, with a 7 percent higher probability (ILO, 2016a). Even when they are employed, on the world's average, they can only earn 77 percent of what men earn (ILO, 2016a). The inequalities are also prominent in sectoral comparison. The share of women in service sector employment is 61.4 percent, while the ratio is 13.5 percent in industry and 25 percent in agriculture (Economic and Council, 2016). A woman spends higher than 4 hours for unpaid work, including household care, for which a man only spends 1.5 hours per day in developing countries. In developed countries, the hours are 3.5 hours and almost 2 hours for women and men, respectively (ILO, 2016a). Women are also less represented in politics, with a share of 24.5 percent in the parliaments.

Estimations show that the world economy would produce 28 trillion dollars more if women participated equally to men (ILO, 2016b) from a macro perspective. From the micro perspective, the problem seems more severe than the GDP loss when a closer examination into households is conducted. The lower social status of a mother can lead to nutrition problems for her babies during and after pregnancy since the mother bargain with her husband not only on behalf of herself but also on behalf of the baby or child over economic resources. The lower the status against her husband is the lower resources she can take for the baby (Smith et al., 2003). This means that lower economic status can create some intergenerational problems. The children raising in such families start their life in disadvantaged positions. If the child is a girl, the problem will be more severe. Malnutrition is not the only intergenerational problem created by domestic violence against women. Pollak (2004) suggests that the fathers who spent childhood in a family with a violent father are more likely to use violence against their wives, while the women who witnessed their mother beaten by their father are more likely to endure the violence from their abusive partners. Therefore, violence can create a vicious cycle of violence by contaminating the younger generations witnessing domestic violence. Thus, governments from different regions of the world implemented some women empowerment policies in order to increase the development level of their countries.

Turkey, as a developing country which initiated its modernization process in the 19th century and accelerated it in the 20th century to overcome the destiny created by its geography somewhere between the Middle East and Europe, still has severe problems in the inequality between men and women. The country's culture is also somewhere between Europe and the Middle East. This means that some patriarchal mechanisms against women are still at work, and these mechanisms are more prominent in some regions. Turkish Statistical Office (TurkStat) shows that the female labor force participation rate in the country is 36.5 percent, which is less than half of the rate for men in the country. The employment rate is also less than half of men, which is 30.5 percent. The unemployment rate among women is 16.5 percent, which is 3.6 percentage points higher than the rate among Turkish men. Turkish men earn higher than women in all education categories in Turkey, with a gap of 19.6 percent for college and 14.3 percent for high school graduates. The overall earning gap between women and men is 7.7 percent. The share of women in parliament seats is 17.1 percent, which is lower than the world average reported above, but a more upsetting fact is that it is even lower than some less developed Middle East and North African Countries.

The intriguing evidence from the world and Turkey underlined above shows how much women fall behind men in economic activities. It is also important to know how women are trapped in this circle. Among the mechanisms, violence with its variety of forms comes to mind as one of the most important factors. The violence comes into existence in the family in its variety of forms. Men use physical, psychological and economic violence in order to distract financial resources from women (Chin, 2012), in order to control them in bargaining over household resources (Eswaran and Malhotra, 2011). Another form of domestic violence is sexual violence, which can also lead to the exclusion of women from socioeconomic activities.

Intimate partner violence against women is not only the result of the evidence presented above. It is also one of the reasons for the picture. Thus, empowerment policies targeting women are essential to prevent intimate partner violence. However, the policies do not guarantee success in reducing violence against women. In some cases, a policy designed to empower women even increase intimate partner violence and domestic violence by triggering some other mechanisms, such as male backlash, especially in developing countries. Therefore, an analysis of whether a specific measure is beneficial in reducing violence against women will contribute to literature and policy designers. This study focuses on an experiment of violence prevention centers (SONIMs) which are founded in 2013 in 14 pilot regions in Turkey and extended to country-wide implementation, possibly after having proven its success in the following years. A difference-in-difference approach is used to analyze the effects of these centers in the cities hosting them. As far as it is known, there is no study analyzing the impacts of the SONIMs in an empirical framework as used in this study. The study is designed as follows: In the following section, the literature that connects intimate partner violence to the empowerment of the women will be discussed. In the second section, the institutional framework under which the SONIMs are established will be provided. Then, the data and methodology of the study will be explained. In the fourth section, the results will be exposed. In the last section, the conclusions and policy implications are drawn.

2 Literature Review

The standard expectation in the literature on intimate partner violence against women is that improvements in the lives of women reduce domestic violence. To illustrate, Aizer (2010) and Hidrobo et al. (2016) show a better labor market and financial opportunities reduce the probability of intimate partner violence on them. Aizer (2010) suggests that narrowing in the gender wage gap also reduces domestic violence. The main explanation of her from a Nash Bargaining Model is that the husband, whose utility function is supposed to be increasing in the violence level used on the wife, is forced to reduce the level of violence on the wife in order to prevent her from divorcing when outside options of the wife become better. She states that the wife does not, indeed, need to be active in the labor market since the potential wage matters rather than the actual wage, so a non-participant wife also benefits from the declines in the gender wage gap in the labor market. Aizer (2010) also confirms the negative relationship between declines in the gender wage gap and domestic violence by presenting empirical evidence on the matter by using the variations in the gender wage gap in the labor market in the counties in California. Azier's findings are inconsistent with the male backlash and instrumental theories of violence.

However, there is also evidence that the changes in the lives of women that seem to be improvements at the first look may increase domestic violence on them through some mechanisms. Chin (2012) shows that there is evidence that shows that participation in the labor market can increase the likelihood of violence. Three inter-related factors can explain this phenomenon. The first is that the man has learned to program himself to guarantee that he is the biological father of the baby given birth by his partner (Eswaran and Malhotra, 2011). For this reason, he has learned to use violence in order to decrease the contacts of the woman with the outside world. According to him, the work can increase the outside contacts, and then it can trigger violent behaviors against the partner. The second mechanism is called as male backlash which is related to first, but also emphasizes the role of men in society more. The social norms are formed to satisfy the fatherhood instinct of the men in patriarchal societies. Thus, the male backlash effect has its origins in the evolution process. A man can evaluate the progressive steps taken by a woman as a threat to his traditional leadership role in a patriarchal society. The third mechanism emerges in bargaining over the household resources. Men use violence to be more dominant in the household bargaining. Therefore, domestic violence can increase as a result of the empowerment of women.

A more detailed analysis can highlight the mechanisms that can work in an opposite direction to the standard view about domestic violence. In these mechanisms, a male can respond to the better status of the wife in retaliation since he sees the improvements as threats to his traditional leading role. In addition to work, income, and wealth of women, as irrelevant to whether she works, can also increase intimate partner violence. The male partner can use violence in order to grab the financial assets of her or even her family. Chin (2012) explains that one of the reasons for partner violence on the woman is to extract her financial resources. Chin (2012) shows that both exposure reduction and male backlash effects function at the same time in India, contrary to Aizer (2010). She finds that the domestic violence level reduces in the rural regions of India, as the female employment increases, thanks to the domination of exposure reduction[1] on male backlash effects. Chin indicates that improvements in the life of females in a patriarchal country may not be sufficient to increase the bargaining power of the wife, as long as the progress is far from making divorce a feasible option for her. Bloch and Rao (2002) show that the male uses violence to get benefit from the wealth of the family of her

1 Chin (2012) states that the violence decreases if the time that couples spend together decreases, according to exposure reduction hypothesis. Otherwise, if the duration of time that a partner is exposed to the other increases, the violence increases. This theory gained has gained importance since the isolation due to COVID-19 pandemic increases the exposure time among the couples, especially married ones.

wife in India. This is due to the fact that the dowry payments are paid from the women's family. Then, men can use violence to increase their bargaining power to father-in-law and mother-in-law. Implicitly or explicitly, he forces them to finance the marriage more in exchange for lower violence on their daughter.

The attempts to improve women's life stemming from legislation and law can also increase the intimate partner violence through backlash mechanisms. This means that improvements with no direct relation to financial issues can also be a reason for partner violence. Iyengar (2009) reports that mandatory arrest laws that enable the police to arrest the abuser in domestic violence cases without a warrant indeed increased the female partner homicides. Two possible factors are explained by the study: Firstly, the victims become less reluctant to report abusive behaviors from their partners in order to avoid the detention of their partners. Secondly, arrestment may have provoked the abusers who can retaliate in return. Iyengar (2009) suggests that underreporting is the main reason for the increase in domestic homicides. Farmer and Tiefenthaler (1996) analyze the effect of applying to the police and going to the shelter protection on domestic violence, with a motivation to account for why some violated women forgive their husbands by dropping the charges even though they called the police or sought shelter protection. They suggest that a wife can take such actions, not only for getting help and security against domestic violence but also as a means to send signal threat points to the husband even when she is not determined to divorce. However, this process may end with a higher level of violence if this bluff is realized by the husband. The overall success of the services for victims is undermined by the number of women who incredibly threaten their husbands. Some women benefit from increasing threat points caused by the services even without the use of services, in addition to the women using services as successful bluffers and being determined to divorce. One other attempt that is implemented to empower women but triggered male backlash at the end is experienced in Turkey. This is a panic button measure taken in two pilot cities in Turkey, Adana and Bursa. Panic buttons are distributed to women dwelling in these cities so as to push the button in a case of violence against them. The buttons are linked to police stations via a GSM system. This security measure in Turkey increased domestic violence incidence by triggering male backlash effects, according to Tumen and Ulucan (2019).

The studies using the perspective of the instrumental theory of violence emphasize the pragmatic utilization of violence to take away the household resources from the wife rather than evaluating the violence as a mechanism that increases the utility of the man by itself, and so describing the man as sadistic.

As Eswaran and Malhotra (2011) show, theoretically and empirically, that violence is used by the husband as a tool to acquire more power in bargaining for household resources, then violence may increase when the autonomy of the wife rises. Bloch and Rao (2002) show that violence on the wife can also be used as a tool to extract income from the family of her, and so the more the income level of the family in law is, the more the violence level he used against the wife.

Erten and Keskin (2018) investigate the causal relationship between intimate partner violence against women and the education of women by using the exogenous variation created by a policy reform made in 1998 that increases the mandatory years of education from 5 to 8 years in Turkey. By using the regression discontinuity design framework, they show that women's completed years of education are increased by 0.9, and their probability of graduating from high school is increased by 19 percent in rural areas thanks to the reform. However, the increase in education triggered the incidence of psychological violence against women residing in rural areas. The financial control behavior on these women is also raised as a result of the reform. Physical and sexual violence is not influenced by the policy reform, according to the study. On the other hand, they report that they find no significant effect of the reform on the schooling of the girls living in urban regions. The results validate the instrumental theories of domestic violence and also show that the male backlash mechanisms are still at work in the country.

Another exogenous variation influencing the bargaining power of women experienced in more recent years in Turkey is also analyzed by the same authors by using the instrumental variable framework. Turkey has received a massive influx from Syria due to the civil war since 2011. This influx may have excluded some women from the labor market because women in Turkey are mostly employed in the informal sector, which is also the place where Syrian people firstly look for jobs. Erten and Keskin (2019) show that the influx deteriorated the labor market conditions of women. However, as being excluded from employment, women experienced less domestic violence incidents, especially in areas where the number of refugees is more.

The studies on Turkey, Tumen and Ulucan (2019), Erten and Keskin (2018) and Erten and Keskin (2019) have a common finding that the theories suggesting that men can use violence in household bargaining are consistent with the evidence from Turkey. Therefore, studies show that the factors that initially empower women also increase the violence on them finally. This also shows that backlash mechanisms are also important in explaining the intimate partner violence against women in Turkey.

3 Violence Prevention Centers: Institutional Setting

Turkish Parliament adopted the law on Protection of Family and Prevention of Violence against Females in 2012. Violence prevention centers (SONIMs) were established under this law in 14 provinces in 2013 (Tumen and Ulucan, 2019). These centers are designed to provide education, consultancy, and rehabilitation services to intimate partner and domestic violence victims and their partners or husbands. The number did not change during 2014. The number has changed since 2015, and each province in the country has a SONIM currently. Republic of Turkey Ministry of Family and Services (2016) states that SONIM's provinces are pilot regions, which indicates that policy was experimental at the beginning. Nationwide expansion of the institutions shows that the experiment was probably regarded as effective in reducing the violence by the Government. The panic button, another measure, was initiated in two pilot regions, Adana and Bursa, at the same time when SONIMs were established. Being contrary to the success of SONIMs, the panic button policy was removed by the Government due to the failure in reducing the violence (Tumen and Ulucan, 2019).

4 Methodology and Data

A difference-in-differences (DID) approach is used to find the effect of the SONIM in the analyzed province. DID approach is generally used when the variable of interest changes at a more aggregated level, such as provinces, states, or cohorts (Angrist and Pischke, 2008). The case study by Card and Krueger (1994) analyzing the effects of the minimum wage rise in New Jersey is one of the leading examples of the application of the method. DID method is based on a comparison of the unit of observation that is exposed to a change in a time interval with another similar unit without that change in the same time interval. The assumption is that only the change in the variable of interest makes the difference between the compared units; otherwise, they would be the same or very close. Therefore, the methodology requires to find two comparable units with a common history before the change in the variable of interest. This is called "the common trend assumption." The common trend assumption can be smoothed by employing the neighboring units as control groups, synthetic control methods, or employing an interaction term if the DID is conducted under a regression when the history before the change is impossible to observe. Card and Krueger (1994) compares New Jersey with

Pennsylvania in order to find the effects of the minimum wage hike on the employment.

2008 and 2014 waves of the Turkish National Research on Domestic Violence against Women data sets presented by the Turkish Statistical Office (TurkStat) are used in the study. The data is cross-sectional and provides information on personal and socioeconomic characteristics of 20,116 women aged between 15 and 59 in Turkey. The survey contains detailed information on intimate partner violence against women in a variety of categories, such as physical, psychological, sexual, and economic violence. Two waves of the survey are from 2008 and 2014, and there is no survey of violence against women before 2008. Therefore, the provinces where SONIMs are founded are taken as the treatment group. The neighboring provinces that are thought to have similar socioeconomic characteristics with the treatment provinces are defined as controls. The causal effect of the SONIMs is calibrated by subtracting the changes in the violence rate in the control provinces from the provinces of treatment. Neighboring provinces to the treatment provinces defined as the control group can be seen from Tab. 12.4. In the choice of the control groups, the similarity between treatment and control group is important. Table 12.1 shows provincial per capita domestic product in dollars, and this table can be checked to compare the income levels of control and treatment provinces.

The focus is placed on two variables. The first is the intimate partner violence variable. The information on whether physical violence is used by the male partner on the surveyed individual in the last year (from the survey date) is employed to create a binary violence variable in the study. The second essential variable is a labor market variable. The information on whether the surveyed woman worked last week (from the survey date) is used to create the employment variable for women.

The first map in Fig. 12.1 represents the cities where SONIMs were founded in 2013. The second map shows the cities covered by this study. Istanbul, Ankara, and Izmir are excluded from the analysis since these cities are the biggest metropolises in Turkey. They are each so unique that it is hard to find a city to make a comparison. Thus, Istanbul, Ankara, and Izmir are excluded from the analysis. Adana and Bursa were the centers of the panic button measure, and the SONIMs in these cities mostly worked to serve for the panic button policy rather than serving as the other SONIMs. Adana and Bursa are also excluded from the analysis due to the different functions of SONIMs in these cities.

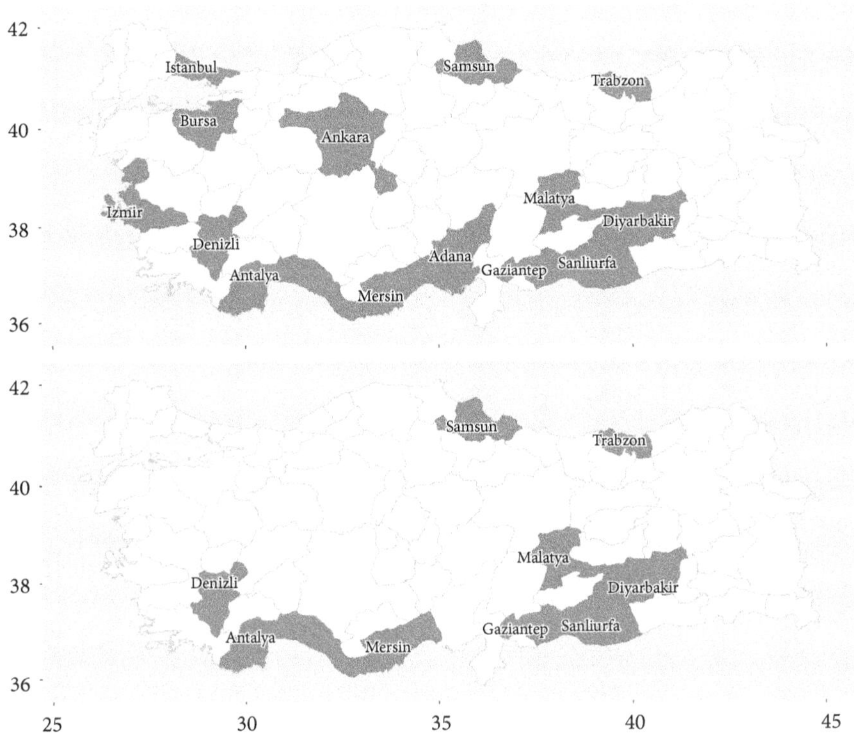

Fig. 12.1: Cities of treatment.

Source: Author's own

Note: The first map shows the cities where the SONIMs were founded in 2013. The second map refers to the cities included in the analysis of this study. The treatment cities are Samsun, Trabzon, Malatya, Diyarbakır, Gaziantep, Şanlıurfa, Mersin, Antalya and Denizli.

5 Results

The cities where SONIMS are founded are compared with the neighboring cities without SONIMs in a difference-in-differences approach. Istanbul, Ankara, and Izmir are excluded from the analysis as explained in the previous section. In Adana and Bursa, SONIMs provide services for the the panic button policy such as receiving applications for panic buttons and choosing the women to give buttons. Thus, we exclude Adana and Bursa from the study, since SONIMs in these cities have completely different functions. The treatment in these

Tab. 12.1: Regional Domestic Products in Dollars for 2008 and 2014

Province	2008	2014	Province	2008	2014
Istanbul	18,622	19,957	Zonguldak	6,822	8,436
Tekirdag	13,823	15,208	Karabuk	8,154	9,632
Edirne	9,460	10,675	Bartin	6,567	7,899
Kirklareli	11,319	12,744	Kastamonu	8,170	9,107
Balikesir	9,738	10,150	Cankiri	7,817	8,703
Canakkale	11,075	12,179	Sinop	6,975	7,835
Izmir	12,954	14,257	Samsun	7,770	8,790
Aydin	7,982	8,743	Tokat	5,910	6,444
Denizli	9,923	11,327	Corum	7,117	7,812
Mugla	11,586	12,374	Amasya	7,923	8,649
Manisa	9,885	11,112	Trabzon	8,598	10,093
Afyon	7,269	8,331	Ordu	6,112	6,665
Kutahya	8,382	9,053	Giresun	6,667	6,844
Usak	8,203	10,021	Rize	8,333	10,210
Bursa	12,706	13,693	Artvin	9,550	10,059
Eskisehir	11,973	13,180	Gumushane	7,225	8,394
Bilecik	14,180	14,908	Erzurum	5,656	7,061
Kocaeli	17,396	19,900	Erzincan	8,790	10,493
Sakarya	9,894	11,139	Bayburt	5,504	7,249
Duzce	9,569	10,989	Agri	3,066	3,880
Bolu	12,684	14,025	Kars	4,535	5,685
Yalova	10,649	13,040	Igdir	5,865	6,280
Ankara	17,338	16,772	Ardahan	4,981	6,360
Konya	7,943	9,594	Malatya	6,223	6,954
Karaman	9,744	11,181	Elazig	6,965	7,749
Antalya	13,748	13,577	Bingol	4,429	5,858
Isparta	9,111	9,591	Tunceli	8,089	10,198
Burdur	10,146	10,673	Van	3,737	4,533
Adana	7,632	8,862	Mus	4,227	5,366
Mersin	8,778	9,702	Bitlis	4,079	5,517
Hatay	6,697	7,637	Hakkari	4,735	5,331
Kahramanmaras	6,297	7,208	Gaziantep	6,949	8,591
Osmaniye	5,674	7,260	Adiyaman	4,920	6,196
Kirikkale	7,816	8,959	Kilis	5,136	6,241
Aksaray	6,586	8,335	Sanliurfa	4,007	4,469
Nigde	6,529	7,998	Diyarbakir	4,848	5,853

Tab. 12.1: Continued

Province	2008	2014	Province	2008	2014
Nevsehir	7,283	8,678	Mardin	4,384	6,075
Kirsehir	6,789	8,057	Batman	5,187	5,393
Kayseri	9,636	10,576	Sirnak	4,431	5,572
Sivas	6,897	8,450	Siirt	4,056	5,593
Yozgat	5,857	7,174			

Source: Turkstat http://www.tuik.gov.tr.

cities is analyzed by Tumen and Ulucan (2019). The evidence presented in Tab. 12.4 shows that SONIMs made a difference in both reducing the violence and increasing the work rate among the women in the whole country. The change in the rate of intimate partner violence is reduced by 2.4 percent in the provinces with SONIMs. The decrease was slightly higher than the provinces without SONIMs. In a simple analysis taking the other cities as the control group, the treatment effect of SONIMs in the whole country is a 0.2 percent decrease. The effect on employment is stronger; the change in the worked women in the provinces with SONIM is 6.8 percent while the rate for the other provinces is 1.7 percent. This means that the average treatment effect is a 5.1 percent increase in an analysis taking the other provinces as the control group.

The initial direction of causality is supposed to be from the effect of the violence through work decisions. The assumption is realistic because the centers' primary aim is to prevent women from violence. Work effect can be a side effect depending on the success in reducing the violence. Finally, the effect of the work can create a new effect on violence. This means that a woman can start to work after being empowered by the policy. However, the male partner who did not choose to use violence at the beginning can rely on violence against an employed female partner in order to extract her income from her job or only due to the backlash effect. In the analyses, the northern cities of Turkey, Samsun and Trabzon are covered firstly. Then, the cities in the east and southeastern regions, Diyarbakir, Malatya, Gaziantep, and Sanliurfa, are analyzed. Then, the cities from the south, The Mediterranean sea region, Mersin and Antalya, will be analyzed. The last city in the analysis is Denizli.

The rates of the women who are violated by intimate partners and the women who worked last week before the time of the survey are provided in the province level in Tab. 12.2 and Tab. 12.3. The average rates among the women living in the neighboring provinces are given in Tab. 12.4, together with their corresponding treatment effects in the treated provinces.

5.1 The Effect on Violence Decisions of Women

The changes in the violence rates in the provinces can be observed in Tab. 12.2. Samsun[2] experienced a 0.3 percent reduction in the incidence of domestic violence while all neighboring cities without a SONIM except Corum experienced an increase in the average probability of domestic violence. The women living in all bordering regions are violated more by 1.2 percent. If the control group is designed by including all these women, the average treatment effect is computed as −1.5 percent, as can be seen in Tab. 12.4. This means 15 women out of 1,000 were not violated by their partners or husbands, thanks to SONIM in Samsun. In a more detailed analysis by comparing Samsun with the other bordering cities from the region, Samsun's better performance can be observed. Domestic violence increased in Ordu by 0.013, which means that SONIM causally reduced domestic violence incidence by 0.016 if we take the women in Ordu as a control group. Amasya, another city near Samsun, witnessed a 0.008 increase, indicating the treatment effect of SONIM in the Samsun is the reduction of domestic violence incidents by 0.011. Sinop experiences a 0.014 increase in the share of women who faced physical violence last year, −0.018 is a treatment effect. SONIM in Samsun seems to contribute to the fight with domestic violence.

Table 12.2 shows that in Trabzon,[3] violence against women reduced by 1.75 percent, which is a higher remarkable decrease in violence rates than its neighboring provinces except Giresun. Table 12.4 shows that the average treatment effect calculated by designing the control group as all women living in the bordering provinces in the region is equal to −0.002. This means that the SONIM in Trabzon prevented 2 women out of 1,000 from being violated by their partners. The treatment effect is a 0.019 reduction when the control group is the women in Gumushane. The effect is −0.045 and −0.014, when control is the women in Bayburt and Artvin, respectively. Therefore, it can be noted that SONIM contributed to the reduction in violence against women in Trabzon.

Diyarbakir[4] experienced a decline in the violence, but the value is slightly lower than the bordering provinces, which suggests that the policy in

2 Sinop, Ordu, Amasya, Tokat, and Corum are the neighboring provinces of Samsun.

3 Giresun, Gumushane, Bayburt, and Artvin are the neighboring provinces of Trabzon.

4 Bingol, Adiyaman, Mus, Batman, Mardin, and Elazig are the neighboring provinces of Diyarbakir.

Tab. 12.2: The Changes in the Shares of the Violated Women

Province	2008	2014	Diff.	Province	2008	2014	Diff.
Adana	0.086(0.28)	0.086(0.281)	−0.0008	Gumushane	0.065(0.25)	0.067(0.25)	0.002
Ankara	0.104(0.30)	0.067(0.25)	−0.0373	Hakkari	0.000(0.000)	0.056(0.236)	0.0556
Antalya	0.081(0.27)	0.066(0.25)	−0.0147	Hatay	0.097(0.296)	0.074(0.262)	−0.023
Bursa	0.051(0.22)	0.069(0.25)	0.018	Igdir	0.173(0.380)	0.161(0.371)	−0.012
Denizli	0.041(0.20)	0.179(0.38)	0.138	Isparta	0.067(0.258)	0.026(0.160)	−0.041
Diyarb.	0.133(0.34)	0.091(0.28)	−0.0422	K. Maras	0.181(0.387)	0.062(0.242)	0.1194
Gaziant.	0.203(0.40)	0.075(0.26)	−0.1275	Karabuk	0.000(0.000)	0.042(0.204)	0.0417
Mersin	0.109(0.31)	0.055(0.22)	−0.0543	Karaman	0.167(0.389)	0.167(0.379)	0.0000
Istanbul	0.081(0.27)	0.089(0.28)	0.0081	Kars	0.147(0.355)	0.073(0.262)	−0.073
Izmir	0.046(0.20)	0.057(0.23)	0.0114	Kastamonu	0.071(0.258)	0.109(0.315)	0.0383
Malatya	0.095(0.29)	0.071(0.25)	−0.0245	Kayseri	0.126(0.332)	0.116(0.322)	−0.009
Samsun	0.064(0.24)	0.061(0.23)	−0.0031	Kilis	0.105(0.315)	0.000(0.000)	−0.105
Sanliurfa	0.141(0.34)	0.051(0.22)	−0.0902	Kirikkale	0.127(0.335)	0.071(0.261)	−0.055
Trabzon	0.050(0.21)	0.033(0.17)	−0.0175	Kirklareli	0.111(0.323)	0.037(0.191)	−0.074
Adiyam.	0.125(0.33)	0.043(0.20)	−0.0821	Kirsehir	0.144(0.353)	0.000(0.000)	−0.144
Afyon	0.172(0.38)	0.152(0.36)	−0.0209	Kocaeli	0.054(0.227)	0.051(0.221)	−0.004
Agri	0.144(0.35)	0.069(0.25)	−0.0750	Konya	0.086(0.280)	0.101(0.303)	0.0157
Aksaray	0.071(0.26)	0.113(0.31)	0.0415	Kutahya	0.080(0.272)	0.154(0.364)	0.0737
Amasya	0.057(0.2)	0.065(0.25)	0.0081	Manisa	0.034(0.182)	0.063(0.244)	0.0286
Ardahan	0.133(0.35)	0.029(0.17)	−0.1039	Mardin	0.123(0.330)	0.042(0.201)	−0.081
Artvin	0.043(0.20)	0.040(0.19)	−0.0029	Mugla	0.036(0.188)	0.167(0.377)	0.1305
Aydin	0.037(0.19)	0.019(0.13)	−0.0178	Mus	0.129(0.341)	0.026(0.160)	−0.103
Balikesir	0.053(0.22)	0.108(0.31)	0.0548	Nevsehir	0.069(0.258)	0.036(0.189)	0.0326
Bartin	0.000(0.00)	0.058(0.23)	0.0577	Nigde	0.145(0.354)	0.120(0.328)	0.0246
Batman	0.200(0.41)	0.091(0.29)	−0.1091	Ordu	0.054(0.226)	0.067(0.251)	0.0130
Bayburt	0.000(0.00)	0.028(0.16)	0.0278	Osmaniye	0.000(0.000)	0.091(0.292)	0.0909
Bilecik	0.111(0.33)	0.042(0.20)	−0.0694	Rize	0.010(0.100)	0.025(0.156)	0.0148
Bingol	0.081()	0.034(0.18)	−0.0463	Sakarya	0.020(0.141)	0.024(0.154)	0.0041
Bitlis	0.214(0.41)	0.063(0.24)	−0.1508	Siirt	0.235(0.437)	0.000(0.000)	−0.235
Bolu	0.060(0.23)	0.042(0.20)	−0.0179	Sinop	0.048(0.216)	0.063(0.244)	0.0149
Burdur	0.083(0.28)	0.000(0.00)	−0.0833	Sirnak	0.173(0.379)	0.067(0.258)	−0.106
Canakk.	0.020(0.13)	0.088(0.28)	0.0679	Sivas	0.098(0.299)	0.067(0.251)	−0.031
Cankiri	0.176(0.38)	0.100(0.30)	−0.0765	Tekirdag	0.000(0.000)	0.063(0.244)	0.0630
Corum	0.096(0.29)	0.080(0.27)	−0.0160	Tokat	0.059(0.236)	0.099(0.300)	0.0397
Duzce	0.087(0.28)	0.054(0.22)	−0.0329	Tunceli	0.000(0.000)	0.118(0.332)	0.1176
Edirne	0.049(0.21)	0.048(0.21)	−0.0018	Usak	0.273(0.467)	0.000(0.000)	−0.2727
Elazig	0.094(0.29)	0.076(0.26)	−0.0184	Van	0.121(0.326)	0.044(0.206)	−0.0769

(continued on next page)

Tab. 12.2: Continued

Province	2008	2014	Diff.	Province	2008	2014	Diff.
Erzincan	0.101(0.30)	0.034(0.18)	−0.0668	Yalova	0.200(0.447)	0.000(0.000)	−0.2000
Erzurum	0.115(0.31)	0.061(0.23)	−0.0540	Yozgat	0.094(0.292)	0.109(0.313)	0.0158
Eskisehir	0.076(0.26)	0.045(0.20)	−0.0306	Zonguldak	0.062(0.242)	0.058(0.234)	−0.0043

Note: The rate of the women violated by their intimate partner in the provinces are represented by the second, third, sixth, and seventh columns. The fourth and eighth columns represent the differences in the rates from 2008 to 2014. The fourteen provinces written boldly in the first column are the provinces where SONIMs are founded. Standard errors are represented in parentheses.

Diyarbakir was not effective for Diyarbakir to go beyond the positive trend in violence against women in the region. Table 12.4 shows that the treatment effect for Diyarbakir is 1 percent when all women in neighboring regions are defined as a control group. This means that SONIM in Diyarbakir is not effective in reducing intimate partner violence. The fall in Diyarbakir is 4.2 percent. Batman, Mus, Adiyaman, and Mardin were the provinces realizing higher falls in intimate partner violence, such as 10, 10.3, 8.2 and 8 percent, respectively. Bingol's fall is very close to Diyarbakir, implying a treatment effect close to zero in the case when Bingol is defined as the control. Only Elazig falls behind in the decrease in the violence rates, as compared to Diyarbakir. The comparison with Elazig only gives a negative treatment effect for Diyarbakir.

In Sanliurfa,[5] from 2008 to 2014, the women faced with physical domestic violence in the survey year were decreased by 0.09, which is a higher reduction than its neighboring cities without a SONIM, Mardin and Adiyaman. The violence on the women in the bordering regions without a SONIM decreased by 8.2, which can be seen in Tab. 12.4. This means that the average treatment effect of SONIM in Sanliurfa is slightly low, and equal to −0.0075, indicating that the SONIM prevented 75 women from being violated out of 10,000 women. The policy was successful in reducing domestic violence in Sanliurfa, although the effect is low.

In Malatya,[6] the share of the women violated by their partners decreased by 2.5 percent, but the bordering cities experienced declines at higher rates,

5 Adiyaman and Mardin are Sanliurfa's two neighboring provinces without a SONIM.

6 Sivas, Erzincan, Tunceli, Adiyaman, K.Maras, Elazig are the neighboring provinces of Malatya 12 Adiyaman, Hatay, Osmaniye, K.Maras, and Kilis are the bordering provinces of this city.

indicating the ineffectiveness of the policy in Malatya. The intimate partner violence on the women living in the region fell by 4.7 percent, which indicates a 2.1 percent increase as the average treatment effect of SONIM, which can be seen in Tab. 12.4. This result may suggest that the SONIM in Malatya may have triggered the backlash effects on the men. This can be seen as reasonable when the patriarchal social norms in the region are taken into account.

In Gaziantep[12], the rate diminished from 20.2 percent to 7.5 percent, corresponding to a 12.7 percent decline. The rate in the bordering cities decreased by 5.6 percent. This corresponds to a negative 7 percent average treatment effect if the control group is designed from the women in the bordering provinces to Gaziantep in the region. Osmaniye is the only city in the region that experienced an increase in the violence rate. There is no city that achieved a lower decline than Gaziantep in the region. Kahramanmaras was the closest city with an 11.9 percent decline in the violence rate. It is followed by Kilis with a 10 percent decline, Adiyaman with 8.2 percent decline, and Hatay with a 2.3 percent decline. Therefore, the success of the policy in Gaziantep is very prominent.

Mersin[7] recorded a 5.4 percent decline in violence rate against women, while the bordering cities experienced an increase of 1.6 percent, opposingly. This corresponds to a negative 7 percent average treatment effect of SONIM in Mersin. A more detailed investigation of the bordering cities shows that Nigde is the only bordering city to Mersin, achieving a decline in the violence rate, while Konya experienced an increase. On the other hand, there was no change in the ratio in Karaman from 2008 to 2014. In Antalya,[8] one of the leading provinces in the Mediterranean region in the country in tourism and industry, the rate of violence against women decreased by 1.4 percent. A 2.5 percent increase is observed in for the women dwelling in the bordering cities, pushing the average treatment effect to –3.9 percent for the SONIM in Antalya. Therefore, in the Mediterranean sea region of Turkey, the SONIMs in Mersin and Antalya were effective in reducing the violence.

Among the cities where the SONIM project was not effective, Denizli[9] is the city with the highest increase in the rate of violence against women. Denizli is one of the leading provinces in the relatively industrialized south-west region of

7 Karaman, Konya, and Nigdes are the bordering provinces without SONIMs.
8 Karaman, Konya, Mugla, Isparta, and Burdur are neighboring cities of Antalya 15 Afyon, Aydin, Usak, Burdur, Mugla, and Manisa are the neighboring cities.
9 Afyon, Aydin, Usak, Burdur, Mugla, and Manisa are the neighboring cities of Denizli.

the country. Denizli experienced a 13.8 percent increase in intimate partner violence, which is 10.8 percent higher than the overall increase in the violence ratio in the bordering cities to Denizli in the region. In the region, Usak achieved a 27 percent decline, one of the highest reductions in the data. Burdur, Afyon and Aydin recorded a –8.3, –2 and –1.7 percent declines, respectively. On the other hand, Mugla and Manisa experienced increases as 13 percent and 2.8 percent, respectively, driving the mean of the region to a 2.9 percent increase.

Analysis of tables indicates that the policy is effective in more underdeveloped regions in the country, which have more patriarchal social norms. Geographically, the policy was more successful in the eastern and northern regions of the country with a more traditional economic structure. In few provinces, the policy even seems to increase the likelihood of intimate partner violence against women, which can be related to backlash effects or bargaining mechanisms explaining some cases in which partner violence on women can increase.

5.2 The Employment Decisions of Women

The effect of SONIMs on the work decisions of women is analyzed by using the information on whether the corresponding individual worked last week of the time when she was surveyed. Firstly, the issue is investigated at the regional level by comparing the changes in the provinces with and without SONIM. The women who worked last week in the treated provinces are increased by 6.8 percent, overall. On the other hand, on average, employed women increased by 1.7 percent. This evidence clearly shows that SONIMs empowers women in terms of their work decisions.

A more detailed investigation by using Tab. 12.4 shows that the highest increase was experienced in Denizli with 23 percent. Denizli is followed by Trabzon with a 13 percent increase and Adana with a 7 percent increase. Denizli achieved a higher increase than its neighbors who have common socio-economic characteristics. In Aydin, the change is even a decrease of 10 percent, which pushes the treatment effect above 30 percent when the control group is designed by choosing the women in Aydin. Among the women in Manisa, there was an increase of 18 percent, following Denizli. The entire change in the neighboring provinces of Denizli is an increase of 14 percent. This means that the treatment effect of the SONIM in Denizli is 9 percent when the sum of the women in the neighboring provinces, Afyon, Aydin, Burdur, Manisa, Mugla and Usak, is taken as a control group. The increase in employment accompanied by an increase in violence against women can be attributed to the backlash effects and bargaining mechanisms in the household. The women may have started to engage in the labor market, as being empowered by the policy. However, this increase may have triggered men to use violence due to the backlash effect on men. Besides, men have used violence as a tool to offset the bargaining power of their wives in households.

In Samsun, the share of the women who worked last week increased by 11 percent, which is higher than the 1.6 percent increase among the women living in neighboring provinces of Samsun. This means that the treatment effect of SONIM in Samsun is around 9 percent on the employment of women. A more detailed analysis of the bordering cities shows that Sinop and Corum achieved to increase employment by 10 and 14 percent, respectively. The other neighboring cities experienced falls in female employment. The analysis of violence against women and female employment shows that SONIM in Samsun contributed to increasing female employment when it lowers the violence against women. The improvement in both female employment and violence indicates that the case of Samsun is consistent with the predictions of bargaining theory used by Aizer (2010) in which an increase in the potential of woman in labor market is shown to decrease the violence from her partner in order to avoid her exit from the relationship. More potential in the labor market increases the outside opportunities of the women by allowing them to consider the exit from marriage or relationship. The industrial composition of Samsun may also have played a role in the realized. If the increase in women's employment is absorbed by the agricultural sector or other low-paid works, backlash effects are expected to be lower. Nonexistence of the backlash effects can be due to the dominance of the agriculture sector in the region. The women in Trabzon who worked last week when the survey is conducted increased from 0.18 to 0.31. This 13 percent increase indicates a high average treatment effect because it is higher than the bordering provinces of Trabzon. The change in the women living in the neighboring provinces is an increase by only 1.8 percent, which allows us to compute treatment effect as 11 percent. Trabzon is similar to Samsun in terms of the empowerment of the women in the region in both the household and labor market. This can be attributed to the common structural characteristics of both cities in the region.

In Malatya, the change in female employment is 2.8 percent and positive, but it is lower than the increase in the women living in the bordering provinces to Malatya, providing a negative treatment effect for Malatya. The overall increase in the region was 4.2 percent, and then the treatment effect of the SONIM in Malatya is –1.4 percent. The improvement in violence is accompanied by lower empowerment in the labor market than the other cities in the region. This opposite move can be explained by the strength of patriarchal social norms in the region. In such regions, improvement in both the violence side and the labor

Tab. 12.3: The Changes in the Shares of the Employed Women

Province	2008	2014	Diff.	Province	2008	2014	Diff.
Adana	0.109(0.312)	0.183(0.388)	0.0738	Gumushane	0.129(0.341)	0.167(0.379)	0.0376
Ankara	0.142(0.349)	0.275(0.447)	0.1330	Hakkari	0.077(0.277)	0.000(0.000)	−0.0769
Antalya	0.372(0.484)	0.342(0.478)	−0.0304	Hatay	0.134(0.342)	0.180(0.386)	0.0459
Bursa	0.153(0.361)	0.266(0.443)	0.1132	Igdir	0.048(0.215)	0.071(0.260)	0.0234
Denizli	0.184(0.391)	0.418(0.497)	0.2342	Isparta	0.067(0.258)	0.436(0.502)	0.3692
Diyarbakir	0.080(0.272)	0.136(0.344)	0.0559	K. Maras	0.072(0.260)	0.185(0.391)	0.1127
Gaziantep	0.095(0.293)	0.105(0.308)	0.0107	Karabuk	0.227(0.429)	0.250(0.442)	0.0227
Mersin	0.178(0.383)	0.229(0.422)	0.0512	Karaman	0.083(0.289)	0.333(0.479)	0.2500
Istanbul	0.173(0.379)	0.264(0.441)	0.0910	Kars	0.093(0.290)	0.113(0.318)	0.0207
Izmir	0.241(0.428)	0.224(0.418)	−0.0167	Kastamonu	0.317(0.467)	0.156(0.366)	−0.1607
Malatya	0.106(0.309)	0.135(0.342)	0.0282	Kayseri	0.078(0.268)	0.185(0.389)	0.1074
Samsun	0.147(0.355)	0.258(0.438)	0.1102	Kilis	0.053(0.229)	0.000(0.000)	−0.0526
Sanliurfa	0.085(0.279)	0.064(0.245)	−0.0210	Kirikkale	0.082(0.275)	0.190(0.397)	0.1087
Trabzon	0.182(0.386)	0.315(0.466)	0.1334	Kirklareli	0.389(0.502)	0.352(0.482)	−0.0370
Adiyaman	0.089(0.288)	0.186(0.392)	0.0964	Kirsehir	0.135(0.343)	0.065(0.250)	−0.0706
Afyon	0.172(0.384)	0.258(0.441)	0.0852	Kocaeli	0.244(0.431)	0.152(0.361)	−0.0924
Agri	0.040(0.196)	0.028(0.164)	−0.0124	Konya	0.171(0.377)	0.304(0.461)	0.1326
Aksaray	0.071(0.267)	0.210(0.410)	0.1382	Kutahya	0.203(0.403)	0.246(0.434)	0.0433
Amasya	0.257(0.443)	0.239(0.431)	−0.0180	Manisa	0.169(0.377)	0.388(0.490)	0.2180
Ardahan	0.067(0.258)	0.206(0.410)	0.1392	Mardin	0.098(0.298)	0.125(0.333)	0.0271
Artvin	0.200(0.403)	0.320(0.470)	0.1200	Mugla	0.169(0.377)	0.286(0.457)	0.1170
Aydin	0.259(0.447)	0.250(0.437)	−0.0093	Mus	0.161(0.374)	0.078(0.270)	−0.0834
Balikesir	0.302(0.460)	0.257(0.438)	−0.0455	Nevsehir	0.138(0.351)	0.164(0.373)	0.0257
Bartin	0.200(0.422)	0.154(0.364)	−0.0462	Nigde	0.072(0.261)	0.200(0.404)	0.1277
Batman	0.133(0.352)	0.091(0.291)	−0.0424	Ordu	0.276(0.448)	0.244(0.431)	−0.0324
Bayburt	0.000(0.000)	0.111(0.319)	0.1111	Osmaniye	0.100(0.305)	0.061(0.242)	−0.0394
Bilecik	0.333(0.500)	0.333(0.482)	0.0000	Rize	0.139(0.347)	0.346(0.479)	0.2071
Bingol	0.051(0.220)	0.103(0.307)	0.0529	Sakarya	0.160(0.370)	0.120(0.328)	−0.0395
Bitlis	0.000(0.000)	0.111(0.317)	0.1111	Siirt	0.059(0.243)	0.057(0.236)	−0.0017
Bolu	0.381(0.489)	0.250(0.442)	−0.1310	Sinop	0.143(0.354)	0.250(0.436)	0.1071
Burdur	0.333(0.492)	0.556(0.527)	0.2222	Sirnak	0.073(0.260)	0.000(0.000)	−0.0726
Canakkale	0.196(0.399)	0.350(0.480)	0.1539	Sivas	0.107(0.311)	0.151(0.360)	0.0441
Cankiri	0.088(0.288)	0.067(0.254)	−0.0216	Tekirdag	0.125(0.333)	0.268(0.445)	0.1427
Corum	0.085(0.279)	0.232(0.424)	0.1473	Tokat	0.247(0.432)	0.264(0.443)	0.0163
Duzce	0.217(0.422)	0.081(0.277)	−0.1363	Tunceli	0.150(0.366)	0.176(0.393)	0.0265
Edirne	0.173(0.379)	0.274(0.449)	0.1010	Usak	0.091(0.302)	0.833(0.408)	0.7424
Elazig	0.109(0.312)	0.092(0.291)	−0.0165	Van	0.054(0.226)	0.101(0.302)	0.0466
Erzincan	0.137(0.345)	0.169(0.378)	0.0328	Yalova	0.400(0.548)	0.500(0.548)	0.1000

Tab. 12.3: Continued

Erzurum	0.080(0.271)	0.099(0.299)	0.0192	Yozgat	0.094(0.292)	0.156(0.365)	0.0627
Eskisehir	0.163(0.371)	0.227(0.421)	0.0642	Zonguldak	0.205(0.405)	0.231(0.423)	0.0264
Giresun	0.289(0.455)	0.282(0.452)	−0.0068				

Note: The rate of the women who worked in the last week before the survey are represented by the second, third, sixth, and seventh columns. The fourth and eighth columns represent the differences in the rates from 2008 to 2014. The fourteen provinces written boldly in the first column are the provinces where SONIMs founded. Standard errors are represented in parentheses.

market is very hard to achieve because men generally respond to better labor market conditions by using violence due to backlash effects in such regions. The SONIM empowers women in households, but this change was not enough to go beyond the barriers of the patriarchal norms.

A similar case to Malatya emerged in the same region, in Sanliurfa. Female employment decreased by 2.1 percent. The increase in the bordering provinces without SONIM was 5.6 percent indicating an average treatment effect of the SONIM on employment as −7.7 percent. Another case in which improvement in violence is accompanied by a delay in the labor market was experienced in Antep, which is a city possessing similar patriarchal social norms in the Southeastern region of the country. Female employment increased by 1 percent, which is lower than the overall increase in the bordering cities in the region, 6.5 percent. Thus, the average treatment effect in Gaziantep is −5.5 percent.

Diyarbakir is the only province in its region that achieved a higher increase in female employment than the bordering provinces in the region. The increase in the employment of the women living in the bordering regions was 1 percent. The increase in Diyarbakir was 4.4 percent higher than the bordering regions. Diyarbakir is more modernized than the other cities in the region. This can be a reason for the positive average treatment effect in employment. The male backlash mechanisms are one of the possible reasons for the positive treatment effect in the violence accompanied by the positive treatment effect in work. The use of violence by men as a tool to be dominant in the household bargaining over the resources can be another reason.

In Mersin, the increase in female employment was 5.1 percent, while in the bordering cities from the region, the change was an increase of 13 percent, indicating that the average treatment effect is negative and equal to 8 percent. Another city from the region sharing a border with Mersin, Antalya, experienced a decrease in female employment by 3 percent. The change was a 16 percent increase for the bordering cities. Then the average treatment effect for Antalya is −19 percent.

Tab. 12.4: Treatment Effects of SONIMs on Violence and Work

Province	Controls	ATEV	ATEW	Province	Controls	ATEV	ATEW
Samsun	Sinop Amasya Ordu Tokat Corum **Change in vio.:0.012** **Change in work.:0.016**	−0.0150	0.093	Trabzon **Change in work.:0.018**	Giresun Gumushane Bayburt Artvin **Change in vio.: −0.015**	−0.002	0.11
Malatya	Sivas Erzincan Tunceli Elazig Adiyaman Maras **Change in vio.: −0.047** **Change in work.:0.042**	0.21	−0.014	Diyarbakir	Elazig Bingol Adiyaman Mus Batman Mardin **Change in vio:−0.053** **Change in work:0.010**	0.01	0.044
Denizli	Afyon Aydin Mugla Burdur Manisa Usak **Change in vio: 0.029** **Change in work: 0.0143**	0.108	0.09	Antalya	Mugla Burdur Isparta Konya Karaman **Change in vio: 0.025** **Change in work: 0.161**	−0.39	−0.191
Mersin	Konya Karaman Nigde **Change in vio:0.016.** **Change in work: 0.132**	−0.070	−0.081	Sanliurfa	Adiyaman Mardin **Change in vio:−0.082** **Change in work:0.056**	−0.0075	−0.077

Tab. 12.4: Continued

Province	Controls	ATEV	ATEW	Province	Controls	ATEV	ATEW
Antep	Hatay	−0.705	−0.055	SONIM	Other	−0.002	0.051
	Osmaniye			Provinces	Provinces		
	K. Maras			Change	Change		
	Kilis			in vio:	in vio:		
	Adiyaman			**−0.024**:	**−0.022**		
	Change in vio.: −0.056			in work:	in work		
	Change in work: 0.065			**0.068**	**0.017**		

Note: ATEV shows the average treatment effect of SONIM on the rate of intimate partner violence in the provinces. ATEW shoes the average treatment effect of the SONIM on the employment of the women living in the province. The second and sixth columns represent the neighboring cities of the city which are designed as the control group. The average treatment effect is found by subtracting the difference in the rate in the treated city from the difference in the rate of neighboring provinces.

6 Conclusion, Discussion and Recommendations

This study presents the evidence behind the switch from a pilot region implementation to a nationwide enlargement of a policy measure, establishment of the violence prevention centers, in a quasi-experimental design. The effectiveness of the policy is very clear from the fact that the improvement in at least one of the areas, in violence or employment, is recorded in all provinces except Malatya. The violence prevention centers (SONIMs) was effective in reducing the violence in five cities, Samsun, Trabzon, Sanliurfa, Gaziantep, Antalya, and Mersin. Among these cities, the improvements in the violence are accompanied by improvements in female employment in Samsun and Trabzon. One of the interesting features of the findings is that, in most provinces, improvement in either one of the two areas is accompanied by a deterioration in the other area, indicating the power of male backlash mechanisms or usage of violence by the male partner as a tool to dominate women in the household bargaining process. This shows that this study is consistent with the other studies on intimate or domestic violence against women in Turkey, Tumen and Ulucan (2019), Erten and Keskin (2018) and Erten and Keskin (2019). As a result of the mechanisms, initial improvement in the violence can be reversed if women start to work. This shows that the institutions should consider further mechanisms and protections for the women who start to work.

References

Aizer, A. (2010): "The gender wage gap and domestic violence," *American Economic Review*, 100, 1847–1859.

Angrist, J. D. and J.-S. Pischke (2008): *Mostly harmless econometrics: An empiricist's companion*, Princeton University Press.

Bloch, F. and V. Rao (2002): "Terror as a bargaining instrument: A case study of dowry violence in rural India," *American Economic Review*, 92, 1029–1043.

Card, D. and A. B. Krueger (1994): "Minimum wages and employment: A case study of the fast food industry in New Jersey and Pennsylvania," *The American Economic Review*, 84, 772–793.

Chin, Y.-M. (2012): "Male backlash, bargaining, or exposure reduction?: Womens working status and physical spousal violence in India," *Journal of population Economics*, 25, 175–200.

Economic, U. and S. Council (2016): "Womens economic empowerment and the changing world of work: Report of the Secretary-General," Tech. rep., E/CN-6/2017/3, December 30. New York: United Nations.

Erten, B. and P. Keskin (2018): "For better or for worse?: Education and the prevalence of domestic violence in turkey," *American Economic Journal: Applied Economics*, 10, 64–105.

Erten, B. and P. Keskin (2019): "Female employment and intimate partner violence: Evidence from Syrian refugee inflows to Turkey".

Eswaran, M. and N. Malhotra (2011): "Domestic violence and women's autonomy in developing countries: Theory and evidence," *Canadian Journal of Economics/Revue canadienne d'economique*, 44, 1222–1263.

Farmer, A. and J. Tiefenthaler (1996): "Domestic violence: the value of services as signals," *The American Economic Review*, 86, 274–279.

Hidrobo, M., A. Peterman, and L. Heise (2016): "The effect of cash, vouchers, and food transfers on intimate partner violence: Evidence from a randomized experiment in Northern Ecuador," *American Economic Journal: Applied Economics*, 8, 284–303.

ILO (2016a): *Women at work: trends 2016*, ILO, Geneva.

ILO (2016b): "World employment social outlook: Trends 2016," Tech. rep., ILO.

Iyengar, R. (2009): "Does the certainty of arrest reduce domestic violence? Evidence from mandatory and recommended arrest laws," *Journal of public Economics*, 93, 85–98.

Pollak, R. A. (2004): "An intergenerational model of domestic violence," *Journal of Population Economics*, 17, 311–329.

Republic of Turkey Ministry of Family, L. and S. Services (2016): "Kadina Yonelik Siddetle Mucadele Ulusal Eylem Plan 2016–2020," Tech. rep., Republic of Turkey Ministry of Family, Labour and Social Services.

Smith, L. C., U. Ramakrishnan, A. Ndiaye, L. Haddad, and R. Martorell (2003): "The importance of women's status for child nutrition in developing countries: International. Food Policy Research Institute (IFPRI) research report abstract 131," *Food and Nutrition Bulletin*, 24, 287–288.

Tumen, S. and H. Ulucan (2019): "Empowered or Impoverished: The Impact of Panic Buttons on Domestic Violence," IZA DP No. 12847.

Section 6 International Theoretical Researches on Gender Issues

Omca Altın

Regulations and Their Effectiveness to Prevent Gender Discrimination in the European Union Labor Market

1 Introduction

Women's participation in the labor market today is very important for the balanced and sustainable development of countries. The increase in women's participation in the labor market increases economic growth while also having a positive impact on women's status in society and contributing to their social and cultural development.

According to the changing conditions in the historical process, women who take part in every stage of production have achieved their current position in the labor market especially after the hard struggles they have given. But despite all this, women have faced many problems in labor markets almost everywhere in the world. The most prominent of these problems were problems related to gender discrimination. Therefore, gender discrimination is one of the most important problems in labor markets. Unequal practices, especially in the areas of women's participation in certain sectors, recruitment, employment, dismissal, pay, promotion, etc., are the problems that women face in the context of gender discrimination.

Economic factors have an important place on the basis of these gender-based discrimination. In particular, reducing costs is the reduction of a single cost, in other words, the cost of the worker, rather than the common costs, in line with the desire to increase profits to the highest level. Wages and social security are the factors that are considered to be a serious cost, and therefore efforts are made to reduce or even eliminate them. Gender discrimination at this point is an important tool used to lower cost(s).

For economic prosperity and also sustainable development, women should not be subjected to gender discrimination and should have the same rights and freedoms as men, especially in economic life. Based on this requirement, the EU has implemented many policies and treaties, directives and regulations in order to prevent gender-based discrimination faced by women, especially in the labor markets.

However, all arrangements made by the EU to be able to prevent gender discrimination in the labor market, in other words, to give an end to all the unequal practices between men and women seems to be inadequate, thus the discrimination that women face in the labor market continues..

2 Gender Discrimination, Its Main Causes and Tools

Discrimination is characterized as unequal forms of behavior and practices for both individuals and groups, based on elements such as race, ethnicity, language, age, religion and gender in society (Akpınar, 2005: 2). Especially in the labor market of individuals with similar human capital, individuals are subjected to serious discrimination based on specified elements (Çolak and Altan, 2003: 203); the kind of discrimination based on gender are among the most discussed topics lately by various dimensions (Dalkiranoglu and Çetinel, 2008: 278).

Gender discrimination is defined as the treatment of persons who are equal in quality only because of their gender (Alparslan, Bozkurt and Özgöz, 2015: 68). Gender discrimination is carried out in two ways. These are overt and implicit sex discrimination (Gutek, Cohen and Tsui, 1996). When we look at explicit gender discrimination, it is clear that there is a direct discrimination between men and women. In particular, the fact that only men are required to apply for job advertisements, that men are paid more than women, and that women are dismissed because they are pregnant are examples of explicit sex discrimination (Dalkıranoğlu and Çetinel, 2008: 279). On the other hand, although there is no obvious situation to suggest discrimination, there are inequalities concerning women, especially in the case of implicit sex discrimination, which is characterized as having a negative impact on a gender group (Arısoy and Demir, 2007: 713). In other words, although there are no visible discriminatory elements in implicit sex discrimination, there are regulations that lead to discrimination in practice (Cox, 1993: 48; Manolkidis, 1997: 90). Situations such as recruiting single women especially for some jobs that require much travel (Alparslan Bozkurt and Özgöz, 2015: 69) elimination of women who have young children during recruitment, in case of dismissal, employers choice to often use incentive toward part-time working women, giving full-time employees the priority to claim incentive bonuses and thus for the working women, who usually work part time, to not have this benefit are among the examples of implicit gender based discrimination (Dalkiranoglu and Çetinel, 2008: 279–280).

Therefore, within the context of gender discrimination, women are less able to benefit from opportunities such as education and work than men (Johansson,

Katz and Nyman, 2001: 4), and they face different practices on issues such as wages, raises, promotions, appointments, dismissals. Working women have to work much harder and wait much longer before they can progress where they work compared to men (Mercanlıoğlu, 2009: 36), and although they progress equally with men in their careers, they are paid less than men (Stockford, 2004). On the other hand, factors such as the employment of working women in jobs that do not require much qualifications, having low levels of education, and obligations within the family make their promotion impossible (O'Mahony and Sillitoe, 2001).

Among the reasons for all these discriminations, especially in labor markets, economic factors are at the forefront, and gender discrimination is seen as a tool to reduce labor costs. In particular, patriarchy and the fact that women have fertility characteristics are the most fundamental elements of gender discrimination. In a patriarchal society, especially women's duties are restricted to the house and women are obliged to do household tasks. At the same time, women bear the responsibility of caring for the child as well as giving birth to children. In the same structure, men have the role of working outside and meeting the needs of the house. The men who meet the needs of the house are both seizing the authority within the house and become the sole owner of income. Therefore, women remain in a secondary position in terms of social status (Akpınar, 2005: 4–5), this is the most important factor that determines the place of women in the labor market. Thus, women are positioned in the labor market in jobs that are paying less, do not require much qualifications, where working conditions are worse off (Anker, 1997: 324; Mackintosh, 1981: 4–13).

3 Dimensions of Gender Discrimination in the EU Labor Market

Labor force participation, employment, unemployment rates, earnings and working times play an important role in determining the extent of gender discrimination in the EU labor market (Akpınar, 2005: 6); these factors include labor force participation, in other words, labor force participation rate (which includes those employed and also unemployed) is determined by calculating the share of labor force within the population of people of 15 years of age and older (T.C. Ministry of Family and Social Policies General Directorate for The Status of Women, 2014: 22). When we look at the average labor force participation rates between the ages of 15 and 64 and 15 and 24 in the EU in 2014, it is seen that men in both the 15–64 age group and the 15–24 age group are more involved in the labor market than women. Especially in EU member states such as Sweden, Denmark, Finland, the Netherlands, Germany, Latvia, Lithuania, the United Kingdom and Estonia in 2014, women are more involved in the labor market than men. Greece, Malta, Romania and Italy are the weakest EU member states in terms of women's participation in working life. On the other hand, in the Netherlands, Denmark, Sweden and Finland, it is observed that the participation rate of young women in the labor force is higher than that of young men. The EU member states with the weakest participation in working life in the 15–24 age range are Bulgaria, Hungary, Slovakia, Italy and Luxembourg (Kırkpınar, 2016: 79–80).

Employment, which is another element, is defined as the fact that the individual is engaged in a direct income-generating work activity or that the institution he works for is engaged in an income-generating activity (T.C. Ministry of Family and Social Policies General Directorate for The Status of Women, 2014: 26). Looking at the overall employment rates in the 15–64 and 15–24 age range in 2014, it is seen that men are more advantageous than women in EU member states. In some EU member states, the difference between men and women in terms of the overall employment rate is seen to be quite high, while in others it is less. Especially in EU member states such as Spain, Croatia, Italy and Greece, Malta, Italy, Romania and the Czech Republic are EU member states where the employment gap between men and women is very high. While the EU member states Sweden, the Netherlands, Malta, Cyprus, Denmark and Finland are countries where women especially among young people have a higher employment rate, EU member states where more women are employed; Greece, Italy, Bulgaria and Slovakia are the EU member countries with the lowest employment rates for young women. On the other hand, as education levels rise, the employment rates of both women and men increase, and the difference in employment rates between men and women decreases even more. However, no matter what level of education women's employment is lower than men's. At the same time, in the vast majority of EU member states, women are employed in part-time jobs more than men. Therefore, women's earnings are less than men's. In particular, part-time female employment rates in EU member states such as the Netherlands, Austria, Germany are seen to be quite high in 2014 (Kırkpınar, 2016: 80–82).

The 2018 report on gender equality in the EU states that although it is less, the female employment rate continues to grow without losing momentum over the years, especially in the third quarter of 2017, this rate is 66.5 % (Özcan, 2019: 33). According to the report, women are more employed in the EU in the areas of cleaning staff, sales staff, personal care staff, preschool and primary school teaching (OECD, 2017). In addition, women's employment in areas such as health and human resources increased, while women's employment in areas such as engineering and information technology was observed to be very low. The report also stated that the employment rate gap between men and women has been around 11 % in recent years, and that there has been no significant convergence in the member states. According to the report, the EU member states with the highest female employment in the EU in 2017 are Sweden and Germany, while Italy and Greece are the EU member states with the lowest female employment in the EU (Özcan, 2019: 33).

The individuals of 15 years of age and above, who were not employed during the reference period and were looking for a job for the last 4 weeks through various channels and able to start working within 15 days are considered unemployed. Therefore, the unemployment rate is determined by determining the proportion of the population that is considered unemployed in the labor force (T.C. Ministry of Family and Social Policies General Directorate for The Status of Women, 2014: 27). In 2014, it is seen that Greece is one of the EU member states with the highest unemployment rate among men and women (Kırkpınar, 2016: 84).

One of the most important indicators of gender discrimination in labor markets is the wage gap between men and women. Another is the gender pay gap. The gender pay gap is expressed as the percentage of the current pay gap between men and women within men's pay, and the calculation of this indicator is based on the average hourly, monthly or annual wage. The gender pay gap seeks to identify the impact of three factors on the average wages of all working-age women, whether working or not. These are the average hourly wages, the weekly average of the number of paid hours, and the employment rate. In 2014, on the basis of monthly and hourly wages, wage differences were found to exist between men and women when the average of EU countries was taken into consideration. While Slovenia, Latvia and Lithuania have the lowest rates especially in terms of wage differences between women and men in EU member states; it has been observed that Malta, the United Kingdom, Austria and the Netherlands are EU member states with the highest rates in wage differentials (Kirkpinar, 2016: 85). In EU member states, the gender pay gap was mainly due to the low wages of married women with children, the low wages of women with high educational attainment in part-time and high-level jobs and women working mainly in low-wage sectors (European Commission, 2002).

Men are paid more than women per every hour they work, according to the 2018 report on gender equality in the EU. Especially in 2016, this difference was 16.2 %. The report stated that the EU member states with the highest gender-based average hourly wage gap were Estonia, Czech Republic and Germany, while the EU member states with the least wage gap were Luxembourg, Italy and Romania. As we can see, the EU has not yet reached the desired level of wage transparency (Özcan, 2019: 34).

Even though some EU member states has proven to be successful in the fight with gender-based discrimination against women in the labor market, it is observed that some EU member states are lagging behind in the goal of achieving gender equality in the labor market, in other words still have serious gender-based discrimination toward women, across the EU. Therefore, when looking at the EU average, the desired level has not been reached in this regard.

4 Regulations and Their Effectiveness to Prevent Gender Discrimination in the European Union Labor Market

The aim of the EU, which is based on economic principles, is one of the most important objectives of the EU for women and men to take part in the economic field. However, the EU has made many arrangements to address the inequalities in these areas (Kırkpınar, 2016: 73), being aware that this will be possible by eliminating the inequalities that women face in economic life in employment, workplaces and wages.

The Article 119 of the Treaty of Rome, which created the European Economic Community, was the beginning of the struggle for equality of men and women in the EU. Other men and women receive equal pay for the same work that they do based on this item with any gender without discrimination, workers' wages are being taken to secure equality in the same job for the same fee paid per piece by the measurement unit based on the calculation time of a paid worker's wages were tied to make equal for similar work (Tekinalp and Tekinalp, 2000: 641). However, the Treaty of Rome on ensuring gender equality was limited only with wage equality, and the Treaty has been very limited in the field of social policies (Birk, 1992: 3; Hepple, 1997: 138; Hantrais, 2000: 113; Heide, 1999: 384). Although the Treaty of Rome obliges EU member states to cooperate, particularly in the social sphere, the authority of the Community to introduce binding arrangements in this area is very limited. Regulations on the basis of equal pay to working women and working men, in particular, have been one of the few areas where the Community has the authority to make binding arrangements (Gülmez, 2003: 9–22).

On the other hand, with the article 13 of the European Community Treaty on the Prohibition of General Discrimination, various measures have been taken to combat discrimination based on gender and it is aimed that gender equality in all EU institutions should be observed in all policy areas such as education, employment and youth. At the same time, equality of opportunity has become everyone's priority (Kırkpınar, 2016: 74). The article 2 of European Community Treaty, which contains the community objectives, emphasizes the equality of men and women. Another article of the European Community Treaty on equality of women and men is article 3, which states that equality of women and men shall be observed when implementing all activities towards the Community. Therefore, this approach to equality of women and men in the European Community Treaty has shown that equality between men and women is not only considered in material terms, but also in the economic and social aspects as well as the human rights side (Tekinalp and Tekinalp, 2000: 642–643). At the same time, with the article 141 of the Treaty of the European Community, article 119 of the Treaty of Rome, in which equality between men and women is addressed, has been amended and in article 114, there are also regulations for equality of opportunity and equality of treatment at work at the point of access to employment opportunities, in addition to the regulations in article 119 for equality in wages between men and women (Cansevdi and Hermans, 2001: 15).

While the founding treaties of equality of women and men were included in this way, the directives issued by the EU also aimed to prevent the difficulties and obstacles that women faced in relation to social security during work and after work life, and to provide balance between the work and family life of women. In this context, directive 75/117 regarding the principle of equal pay for the same job, directive 76/207 for the implementation having equal rights during the employment of women, during the training of the profession, working conditions, advancement in work, directives 80/807 and 86/378 containing the provisions for reshaping the social security system to have equal rights a way to ensure equality between men and women, directive 86/613 to prevent the victimization of women at workplaces in which their spouse's independently work, directive 92/85 to ensure the safety of women who are pregnant, in maternity leave and breastfeeding in their work place, directive 96/34 containing the provisions for parental permissions are legal arrangements within the EU legislation to prevent gender based discrimination against women (Tekinalp and Tekinalp, 2000: 644–648).

In 1989, The Charter of Fundamental Social Rights of Workers, which was created to institute minimum standards at the EU level other than the founding treaties and directives, stated in the of article 16 within the header "Fundamental Social Rights of Workers" by focusing onto especially for the women and men to be treated equally, creation of equal opportunities between women and men, practices should be adopted to ensure equality of women in employment, wages, working conditions, social protection, education, vocational training. At the same time, measures to help women and men balance their work and family lives have been highlighted in the Charter (Kırkpınar, 2016: 75).

The Charter of Fundamental Rights of the European Union signed in 2000 includes economic, political, social and civil rights, and in this charter it is emphasized that the EU will evaluate the equality of men and women and the problems related to the issue from an individual standpoint, and it is stated that discrimination based on sex should be considered within the scope of discrimination based on any principles and such discrimination should be prohibited. On the other hand, the Charter states that men and women must be equal in all areas, including work opportunities, work environment and wages (Kırkpınar, 2016: 75).

Further progress has been made in this area through various programs in addition to these legislative arrangements for the equality of men and women carried out by the EU. Since the 1970s, EU policies that contributed to the issue of equality in the EU have focused more on women and community initiatives on women's participation in the labor market have been implemented. In particular, the NOW initiative, which came into force in 1990, aims to support women in employment and vocational education. On the other hand, the Equal Pay Day Initiative, which has been held annually since 2011 and the Rights, Equality and Citizenship Program, which includes the years 2014–2020 and whose aim is to ensure equality of men and women, are among the EU's community initiatives (Kırkpınar, 2016: 75).

The White Book of 1994, prepared by the EU Commission, contained recommendations for balancing women's working and family lives, and it was also decided to publish the Equality Report every year to understand the degree of progress the community has made in its activities in the context of gender discrimination prevention. These reports have been published since 1996. The integration of the gender side with all the policies of the community, which were adopted since 1996, has been very important for the EU. It was decided that the interests of women and men should be taken into consideration and that the needs of both women and men should be met (Zengingönül, Kırkpınar, 2004: 14).

At the Vienna Summit held in 1998, it was stated that the creation of equal opportunities for women and men in employment was very important and that new alternatives would be created that would enable women to be competitive in the labor market. On the other hand, by 2010, women's employment had increased to 60 % at the community level, and it was aimed that women would be more involved in the labor market (Kırkpınar, 2016: 76).

By 2000, a framework strategy on gender equality was prepared, which included activities in the years 2001–2005. With his strategy, it is aimed by the EU to integrate the gender-based side of the struggle for prevention of gender inequality between men and women with all policies of the Community and to regulate all policies and actions toward gender equality under one roof by emphasizing the benefit of women (Commission Communities, 2000).

Another of the documents adopted within the framework of ensuring equality between women and men is the Equality Strategy for women and men in the period 2010–2015 prepared by the European Commission. The strategy aims to ensure equality between women and men in terms of economic independence, equal pay for the same job, equality during decision-making, as well as preventing gender-based violence, promoting gender equality in terms of gender, as well as ensuring gender equality in all policies (Kırkpınar, 2016: 75). The strategic participation document for Gender Equality 2016–2019, published by the Commission in 2015, is an extremely important document developed under the scope of gender discrimination prevention. Strategic Participation Certificate for Gender Equality is based on the European Parliament EU Strategy Decree for achieving gender equality after the year of 2015 and the European Pact for gender equality for the period of 2011–2020 and at the same time, the 2010–2015 Strategy for Equality Between Women and Men, and adopts the Commission's initiatives on gender equality, which is the main value of the EU. This strategy focuses on the benefits of gender equality on economic growth and sustainable development, supports the implementation of the Europe 2020 Strategy regarding the social gender equality, aids the priority issues of the Women's Charter and contributes to the experiences of the Roadmap for Equality between Women and Men (European Commission, 2016: 9).

As we can see, the EU has implemented many regulations aimed at preventing gender discrimination between men and women. However, despite all these arrangements made by the EU to prevent gender discrimination, both through the founding treaties, guidelines and other official documents, gender discrimination continues, especially in the labor markets.

5 Conclusions

In the study, which aims to assess the extent to which these regulations are effective in preventing gender discrimination in labor markets, it is observed that despite the policies implemented, women are not equal to men in the labor market in the EU and women are in a secondary position. Although there are countries among the EU member states that have been successful in achieving certain goals in the context of preventing gender discrimination against women in labor markets, there are also EU member states that are far behind in achieving these goals within the EU. Therefore, when looking at the EU average, the desired level has not been reached in this regard.

In particular, data on employment, unemployment, income and part-time work are the most important indicators of gender-based discrimination against women in the EU labor market. In the EU, it has been observed that women have lower qualifications and abilities than men, work for less wages, and that the unemployment rate is higher among women than men. Women have lower rates of participation in employment than men, often employed in part-time jobs. At the same time, women are subjected to gender-based discriminatory practices on issues such as promotion and promotion in the labor market.

In the legal arrangements and policies developed by the EU to prevent discrimination based on gender, it is seen that the EU focuses more on issues such as wages, employment and access to vocational education. However, none of these steps taken by the EU produces a realistic solution. Therefore, the EU must first properly identify the underlying causes of gender discrimination and effectively implement the necessary regulations in this context.

References

Akpınar, T. (2005). AB İşgücü Piyasasında Cinsiyet Ayrımcılığının Boyutları ve Ortadan Kaldırmaya Yönelik Çabalar, *Ankara Üniversitesi Siyasal Bilgiler Fakültesi Dergisi*, 60(4), 1–22.

Alparslan, M., A., Bozkurt, Çetinkaya, Ö. and Özgöz, A. (2015). İşletmelerde Cinsiyet Ayrımcılığı ve Çalışan Kadınların Sorunları, *Mehmet Akif Ersoy Üniversitesi İktisadi ve İdari Bilimler Fakültesi Dergisi*, 2(3), 66–81.

Anker, R. (1997). Theories of Occupational Segregation by Sex: An Overview, *International Labour Review*, 136(3), 315–339.

Arısoy, A. and Demir, N. (2007). Avrupa Birliği Sosyal Hukukunda Ayrımcılıkla Mücadele Kapsamında Kadın Erkek Eşitliği, *Ege Akademik Bakış*, 7(2), 707–725.

Birk, R. (1992), Avrupa İş Hukukunda Güncel Durum ve Gelişmeler, 1990'lı Yıllarda Türk Çalışma Mevzuatının Avrupa Topluluğu Çalışma Mevzuatı Açısından Değerlendirilmesi, Tınar, Yaşar, Mustafa, Çev., İzmir: Dokuz Eylül Üniversitesi Avrupa Topluluğu ve Uluslararası Ekonomik İlişkiler Araştırma ve Uygulama Merkezi Yayını, 1, 1–12.

Cansevdi, H. and Hermans, S. (2001). Avrupa Birliği'nin Sosyal Politikası ve Türkiye'nin Uyumu, İstanbul: İktisadi Kalkınma Vakfı Yayını.

Commission Communities. (2000). *Towards a Community Framework Strategy on Gender Equality (2001–2005)*, Retrieved April 20, 2020, from https://eur-lex.europa.eu/legal-content/EN/TXT/HTML/?uri=LEGISSUM:c10932&from=EN.

Cox, S. (1993). Equal opportunities. In Gold, Michael, ed., *The Social Dimension: Employment Policy in the European Community*, Basingstoke: Macmillan, 41–63.

Çolak, F., Ö. and Altan, Ş. (2003). Sex Discrimination in the Banking Sector: The Case Of Turkey, *Kamu-İş İş Hukuku ve İktisat Dergisi*, 7(2), 1–12.

Dalkıranoğlu, T. and Çetinel, G., F. (2008). Konaklama İşletmelerinde Kadın ve Erkek Yöneticilerin Cinsiyet Ayrımcılığına Karşı Tutumlarının Karşılaştırılması, *Dumlupınar Üniversitesi Sosyal Bilimler Dergisi*, 20, 277– 297.

European Commission. (2002). Employment in Europe 2002: Recent Trends and Prospects, Retrieved April 9, 2020, from http://aei.pitt.edu/40709/1/employment_2002.pdf.

European Commission. (2016). *Report on Equality between Women and Men 2015*, April 12, 2020, from https://op.europa.eu/en/publication-detail/-/publication/2ca44101-173b-11e6-ba9a-01aa75ed71a1.

Gutek, B., A., Cohen, A., G. and Tsui, A. (1996). Reactions to Perceived Sex Discrimination, *Human Relations*, 49, 791–813.

Gülmez, M. (2003). Avrupa Birliğinde Sosyal Politika, Ankara: Türkiye-AB Sendikal Koordinasyon Komisyonu Yayını.

Hantrais, L. (2000). Social Policy in the European Union, Basingstoke: Macmillan Press.

Heide, I. (1999). "Supranational action against sex discrimination: Equal Pay and Equal Treatment in the European Union," *International Labour Review*, 138(4), 381–410.

Hepple, B. (1997). The Principle of Equal Treatment in Article 119 EC and The Possibilities for Reform. In Dashwood, Alan and O'leary, Siofra, eds., *The Principle of Equal Treatment in E.C. Law*, London, Dublin, Hong Kong: Sweet & Maxwell, 137–152.

Johansson, M., Katz, K. and Nyman, H. (2001). *Wage Differentials and Gender Discrimination – Changes in Sweden 1981–1998*, (Working Paper 2001: 15) Retrieved April 8, 2020, from http://www2.ne.su.se/paper/wp01_15.pdf.

Kırkpınar, N. (2016). Avrupa Birliği ve Türkiye'de Kadının Ekonomik Hayattaki Yeri, K*aratahta İş Yazıları Dergisi*, 4, 67–90.

Mackintosh, M. (1981). Gender and Economics: The Sexual Division of Labor and the Subordination of Women. In Young Kate, Wolkowitz, Carol and Mccullagh, Rosalyn, eds., *Of Marriage and the Market: Women's Subordination Internationally and Its Lessons*, London: Routledge, 3–17.

Manolkidis, S. (1997). The Principle of Equality from a Comparative Constitutional Perspective: Lessons for The EU. In Dashwood, Alan and O'leary, Siofra, eds., *The Principle of Equal Treatment in E.C. Law*, London: Sweet & Maxwell, 80–104.

Mercanlıoğlu, Ç. (2009). Cinsiyete Dayalı Eşitsizlik Kadın Yöneticilerin İş ve Özel Hayatlarını Dengeleme Zorlukları ve Bedelleri, Baytekin, Binnaz, Fidan, Fatma, Hazer, Gülsemin, Aygin, Dilek, Yıldırım, Neşide, Hayır, Meryem, Şimşek, Fatih, eds., 5–7 Mart 2019 Uluslararası-Disiplinlerarası Kadın Çalışmaları Kongresi'nde sunulan bildiri, Sakarya: Sakarya Üniversitesi, 35–44.

OECD. (2017). *The Pursuit of Gender Equality: An Uphill Battle*, Retrieved April 15, 2020, from https://www.oecd.org/publications/the-pursuit-of-gender-equality-9789264281318-en.htm.

O'Mahony, G. B. and Sillitoe, F. J. (2001). Identifying the Perceived Barriers to Participation in Tertiary Education among Hospitality Employees, *International Journal of Contemporary Hospitality Management*, 13(1), 21–29.

Özcan, M. (2019). AB Katılım Sürecindeki Türkiye'nin Kadın İstihdamı Karnesi, *İktisadi Kalkınma Vakfı*, https://www.ikv.org.tr/ikv.asp?ust_id=207&id=3393, Date of Access: 10.04.2020.

Stockford, A. M. (2004). The Bellwomen: The Story of the Landmark AT&T Sex Discrimination Case, New Brunswick: NJ: Rutgers University Press.

T.C. Aile ve Sosyal Politikalar Bakanlığı Kadının Statüsü Genel Müdürlüğü. (2014). Türkiye'de Kadın İşgücü Profili İstatistiklerinin Analizi, Ankara: Duygu Matbaacılık.

Tekinalp, Ü. and Tekinalp, G. (2000). Avrupa Birliği Hukuku, İstanbul: Beta Yayınları.

Zengingönül, O. and Kırkpınar, N. (2004). Avrupa Birliği'nin Odak Noktalarından Biri: Kadın İstihdamı, *Gazi Üniversitesi Mesleki Eğitim Fakültesi Mesleki Eğitim Dergisi*, 6(11), 1–26.

Pınar Çuhadar and Behiye Körpe

The Impact of Social Norms on Women's Employment and Gender Policies in the Middle East

1 Introduction

Orthodox economic theories claim to explain the general functioning of economy through the behaviors of individuals isolated from society. However, these theories choose to ignore from their analysis the community-specific norms, values, cultural elements and institutional factors that influence an individual's socialization process in the models they use. However, many norms that ensure individuals to be accepted by the community they are a part of during the socialization process, shape their behavior within the social hierarchy and determine their roles by giving meaning to these behaviors can be more effective than the written rules of law (Ellickson, 1998; Sustein, 1996). As a matter of fact, the norms produced by the collective culture of society encourage socially approved behaviors while preventing those that are not socially approved through sanctions, thus by giving the society control over the individual, they contribute to the continuity of collective life. Norms, the products of shared value systems, are embedded in individual psychology and social culture, allowing individuals to develop internal constraints, thereby eliminating the ambiguities of certain behaviors (Cialdini and Trost, 1998).

In addition to the norms, the division of labor in a society serves as a continuum of communal living, while also providing the influence of some groups on the distribution of economic resources, their political power, and the reproduction of the values created by institutions such as the family. In this respect, norms that appear stable and continuous are becoming an important determinant of individual and collective preferences. Evolutionist approaches also question the process of adaptation of individuals to the norms embedded in the social and psychological system and the factors affecting the change of norms. Social movements and technology are thought to be the most important factors influencing the change of norms (Ostrom, 2000; Kranton, 2016). Therefore, the change and transformation of the norms that shape the life of society through its acceptance and practices requires socioeconomic relations that are redefined by a process of "creative destruction."

Gender roles that have cultural meaning and are passed down from generation to generation along with norms should also be considered as a result of the division of labor between men and women that has been shaped in the historical process. Similarly, the social classes created by the relations of property and production are another element that determines the division of labor within the household. Research in the field of social psychology supports that classes are the determinant of the line between "freedom and constraints" over individual preferences. All social stratification, the prevailing ideology on gender and the cultural codes of the family institution influence the beliefs and behaviors of women and their choices in working life. In this regard, the norms that determine gender roles should be monitored as elements which live on power and the hegemonic relationships, provided a broad consensus in society, affecting the preferences and actions of living practice of women and men within the socio-economic structure (Pearse and Connell, 2016; McGinn and Oh, 2017).

Research on the economies of a number of developed countries, with different characteristics, have demonstrated the impact of norms in regard to the effect on labor supply-labor demand and by evaluating in terms of gender politics by assessing the effect of societal gender roles in women's employment, family ties and family relations, education decisions, career prospects, preferences for having children. In his qualitative research on Japan, Hirsch (2000) observed the influence of norms and belief systems, the bearer of culture, on gender roles and preferences in the labor market. Women have an important place in the Japanese economy but mostly in secondary positions supporting male executives. Indeed, it is observed that women in Japan have a high share in flexible and cheap labor rather than as managers; and are discriminated against in terms of wages. In Japan, social norms place cultural and legal barriers that support men to devote themselves to their firms and have a career-oriented life, which keep women from becoming managers. Campa, Casarico, Profeta (2009) examined the influence of cultural elements in the preferences of firms and individuals in Italy, which have a heterogeneous structure in the employment of women in the labor market. According to the research results, heterogeneity in women's employment in the region cannot be explained by demographics, non-gender factors or the peculiar qualities of the market system. The findings revealed that gender is an important determinant of employment for Italy. Accordingly, heterogeneity in the field of women's employment in the country also stems from heterogeneity in the field of culture.

Again, in the literature, many researches reveal that the place of women in working life, having children, the number of children and children's age have negative effects on women's employment (Kalwij, 2000). There are also research findings that suggest that working women face obstacles in the way of specialization in business life after having children (Becker, 1981). It has also been argued that variables such as the level of education, income and positions at work, and working hours of married women's spouses negatively affect women's working lives (Maume, 2006). Fortin (2005) assessed the impact of gender roles and working values determined by social institutions such as religion and family on the OECD labor market in terms of female employment. Accordingly, the traditional understanding that "the man is the breadwinner, the woman is the keeper of home" is influential in the decisions a woman makes about family, having children, taking part in the labor market. In the formation of this perspective, the family education and religious culture obtained in the early years are especially decisive. In countries where unemployment is high, the idea of giving men the priority to have jobs seems to have an effect on wage disparities between the genders and on women's work trends. However, socially determined behavior patterns and institutional constraints can also be balanced with personal experience over time. At this point, especially women's participation in higher education and the market being open to competition are important variables.

Pfau-Effinger (2012) examined the relationship between social norms and public policies in his research. For this purpose, the factors affecting the employment of women with children under the age of three were examined by comparing between countries. The study argues that there are women who attach different meanings to the concepts of family and career depending on cultural forms, but there is also a tendency for gender culture to change with social developments. Pfau-Effinger (2012) shows that the family policies are also shaped by cultural influences, even though it could be asserted that in countries with low female employment rates high unemployment rates could be observed because of the problematic nature of the labor market in said countries, the data does not support this assertion; however in regards to child care, cultural values are of descriptive nature for the available data. According to the study, the unique nature of each social structure is important in this respect. Dieckhoff, Gash and Steiber (2015) examined the relationship between family policies and women's employment for 18 European countries; they concluded that family policies had an effect on women's employment. Tolciu and Zierahn (2012) demonstrated the impact of social norms on women's employment rates and their severity in terms of attitudes towards gender roles and job commitment following a study conducted in Germany using country data.

Under the influence of social norms in developed industrialized countries, women's employment and gender policies can become the source of greater inequalities in developing countries. The existence of exclusionary social institutions is a barrier to women's empowerment and participation in the labor market on an equal footing with men, especially in developing countries. In fact, social policies such as maternity leave and childcare in relation to these institutions can sometimes be at the center of discrimination against women. In these countries, the shift of women's employment from fragile, that is, non-long-term informal sectors to formal sectors, which is a necessary condition for women's empowerment without the support of the state through social policies, also seems difficult (Cerise et al., 2013). While it is generally accepted that there is an inverse relationship between the level of development of countries and gender discrimination, it is seen that gender discrimination is a phenomenon that we face all over the world. It is also possible to conclude that the reform movements for women to have equal conditions with men in all areas have often not reached the desired outcome. In many developed economies, women are exposed to wage inequality across all sectors, even though they have the same rights to work as men, regulated by the same laws. This disparity is more evident in underdeveloped and emerging economies (Peker and Kubar, 2012). This situation brings other negative consequences for women as well as gender discrimination. Cheaper women's labor leads to increased male dominance and women's exposure to economic violence (Tunç, 2018). One of the main reasons for this continued discrimination is the continued existence of norms supporting society's negative view of women's participation in social and economic life (Berber and Eser, 2008).

The purpose of this study is to examine the Middle East region, which mostly becomes prominent on gender inequality and violations of women's rights, in terms of the effect of social norms on women's employment and gender politics, and to evaluate the period after the Arab Spring, which was born as a freedom movement, in terms of gender politics. For this purpose, the second part will discuss the impact of social norms and policies on women's employment decisions in the Middle East, and the third part will discuss the situation after the Arab Spring. In the conclusion section, a general evaluation will be made, and the findings related to the subject will be summarized.

2 Social Norms, Women's Employment and Gender Policies in the Middle East

Although gender inequality is seen as one of the common problems of countries independent of their level of development, the Middle East stands out as the region where gender inequalities have reached the highest level. Although the historical development processes, social composition, economic resources and production structures of the Middle East countries differ in many aspects, it is observed that the general trend is in this direction. In the Middle East, the term "patriarchal authority" is often preferred when a term is used to generalize the relationship between individual, family, and gender roles. Patriarchy is defined as "a system that historically co-existed with the system of production, in which men predominate over women, where the status of women is determined according to classes based on the division of labour between genders as well as the type of production." One of the important reasons why women are under male control in the Middle East before and after the adoption of Islam and the continuity of this understanding is the desire to control property. The social stratification system and nationalization process formed by the transformation of production structure from agriculture to industry is described as "transition from patriarchy to neo patriarchy." The implementation of planned development strategies in Middle East countries, as in many developing countries in the period between 1950 and 1980 alone, increased the importance given to education; there was a divergence in education and women's participation in social life by taking part in the labor force. Because education affects the age of women to marry and have children, employment allows women to communicate and organize with other women. However, with the change of production structure after the 1980s, the increase in natural resource exports narrowed the employment areas of women, especially those with lower educational attainment, and the withdrawal of the state from the social policy area through globalization and the downsizing of the state accelerated the impoverishment of women. In the same period, the change of economic development strategy as well as the strengthening of religious influences in political movements also affected the place of women in economic and political power relations. But explaining the status of women in the Middle East only through religious political movements is described as simple and superficial. As a matter of fact, the gender perception, which is shaped by religious and cultural norms in the role of women in working life, political movements, family and other social roles, does not seem unique to Middle East geography alone. Christian and Jewish communities who live in the West embracing research also concludes that the relationship between religiousness of women with gender roles (Read, 2003; Metcalfe, 2008; Cherif, 2010; Moghadam, 2013a).

In addition to norms, the impact of labor intensiveness and richness in natural resources are discussed to be other determining factors for women's employment in Middle Eastern countries. According to this, women's employment is higher in Egypt, Lebanon, Morocco and Tunisia, where jobs are labor-intensive and natural resources are scarce, compared to Algeria, Iraq, Syria and Yemen, which are richer in resources and labor. Women's employment rates are higher in labor-importing countries such as Kuwait, Qatar and Bahrain, which have rich natural resources. After the 2000s, women's employment increased, although it varied between countries. The feminization of public employment has a significant impact on this change. In these countries, incentives to support private enterprises are granted only to men, and banking operations cannot be conducted without the supervision of a man. In the Middle East, oil-producing firms also support discrimination by ensuring that resources for professional development and education are allocated to men. Social norms and maternity costs keep women out of the private sector in the related countries (Moghadam, 2004). It is also thought that women adopt traditional values in conditions where they cannot find a place in the labor market, making it easier for them to marry; economic security is also provided through marriage. Poor, low-educated women with limited economic opportunities also tend to maintain marriages that conform to traditional belief systems and perpetuate existing inequalities (Blaydes and Linzer, 2008).

Women's need for a democratic system and their adoption of pluralism seems to be related to their civic consciousness. The reason for the failure of civil society movements in the Middle East is that this consciousness has not yet been formed. Although many civil movements in the region tend to act utilitarianism in order to strengthen the existing clientelist economic, political and social structure instead of the demands of good governance and democratic system, modernist and democratic movements can also be found depending on the status of education and employment. But indicators of gender gap in the region support utilitarianism as dominant to modernism (Çiftçi and Bernick, 2015).

3 Developments during the Post-Arab Spring Period

The impact of the Arab Spring, which emerged in 2011 as a "movement of emancipation" against authoritarian systems, on women's demands for equality has mostly been unsatisfactory, although there have been different results in each country depending on the continuity of the movement (Sjoberg and Whooley, 2015).

The protests, which began in 2010 when Mohammed Buazizi, a university student in Tunisia, burned himself, then spread to several Middle Eastern and North African countries, including Egypt, Libya and Syria, creating a domino effect. The Arab Spring, which soon brought many Arab countries under its influence, is generally regarded as a public protest carried out in the name of democratization. Women and men in these social movements belong to all kinds of social and economic classes and have taken part side by side in the same ranks in this struggle (Aktas, 2012). During the protests, people from all walks of life such as journalists, academics, activists, trade unionists, students and mothers mobilized and took to the streets to gain freedom and respect (FIDH, 2012). Although there were many factors that played a part in the beginning of this mass movement, the economic reasons lie at the root of the protests. In addition, the existence of a political authoritarianism, dominated by dictatorship, especially by bribery, corruption and injustice, the people feeling insecure under the oppressive regime, the forcing of the people to low wages and difficult conditions, even if they have sufficient economic resources, are listed as the factors that ignited this social movement. The main reason for women to flock to the streets during the protests was their demands for democratization as well as their desire to oppose the patriarchal trend of the societies in which they live as women (Ertan and Dikme, 2016).

There are other examples in history where democratization protests, such as the Arab Spring, have had positive effects on women's rights (Viterna and Fallon, 2008). It has been observed in various historical events that women have been given greater political participation, rights and freedoms as a result of such protests (Viterna and Fallon, 2008). The democratization movements that took place in various parts of the world, such as Argentina, Chile, South Africa, the Philippines and Northern Ireland, can be cited as examples that support this thesis. Women's participation in political life has increased after the protests in the said countries and they have become more effective in decision-making and policy-making processes, and/or women have been able to take successful steps in the name of democratization (Moghadam, 2013a).

On the other hand, many studies have shown that following such social movements in which women are actively involved, there have also been negative examples where women's policy making and inclusion in politics have been rather limited (Ertan and Dikme, 2016). As a matter of fact, women's movements in some European countries have had a contrary effect, causing their participation in politics to decline. In addition, such protests have further impacted women's feminine rights: limitations have been imposed on their rights such as motherhood, having children, and abortion (Viterna and Fallon, 2008; Moghadam, 2013b; Roman, 2001; Haney, 1994). Similarly, democratization movements in the Middle East and North Africa have had consequences against the woman who played an active role in these protests. Women were eliminated in politics by not being involved in any post-action negotiations, and even their political rights were limited (Esfandiari, 2012; Al Ali, 2012; Karakir and Aknur, 2015).

Manea (2014) examined the impact of the Arab Spring on women by dividing the process into three phases. In the first phase of the Arab Spring, women had no demands for gender equality. At this stage, the common demand of the peoples of the Middle East was seen as a change of regimes due to lack of economic opportunities, patronage system, corruption and lack of good governance. However, in the following days, all means of physical violence against women began to be used as the initiative turned into a civil war. Libya is cited as the worst example in this regard. Yemen declared a rule banning men and women to get together in public spaces. The second stage was the stage in which elections were held in many countries where insurgencies took place. But women who were at the forefront of the protests during the Arab Spring had no place at the bargaining tables after dictators were toppled, their political representation and rights were restricted. Libya comes to the fore again as a country where social norms, tribes and tribal culture are dominant. Similar results have been observed in Egypt. Tunisia has been cited as a good example of transition, while Morocco and Algeria have taken important steps for women's representation in the parliament. Therefore, after the Arab Spring, there have been some improvements in women's political representation as well as access to education, albeit in a limited number of countries. In the third phase, parties in Tunisia and Egypt insisted on arrangements protecting male-favoring inequalities. Today, many countries in the region are working to provide support to women and children as internal turmoil continues, and many women activists are working to eliminate the violence perpetrated by fundamentalist groups against women. (Manea, 2014; Es. Fandiari and Heideman 2015).

Socioeconomic indicators support that the Arab region does not paint a pleasant post-spring picture. The region currently has the lowest female labor force participation rate in the world, at 18.4 %. This rate is very low compared to the world average of 48.4 %. By contrast, male labor force participation rates are above the global average of 77 %, that is, 75 %. In Arab countries, the female unemployment rate is 15.6 %, which is three times the world average. The proportion of women in administrative positions in the region is also low, compared with the average in the world: only 11 % of people with administrative positions in Arab countries are women (ILO, 2019). In this respect, as Merrill (2017) points out, the change of gender inequality seems to be possible only through the change of norms that affect the thinking and behavior patterns of society in the long term; in this respect, the change is more than the destruction of dictators.

4 Conclusion

Social norms perform many functions as a whole set of rules that contain cultural elements that shape individual preferences. It is some of these functions that individuals' roles and patterns of behavior within the social hierarchy are determined. Gender roles are also embedded in social norms, leading to the behavior and preferences of men and women both in the household and in the society that they belong to. Although this effect can be observed in many societies regardless of the level of development of countries, it is seen to be felt more in developing countries, where traditional patterns remain valid. Considering the relationship between social norms and cultural elements, it can be observed from historical experience that the change of these generally accepted rules took time and was not easy.

The Middle East is one of the geographies where social norms, along with cultural and religious elements, determine the roles of men and women. Middle Eastern countries often have an understanding that patriarchal authority applies and that women are restricted to traditional household roles. This understanding is effective for decision-making of women in many areas from getting higher education, take place in business areas in parallel with their education, to take an active role in political decision-making mechanisms, to marriage and having children. In the Middle East, male-dominated understanding prevails in all social institutions, from family institutions to state institutions, making it difficult for demands for change to be met. Indeed, the experience of the Arab Spring proves that there is a long distance to change in the geography of the Middle East, where concepts such as citizenship awareness and democratic participation have no place in theory and practice.

Like all women in the world, women in the Middle East deserve to have equality, human dignity, democracy and justice. But the data shows that the Arab Spring did not improve women's conditions in most Middle Eastern countries as expected; women's social, economic and political demands were not met; on the contrary, women were dragged into battlefields in many countries by terrorist groups, which in turn resulted in them being enslaved, widowed or condemned. At the end of five years, the only result women achieved with the Arab Spring, in which they played a substantial role, has only been disappointment.

References

Aktaş, M. (2012). The Arab Spring and Women's Rights. *The Journal of EKEV Academy*, 52, 29–43.

Al Ali, N. (2012). Gendering the Arab Spring. *Middle East Journal of Culture and Communication*, 5, 26–31.

Becker, G. (1981). *A treatise on the family*. Cambridge, MA: Harvard University Press.

Berber, M., & Eser Yılmaz, B. (2008). Türkiye'de Kadin İstihdamı: Ülke ve Bölge Düzeyinde Sektörel Analiz. *The Journal of Industrial Relations and Human Resources*, 10(2), 1–16.

Blaydes, L., & Linzer, D. (2008). The Political Economy of Women's Support for Fundamentalist Islam. *World Politics*, 60(4), 576–609.

Campa, P. Casarico, A., & Profeta, P. (2009). Gender Culture and Gender Gap in Employment, CESifo Working Paper, No. 2738, Center for Economic Studies and Ifo Institute (CESifo), Munich.

Cerise, S., Eliseeva, A., Francavilla, F., Mejia, C., & Tuccio, M. (2013). How Do Maternatiy Leave and Discriminatory Social Roles Relate to Women's Employment in Developing Countries? (access: 20.05.2019). Retrieved from https://www.oecd.org/dev/poverty/OECD%20DEV%20(2013)%20%20SIGI%20and%20Maternity%20Leave.pdf.

Cherif, M. F. (2010). Culture, Rights, and Norms: Women's Rights Reform in Muslim Countries. *The Journal of Politics*, 72(4), 1144–1160.

Cialdini, R. B., & Trost, M. R. (1998). Social Influence: Social norms, conformity, and compliance. In D. T. Gilbert, S. T. Fiske, G. Lindzey (Eds.), *The Handbook of Social Psychology* (4th ed., pp. 151–162). Boston, MA: McGraw-Hill.

Çiftçi, S., & Bernick, E. B. (2015). Utilitarian and Modern: Clientelism, Citizen Empowerment, and Civic Engagement in the Arab World. *Democratization*, 22(7), 1161–1182.

Dieckhoff, M., Gash, V., & Steiber, N. (2015). Measuring the Effect of Institutional Change on Gender Inequality in the Labour Market. *Research in Social Stratification and Mobility*, 39, 59–75.

Ellickson, R. C. (1998). Law and Economics Discovers Social Norms. *The Journal of Legal Studies*, 27(2), 537–552.

Ertan, S., & Dikme, R. (2016). Arap Baharı'nın Kadın Haklarına Etkisi. *Turkish Journal of TESAM Academy*, 3(2), 73–108.

Esfandiari, H. (2012). Is the Arab Awakening Marginalizing Women? *Middle East Program Occasional Paper Series, Wilson Center*, 1–4.

Estandiari, H., & Heideman, K. (2015). The Role and Status of Women after the Arab Uprisings. IEMed. Mediterranean Yearbook 2015 (access: 06.07.2019). Retrieved from http://www.iemed.org/observatori/arees-danalisi/arxius adjunts/anuari/med.2015/IEMed_MedYearbook2015_The_Role_and_Status_of_Women_Haleh%20Esfandiari_Kendra%20Heideman.pdf.

FIDH. (2012). Women and the Arab Spring: Taking Their Place? (access: 01.08.2019). http://www.europarl.europa.eu/document/activities/cont/201206/20120608ATT46510/20120608ATT46510EN.pdf.

Fortin, N. M. (2005). Gender Role Attitudes and the Labour-Market Outcomes of Women across OECD Countries. *Oxford Review of Economic Policy*, 21(3), 416–438.

Haney, L. (1994). From Proud Worker to Good Mother: Women, the State, and Regime Change in Hungary. *Frontiers Editorial Collective*, 14, 113–150.

Hirsch, L. J. (2000). Culture, Gender, and Work in Japan: A Case Study of a Woman in Management. *Ethos*, 28(2), 248–269.

ILO (2019). Internatiol Labour Organization. Gender Equality and Non-discrimination (access: 03.08.2019). https://www.ilo.org/beirut/areasofwork/equality-discrimination/lang--en/index.htm.

Kalwij, A. S. (2000). The Effects of Female Employment Status on the Presence and Number of Children. *Journal of Population Economics*, 13, 221–239.

Karakır, İ. A., & Aknur, M. (2015). Devrimler Sonrasında Arap Kadını'nın Siyasi Temsili: Bir Arap Baharı Yanılgısı mı? *The Journal of Ankara University*, 70(1), 131–162.

Kranton, R. (2016). Identity Economics 2016: Where Do Social Distinctions and Norms Come From? *The American Economic Review*, 106(5), Papers and Proceedıngs of the One Hundred Twenty-Eighth Annual Meeting of The American Economic Associatıon, 405–409.

Manea, E. (2014). The Arab Popular Uprisings from a Gender Perspective. *Zeitschrift für Politik*, Neue Folge, 61(1), 81–100.

Maume, D. (2006). Gender Differences in Restricting Work Efforts because of Family Responsibilities. *Journal of Marriage and Family*, 68, 859–869.

McGinn, L. K., & Oh, E. (2017). Gender, Social Class, Women's Employment. *Current Opinion in Psychology*, 18, 84–88.

Merrill, R. C. (2017). The Middle Eastern Gender Gap: The State of Female Political Participation Before, During and After the 'Arab Spring'. *The Arab Spring, Civil Society, and Innovative Activism*, 121–140.

Metcalfe, B. D. (2008). Women, Management and Globalization in the Middle East. *Journal of Business Ethics*, 83, 85–100.

Moghadam, M. V. (2004). Patriarchy in Transition: Women and the Changing Family in the Middle East. *Journal of Comparative Family Studies*, 35 (2), 137–162.

Moghadam, M. V. (2013a). Modernizing Women: Gender and Social Change in Middle East (3rd ed.), Lynne Rienner Publishers: USA.

Moghadam, M. V. (2013b). What Is Democracy? Promises and Perils of the Arab Spring. *Current Sociology*, 61(4), 393–408.

Ostrom, E. (2000). Collective Action and the Evolution of Social Norms. *The Journal of Economic Perspectives*, 14(3), 137–158.

Peker, A. E., & Kubar Y. (2012). Türkiye'de Kırsal Kesimde Kadın İstihdamına Genel Bir Bakış. *The Journal of Afyon University*, 14(2), 173–188.

Pearse, R., & Connell, R. (2016). Gender Norms and the Economy: Insights from Social Research. *Feminist Economics*, 22(1), 30–53.

Pfau-Effinger, B. (2012). Women's Employment in the Institutional and Cultural Context. *International Journal of Sociology and Social Policy*, 32(9), 530–543.

Read, G. J. (2003). The Sources of Gender Role Attitudes among Christian and Muslim Arab-American Women. *Sociology of Religion*, 64(2), 207–222.

Roman, D. (2001). Gendering Eastern Europe: Pre-Feminism, Prejudice, and East-West Dialogues in Post-Communist Romania. *Women's Studies International Forum*, 24, 53–66.

Sjoberg, L., & Whooley, J. (2015). The Arab Spring for Women? Representations of Women in Middle East Politics in 2011. *Journal of Women, Politics & Policy*, 36(3), 261–284.

Sustein, R. (1996). Social Norms and Social Roles. *Columbia Law Review*, 96 (4), 903–968.

Tolciu A., & Zierahn, U. (2012). Women and Work: What Role Do Social Norms Play? *International Review of Applied Economics*, 26(6), 711–733.

Tunç, M. (2018). Kalkınmada Kadın Ayrımcılığı ve Toplumsal Cinsiyet Eşitsizliğinin Rolü: Ülkelerarası Farklı Gelir Gruplarına Göre Yatay Kesit Analiz. *Sosyoekonomi*, 26(38), 221–251.

Viterna, J., & Fallon, K. (2008). Democratization, women's movement, and gender-equitable states: A framework for comparison. *American Sociological Review*, 73(4), 668–689.

List of Figures and Graphs

List of Tables

www.ingramcontent.com/pod-product-compliance
Ingram Content Group UK Ltd.
Pitfield, Milton Keynes, MK11 3LW, UK
UKHW020153290926
15471UKWH00005B/848

9 783631 817919